Oklahoma World War II Veterans Remember

SERVING
our
COUNTRY

Oklahoma World War II Veterans Remember

SERVING
our
COUNTRY

BY TIM STANLEY

Foreword by
RETIRED GEN. TOMMY FRANKS

Editors Debbie Jackson and John Walblay
Designer Steven Reckinger

TULSA WORLD

Copyright 2016 by Tulsa World

Printed in the United States of America

ISBN 978-0-692-79870-6

Library of Congress Control Number 2016957687

Tulsa World
315 S. Boulder Ave.
Tulsa, OK 74103

TABLE OF CONTENTS

TABLE OF CONTENTS

TABLE OF CONTENTS

FOREWORD

Gen. Tommy Franks, retired

It was my honor, my privilege, to serve our country in uniform for almost four decades. I served with great patriots, selfless troopers and many amazing heroes. The stories contained in this book are those of heroes from a different time. Oklahoma heroes — American heroes — from the Greatest Generation. I am humbled to read their stories and reflect on the fact that we call them the Greatest Generation for a reason.

These stories are from the time of Norman Rockwell, literally the America of my father. The men and women who lived the events recorded here left a great legacy of leadership and patriotism. We are in their debt.

In September 1939, Hitler's Nazi Germany marched into Poland, initiating what would become World War II. By 1940, England, our historic ally, was deep in a war for survival against the Nazis. America supported our European allies, but did not join the war until December 1941, with Japan's attack on our forces in Hawaii. At this time literally millions of Americans signed up to serve – to protect our country, their own families and our way of life. More than 16 million served in the military between December 1941 and September 1945. Their service was for "the duration." Most served overseas for an average of 16 months. These are the stories of those who served and those who loved them.

Virtually every family was affected. My family, my wife Cathy's family, our fathers, uncles, cousins and their friends, all served. The families at home made sacrifices but remained committed to the war effort. Ration cards were a way of life. Gasoline was rationed. Tires were rationed. Shoes were rationed. Many planted "Victory Gardens" to help with the food shortages. Americans at home did whatever they could to help the men and women who were fighting.

Mail between families and their loved ones overseas could take weeks, or months. And when letters were received, sometimes they were heavily censored. Families at home got their news about the war from newsreels at the movies, from newspaper reports, and from the radio. Ernie Pyle, with his newspaper column, was highly regarded for capturing the events and the feelings of the regular soldier on the battlefield. Bill Mauldin, as an editorial cartoonist, created characters to represent the ordinary "GI Joe." Both Ernie Pyle and Bill Mauldin were very popular with families at home. Edward R. Murrow was a radio broadcaster followed by millions. He delivered straight talk about the difficulties and dangers of the war. Families would often sit around the radio to listen to Murrow and learn as much as they could about what their own soldier was enduring.

I was born in Wynnewood, Oklahoma, in the summer of 1945, between V-E Day and V-J Day. My earliest memories include stories from my father of his time in the Army Air Corps. He spoke of boot camp, the aircraft maintenance training he had received, his time as an aircraft mechanic with a unit in Panama, his pride in serving, and the friends he had made in the military. I met many of those friends and their families. I remember hunting, fishing and going camping with them. They told great stories that made a significant impact on me. Over the course of the years that followed I came to appreciate the value of my father's service and the many sacrifices my family, along with so many other families, had made to defend America. The Greatest Generation, indeed.

As I read the stories in this book and reflect on memories of my family and my father's service, I realize the importance of sharing these stories with the current generation and with generations to come. We have an obligation to our children and grandchildren to record as many of these stories as we can while these heroes are still living.

The values we see reflected in these stories — patriotism, integrity, loyalty, selfless service, honor, personal courage, to name just a few — are among the values that made America the greatest nation on the earth. The strength of our country is found in the strength of the American people — men and women like those who wrote the stories contained in this book.

I am thankful to Tim Stanley for capturing the remembrances of these great veterans, and reminding us all of the virtues of America during a time of crisis. Tim brings their stories to life. Personal and compelling stories from the front lines. Stories of falling in love. Stories of being wounded. Stories about sacrifice. These are real people with stories to tell. These are Oklahoma World War II veterans. Our own Oklahoma Greatest Generation.

ACKNOWLEDGMENTS

The Tulsa World would like give special thanks to the following for their support and assistance during this project:

Military History Center, Broken Arrow

Tulsa Marine Corps League

Tulsa American Legion Post 1

Tulsa Air and Space Museum

All Veterans Association Inc.

Oklahoma Military Academy Alumni Association

Oklahoma Women Veterans Organization, Tulsa chapter

Circle Cinema

Keith Myers

Eric Sims

Eva Unterman

University Village

Montereau

Oklahoma Methodist Manor

St. Simeon's

Legend Senior Living

Senior Star at Burgundy Place

Inverness Village

Heatheridge

Town Village

Most of all, we'd like to thank the veterans themselves

for sharing their memories, photos and time.

"American Soldiers clearing a Japanese bunker near Buna, New Guinea." U.S. ARMY

INTRODUCTION

Tim Stanley

I like the way Eva Unterman put it:

"Stories make stories. And your story has created a new story."

Unterman, a Holocaust survivor who lives in Tulsa, said this to me in 2016 at a special event we were attending, and in which I was happy to have played a part, albeit unintentionally.

Organized to bring Unterman and two aging World War II veterans together, the idea for the event had been sparked by a story I wrote for our "World War II veterans remember" series on bomber tail gunner Roland Kinzer. Back in 1945, at age 19, Kinzer had been part of a bombing raid on a German city where, as fate would have it, Unterman, 12, was being held with her mother and other Jewish prisoners of war.

Thrilled to read about one of the men she considered her "liberators," Unterman reached out to Kinzer after the story ran. It went from there. A meeting was set for her and Kinzer to have a public "reunion," along with Jack Babbitt, another local veteran of those raids.

More than 70 years after the momentous events in which they had been swept up, three lives intersected again in Tulsa, Oklahoma. And none of them will ever be the same for it. A new story, as Unterman pointed out, was being written right before our eyes.

The Tulsa World began its "World War II veterans remember" story and video project in early 2015 as a way to commemorate the 70th anniversary that year of the end of the war in 1945.

But also motivating us was another impending end: the end of an opportunity. Our time with them being short, we wanted to give surviving area veterans, most of whom are now in their 90s, a chance to tell their stories.

And what stories they've turned out to be. Embraced from the beginning by our readers, the series has become a repository for the memories — the good and bad intermingled — of what has been rightly called our greatest generation, those sons and daughters on whom a nation hung its hopes in its darkest hours.

From the beginning there have been many requests that we collect the stories in a book. This volume is our answer to that. It includes the first 65 stories, with accompanying photos and graphics, from the series, which is now in its second year.

A hundred years from now, when all of us are gone, I am confident the stories of our greatest generation will still be told. In books, on film, in whatever new mediums of expression emerge, they will still be brought to life. With the series and now this book, we at the Tulsa World are happy to have played a small part in ensuring that will be the case for the stories of these Oklahoma veterans.

I can't help thinking of what Unterman said — about stories and how they often make more stories. Having seen that play out firsthand, I can only wonder what stories are going to be sparked by the ones on these pages — what new stories there are to be written.

I hope that prospect excites you as much as it does me.

Battle of Bastogne

Ahrend was a combat engineer with the 101st Airborne

Seeing it for the first time in Washington, D.C., James Ahrend was both impressed and inspired by the National World War II Memorial. But one thing was missing, he felt.

"There weren't any names," the Broken Arrow resident said. "I was looking for some names of buddies who died."

As on the nearby Vietnam Veterans wall, Ahrend — who served with the Army's 101st Airborne in WWII — had been expecting to find the slain from his war listed. He understands, though, why they aren't. "There are just too many," he said. Fortunately, Ahrend's memory has no such limitations.

Preserved there, for whenever he wants to see them, are all of those buddies' names he was looking for, along with their faces. The place names, too, are there: Normandy. Eindhoven. Bastogne. And

70 years later, they still have the power to bring tears to his eyes.

'So cold we couldn't think'

"We were cold. Scared and cold. So cold all you wanted to do was get somewhere that was warm." Ahrend is describing his time at Bastogne, which in the winter of 1944-45 was experiencing its worst conditions in 100 years. They were so bad, he said, you almost forgot about the bigger problem: being surrounded and cut off by the German Army.

"We were so cold we couldn't think too much," he said.

During an October 2015 interview at his home in Broken Arrow, Ahrend, 91, revisited that and other experiences as an Army combat engineer in the war. Known to family by his middle name, Preston, Ahrend picked up another moniker from fellow members of the 326th Engineer Battalion. To them, "a bunch of Yankees," he was "Okie," he said, laughing.

Ahrend's primary duty with the unit, part of the 101st Airborne, was constructing temporary bridges to keep the American forces

— 14 —

moving forward. It was a role that often put him in the thick of the action. Ahrend was involved in four campaigns during the war: Normandy, Central Europe, the Rhineland and the Ardennes (Battle of the Bulge). Bastogne came during the last.

A strategically important site, the fight for the Belgian city would garner Ahrend yet another nickname, this one shared with his fellow 101st Airborne mates. Remembered ever after as the "Battered Bastards of Bastogne" for their heroic stand there, they would take their place among the legendary fighting forces in the history of American warfare.

'The worst place ever'

"We didn't know what we were getting into," Ahrend said of Bastogne. His unit arrived on Dec. 18, 1944. By that time, American units defending the city had been decimated. And it only got worse. After Ahrend and his comrades got there, the Germans soon had the city completely surrounded.

"Bastogne was the worst place ever. Even our cooks had to fight," he said.

Ahrend had an overcoat to wear, but not much else in the way of protection from the cold. Once, he said, "to thaw out a bit," he and some other troops took refuge in a small building. Immediately the Germans, using their rocket guns — "Screaming Mimis" — started shelling it.

Ahrend and another man close to the front door dived through it. Running for cover, Ahrend looked back only to see that the German guns "had got all the rest."

"(Screaming Mimis) make a weird sound," he added. "I can't describe it. It's the sound of death."

The Germans' 88 mm artillery guns were also dreaded. Ahrend had a close call when a shell from one landed next to his fox hole. "It was a dud. Or I'd have been a goner. ... The 88s were devastating."

Trapped in the "doughnut hole," as the troops called the area within the circle of German forces, the Americans would deal with dwindling food and medical supplies as the siege dragged on. At one point, they were told to surrender or face total annihilation. To this, American commander Brig. Gen. Anthony McAuliffe's famous response was both curt and comical: "To the German Commander: NUTS!"

"It surprised us that he said that," said Ahrend, chuckling over what is still one of his favorite stories to tell. At last, after more than a week under siege, 3rd Army forces led by Gen. George Patton broke through to relieve the 101st.

"I think I'm here today because of him (Patton)," Ahrend said. "A lot of young men died there, and never knew why," he added of Bastogne. "They were out there five minutes and were gone."

First action

Ahrend grew up dirt poor, living through the Depression with his family on their farm near Sasakwa in Seminole County. "We survived on what we raised," he said, adding that they kept a garden, hogs and cattle.

After he was drafted into the Army, he was sent overseas as a replacement soldier with the 101st. His first action came on D-Day, June 6, 1945. The 326th flew into Normandy in gliders, which were towed and released by C-47s. From there, they would use gliders again for Operation Market Garden in Holland — although there they would get a much different reception than at Normandy.

Landing in a big field, they had just climbed out when "we heard them coming," Ahrend said. "Sounded like horses. But it was the townspeople coming out to help us — wearing wooden shoes." He said the Dutch people, who had been living under German occupation, were ecstatic to see the Americans.

James Ahrend (far left) with some of his buddies from the 326th Engineer Battalion, 101st Airborne. The 326th became known as the "Battered Bastards of Bastogne," the site of some of the fiercest fighting during the Battle of the Bulge. COURTESY

James Ahrend: Combat engineer

Part of the 101st Airborne Division, Ahrend took part in four campaigns - Normandy, Central Europe, Rhineland and the Ardennes, where he fought during the Siege of Bastogne.

5th Panzer Army

BELGIUM

U.S. front line, Dec. 21-23

Longchamps

U.S. front line, Dec. 25-26

U.S. front line, Dec. 21-23

N

Brussels ☆

Bastogne

101st Airborne Division

Bizory

Longvilly

Neffe

Siege of Bastogne
Dec. 20-27, 1944

Drop zone, Dec. 23

Bastogne

Wardin

Marvie

STRENGTH
101st: 11,000 enlisted; 800 officers
Remaining units: 11,000+
Total: 22,800+
Germany: 54,000+

U.S. front line, Dec. 25-26

Dec. 26

Patton's 3rd Army

LUXEMBOURG

0   2   4

Miles

CASUALTIES AND LOSSES
U.S.: 3,000+ total casualties; (2,000 in the 101st)
Germany: unknown

STEVEN RECKINGER/Tulsa World

But the fighting there was far from done. Ahrend remembers one incident in particular from Holland, when he and some other soldiers were assigned to roust some Germans holed up in a barn. Emerging from the pine trees about 50 or so yards from the barn, they decided to spread out and empty their guns into the building.

"We didn't know how many there were and we hoped to make them think there was more of us," Ahrend explained. The ploy worked. The Germans "came running out, hands over their heads," he said. "We'd caught them asleep."

There were about 20 of them, which would have easily outnumbered Ahrend's small band. Taking their prisoners with them, they marched five miles back through the snow. For its efforts in liberating the country, the 326th would later be recognized with Holland's oldest and highest honor, the Orange Lanyard.

The honors for the unit would pile up. The 326th also would receive the French Croix de Guerre and the Belgian Fourragere, not to mention two presidential unit citations, one each for Normandy and Bastogne.

Live, laugh, love

"Boy, that Statue of Liberty looked so good to me," Ahrend said, describing his arrival back in New York after the war. "A bunch of us kissed the dirt."

Returning to the family farm, he set about trying to readjust. "For a time after I got back," he said, "I'd jump at every big noise."

It didn't take Ahrend long to decide that farm life wasn't for him,

and he left "that cotton-picking farm" behind for California. He stayed there for a while, before returning to begin a long career with American Airlines in Tulsa. He met and married his wife, Clara, and together they raised a family. He retired from American in 1987 after nearly 40 years as a crew chief.

Ahrend's trip to Washington to see the WWII memorial came in 2013, courtesy of the Oklahoma Honor Flights program. It was an opportunity, he said, to reflect on the men he fought with.

"Young soldiers make the best soldiers. They don't worry like older people. They don't realize the danger. I think about them a lot," he added of the friends and comrades who didn't make it home. He said he'd like to tell them that they're the real heroes. "But they're not here to talk about it."

As for why he's here, why he didn't die fighting on foreign soil, Ahrend is pretty sure he knows. "My father in Heaven had better things for me," he said. "I don't see how it could be any other way. ... War is terrible."

Because of his war experience, he is "more thankful for how important life is and how you should live your life. My favorite words are 'live, laugh and love.' But you've got to cry, too. If you can't cry, you can't let the pressure off."

James Ahrend poses with captured Nazi artillery on railcars. Ahrend saw action in four major campaigns in the European theater as a combat engineer.
COURTESY

A painful souvenir

Alspaugh served with the 102nd Infantry Division in Europe

Of all the places on his body he could've been hit, Jim Alspaugh is glad it was one of the "fleshy" ones. "I was fortunate," he said.

When he speaks at schools, he added, "I always ask the kids if they've seen the movie 'Forrest Gump.' Then I tell them Forrest and I are brothers — we were both shot in the buttocks."

Alspaugh was wounded in Germany late in 1944, and it knocked him out of action for several weeks. He still has one of the pieces of shrapnel. A medic gave him the keepsake — about the length and width of Alspaugh's little finger. There was so little in military life to hold onto, Alspaugh said, he decided he might as well keep it. Later on, when he started making presentations about the war, Alspaugh took the shrapnel with him to show off to listeners.

Jim Alspaugh holds the 3-inch piece of shrapnel that wounded him in the back-side. He has kept the shrapnel these 70 years as a souvenir of his war service, and takes it with him to show audiences during his frequent public speaking engagements.   MICHAEL WYKE/Tulsa World

'Going to live forever'

Alspaugh, a native and longtime resident of Tulsa, had to overcome an early loss in life long before he ever saw the war. When he was just 3, his father died. The youngest of five and the only boy, Alspaugh credits the combined influence of family, church and the Boy Scouts, which he joined at age 12, with helping fill the void, as well as preparing him to endure the hardships of war.

After graduating from Will Rogers High School and attending the University of Oklahoma, Alspaugh was drafted into the Army in September 1943.

He remembers attending a Christmas Eve service that year while training at Fort Benning, Georgia. Although aware it could be his last Christmas stateside for a while, he had only vague notions as to what might lie ahead. Young people believe they "are all going to live forever," said Alspaugh, 90, in a recent interview. "I don't know that we were ever aware of the dangers we were going into."

By the time he arrived in France with the Army's 102nd Infantry Division, it was late September 1944, and Allied forces were closing in on Germany. All the trucks were in use, so Alspaugh and his unit traveled to the front by rail in boxcars. From Belgium, they moved through Holland and into Germany, along the way taking their first casualties, including some of his friends.

Officially a rifleman with an infantry platoon, Alspaugh was assigned to communications. As the unit advanced, it laid phone lines, unrolling them directly onto the ground off small spools. Alspaugh's primary job was to maintain those lines. The phones were used principally, he said, "for our riflemen to warn of enemy in the area, or in picking out targets to shoot at." If a line was broken, he either repaired it immediately, or, if an urgent message awaited, he carried it himself to the recipient. These duties kept him out of direct combat. But not out of the line of fire.

"When you hear a mortar go off," Alspaugh said, "it makes, like, a coughing sound. Then they go up high and you don't hear them again until they come down. You have a few seconds to get flat."

For much of November and on into December, Alspaugh's division was involved in Operation Queen, an American effort to capture the Ruhr River and use it to stage an invasion. His part in it, however, would end abruptly.

On Dec. 11, 1944, near Linnich, Germany, Alspaugh headed out to locate a broken phone line. He found it, he said, at a cut in the road. But he never got the chance to fix it. Looking back, Alspaugh believes it was probably a German 88-mm gun that got him.

"I could just picture them waiting, saying, 'Here he comes.' " The shell that the Germans fired at him missed, but two fragments from it struck him in his left buttock.

"It was strange. You feel a heavy hit like someone hitting you with a baseball bat," he said. "I did not bleed heavily ... the heat of the explosion heats the fragment, which tends to cauterize the wound."

He was fortunate: Another inch or two in any direction, and the shrapnel could have shattered bone or severed a major artery. Alspaugh was evacuated to a battalion aid station by medical jeep. He remembers the ride well. Sprawled face down on a stretcher on the hood of the jeep, he was told by the driver "to keep a close watch. They had not swept that road for mines."

At the aid station, medics took two fragments out before sending him on to a division hospital. There, he was greeted by a familiar face. One of the medics was his friend Buddy Quackenbush of Tulsa. Just a few months earlier, the two had worked together at a Brownie's hamburger stand. For the few days Alspaugh was in Quackenbush's hospital, "he would come and see me. It was reassuring to me."

Obligation to return

About that time, back in Tulsa, there was no such reassurance. On Dec. 22, a telegram arrived for Alspaugh's mother that effectively ruined her Christmas.

"It was delivered by a Western Union boy on a bicycle," Alspaugh said. "It said that I had been seriously wounded in action."

That was all it said, he added, except that further information would follow. "I don't know how long it was before she got word that I was all right. But that (first telegram) was pretty hard on her."

Alspaugh, meanwhile, wasn't doing so well. By the time he arrived in England — after stopping in Paris "just long enough to be bathed, fed and have our dressings changed" — his wounds were showing the beginnings of gangrene. Doctors went to work immediately, extracting what the shrapnel had left behind: bits of dirt, straw and fragments of his uniform.

With proper rest and care, and a lot of penicillin, Alspaugh recovered. Again, he was reminded of what a small world it was: One of the medics at the hospital, he was surprised to learn, was from Coweta. What's more, the man was receiving the Tulsa World by mail. He began passing on his copies to Alspaugh.

"It was the first newspaper from home I had seen since I'd been in the service," he said. "That was pretty special to me."

All told, Alspaugh's recovery would take more than three months. Near the end of that time, he said, "the doctor asked me if I thought I could go back," meaning his mental and emotional fitness more than the physical. But instead of taking the opportunity offered to be done with the war, Alspaugh replied in the affirmative.

"I felt an obligation to my friends to go back," he said.

Alspaugh, who received a Purple Heart and Bronze Star in connection with his being wounded, was reunited with his unit on April 28, 1945. Just over a week later, on May 8, the Germans surrendered. The war in Europe had officially ended. For the next year, Alspaugh stayed in Europe with his unit as part of occupying forces.

For the children

As an occupying soldier, Alspaugh found himself preoccupied by the desperate circumstances of the German people.

"We would smuggle peanut-butter-and-jelly sandwiches out of the mess hall and give them to the little German children." He's always had a "strong feeling for the children," he said.

As a father, he would raise four — three of his own, as well as his wife Emily's son from a previous marriage. A war widow, Emily lost her first husband when his B-25 crashed. Alspaugh met her after the war. These days, he still thinks a lot about children. More than anything, he wants to make sure they know about the sacrifices of the generations before them.

Alspaugh, who turned 91 on Jan. 4, 2016, served as secretary of All Veterans of Tulsa, formerly known as WWII Veterans of Tulsa, a group that for the last 20 years has provided speakers for schools and other groups. Alspaugh himself has been a frequent speaker. He made a public appearance on Veteran's Day 2015 at Jarman Elementary School's annual veteran's salute.

For many years, Alspaugh took his shrapnel fragment with him as a visual aid. He keeps it in a medicine bottle, which fits nicely in his pocket. "When we started going to the schools, I thought that would be interesting to them. And it has been."

Alspaugh said he fears kids today are not being taught about the war as they should. "That's why I keep doing what I do," he said.

PAUL ANDERT   ARMY 1940-45

A story to tell

Paul Andert keeps memories alive for younger generations

If you've ever visited his website, or received one of his regular emails — the ones simply signed "Old Paul" — then you know that Paul Andert has adapted to the computer age. In the summer of 2015, the 92-year-old Tulsan took another high-tech step forward.

"It was a first time for us and a first time for them," said Andert of the Skype session he had with high school students in Caen, France. "We exchanged views ... . They wanted to know what parts of France we were in (during the war)." Hosted by Oklahoma Technical College, the "first-time experiment went well," he said. "I hope to do it again soon."

Andert, who's devoted the latter part of his life to telling his World War II story, is happy to take ad-

vantage of any avenue open to him. Over the past 20 years, he's given hundreds of talks around the country to civic and veterans groups, schools and churches. He's appeared on "The Glenn Beck Program" and tackled film as an adviser on the WWII movie "Fury."

He's also written extensively, including "Unless You Have Been There," a book about his war experience. Fame was never his goal, but Andert is fine with a little notoriety — as long as it serves the greater cause: keeping alive the memory of the men and women who fought so bravely for this country.

The 'spaghetti' principle

Spend much time around Paul Andert, and you learn quickly that he's got plenty of opinions. And he can be unapologetically blunt when sharing them. But even when he's setting you straight on God or country or any other of his favorite subjects, his blue eyes never lose their sparkle.

It's the same when he talks about the war. A native of St. Louis, he dropped out of school at 17 and lied

Paul Andert, standing next to a destroyed truck, dodged death many times while serving in Europe. COURTESY

World War II veteran Paul Andert doesn't fudge on the messier facts of his service in Europe. COURTESY

about his age to get into the Army. Andert would be leading his own infantry platoon by the time the U.S. joined WWII. It was a job he took seriously, he said.

Taking his cue from Gen. George Patton — his commander in the 2nd Armored Division — Andert tried to lead by the "spaghetti" principle, he said.

"You can't push spaghetti, as it won't go anywhere," he explained. "You have to get out in front and pull it." In other words, "as a leader you are to show your soldiers you will not ask them to do anything you wouldn't do."

Andert lived by this credo. Even when an injury could have ended his war service, he wasn't about to ask his men to finish the fight without him.

"The doctor said he was going to do me a favor: 'You've been in three invasions, and I'm going to send you home,' " Andert recalled. "But I told him I'm not going home and sit in front of a radio and wonder what's happening to my guys."

'All the times I nearly got killed'

Andert was working on three book projects when he was interviewed by the Tulsa World. Of the two related to the war, one is about his recollections of serving under Patton. The other?

"It's about all the times I nearly got killed," he said.

The premise is simple enough. Still, with three years of front-line warfare experience, the task is anything but. One example will surely make the cut, the one about Andert's being caught between a wall and

a German Tiger tank.

"With nothing to do but hug that damn wall," Andert said he held his breath as the tank fired. The shell missed him. But the force of the explosion did not, and it catapulted him up and over the top of the wall to fall on the other side. A leg injury would cost him the next few weeks in a hospital.

Cheating death, though, can become a way of life. Soon Andert was at it again. An episode near Linnich, Germany, would be the first of three close calls in a row.

First, he was hit by shrapnel from an exploding shell. Then Andert survived the crash-landing of a plane and the sinking of a boat. The plane had been carrying him to England to recover from the shrapnel wounds when it clipped some power lines on its descent. The boat — crossing the channel to take him back to his unit — was accidentally rammed by another vessel. Andert, who came away both times uninjured, can't help laughing about it all now.

"I lucked out again," he said.

The ideal meets the real

Once Andert gets going, listeners are in for a ride. In a rapid-fire delivery that would put his old Thompson submachine gun to shame, he relates one incident after another, barely pausing for a breath. And he doesn't fudge on the messier facts. Recounted along with the brave and heroic are tales of friendly-fire incidents and missions gone wrong.

The treatment of prisoners, too, wasn't always pretty. But as Andert

Army veteran Paul Andert was platoon leader and served under Gen. George Patton in the European Theater. COURTESY

is likely to put it, "unless you have been there" you have no business judging. Also, while the "no man left behind" mantra sounds good, he said, in the field dealing properly with the wounded and dead was often impossible.

He recalls how once the best he could do for a slain friend was "to put his head back with his body and his dog tags." It wasn't much. But at least it would allow him to be identified later. Those memories, Andert added, are the worst. You never get over losing men under your command.

By the end of the war, Andert had participated in seven major campaigns and been decorated many times. He's proud of the medals — chief among them a Silver Star, three Bronze Stars, two Purple Hearts and the French Croix de Guerre.

But as gestures of appreciation, they take a backseat, he said, to something that happened when he first got back to the states. Boarding a bus for home, Andert was surprised and touched when a young girl rose and told him to take her seat.

"That," he said, "was the best homecoming I could get. It meant so much."

Making a difference

Andert had never met the woman before. But what she said after one of his presentations has stuck with him.

"She told me I changed her life," he recalled with a puzzled expression. Don't get him wrong: he was flattered.

"But I don't know how anything I said" could change a life. But as a sign that, just possibly, he's making a difference, Andert will take it.

His favorite responses are those from schoolchildren. Two walls in his home are devoted to the many letters he's received after he visited classes.

"Sometimes, dads will stop by (his home) and bring their sons," he said, "and I'll talk to them about the war and answer their questions." Andert spares his younger listeners some of the rougher details. Instead, they hear stories like the one about how he outfoxed his comrades once to get some confiscated German wieners. The image of Andert, his field-jacket pockets bulging with hot dogs, is one "they always get a kick out of," he said, chuckling.

'Young to be a platoon sergeant'

Another story that gets told often concerns a visit Gen. Dwight Eisenhower paid to Andert's base in England. Standing at attention with other 2nd Armored personnel, Andert was surprised when the future president stopped, looked him in the eye and said:

"Kind of young to be a platoon sergeant, aren't you?" Andert replied, "Yes, sir." "Lied about your age, didn't you?" "Yes, sir."

The two then exchanged some small talk, and Ike moved on. For someone whose service started with a lie, albeit a forgivable one, Andert is all about the truth now.

Which is why he's not about to quit speaking and writing. There's too much of it still to tell. How else, Andert said, will current and future generations know about the real experiences of WWII soldiers? Somebody has to tell them. And who better, he added, than somebody who's "been there."

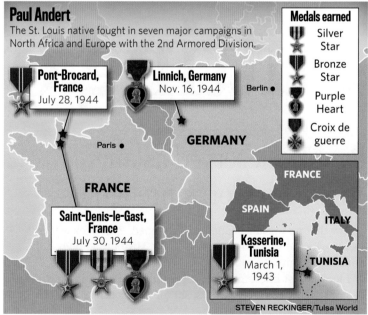

Paul Andert

The St. Louis native fought in seven major campaigns in North Africa and Europe with the 2nd Armored Division.

Pont-Brocard, France
July 28, 1944

Linnich, Germany
Nov. 16, 1944

Berlin ●

Paris ●

GERMANY

FRANCE

Saint-Denis-le-Gast, France
July 30, 1944

FRANCE

SPAIN

ITALY

Kasserine, Tunisia
March 1, 1943

TUNISIA

Medals earned

Silver Star

Bronze Star

Purple Heart

Croix de guerre

STEVEN RECKINGER/Tulsa World

Putting out fires

Paul Beck served as an Army Air Corps firefighter

Now that he was all cleaned and wrapped, Paul Beck couldn't decide what he was more worried about. His burned body or his wounded dignity.

"I looked just like a mummy. ... I couldn't do anything for myself," he said. "I had a slit for my eyes, slit for my mouth, and slit in my backside and around front."

Still, underneath all those bandages, Beck couldn't help but feel grateful. After all, he was alive. The bandages were just there to make sure he stayed that way. Beck wasn't the only one thankful to be alive. Somewhere in that same hospital was the man he had rescued.

Stationed on Guam as an Army Air Corps firefighter, Beck had helped pull a crew member of a downed B-29 from his burning plane. That's how Beck had sustained his own injuries — burns over 65 percent of his body. The man he saved had been seriously wounded, but he survived. For his actions that day, Beck received a Soldier's Medal, which is awarded for "heroism not involving actual conflict with an enemy."

'Easier to fly'

Today, more than 70 years later, the experience remains fresh in Beck's memory. But there's no sign of it on the outside. His burns left little scarring behind. Except, he said, in a couple of places that only he knows about and he's "not going to show."

Beck, 97, a longtime Sapulpa resident, welcomed the Tulsa World to his home in 2016 to share some memories of his World War II service. Born and raised in Cushing, things had been going pretty well for Beck after high school. He had married his high school sweetheart, Ann, a fetching redhead, and was off to a good career with Safeway, working his way into store management.

But then world events intervened. To avoid being drafted and to get his choice of branches, Beck, 25 at the time, elected to volunteer. He chose the Army Air Corps.

Paul Beck was severely burned in this plane fire. COURTESY

"It was easier to fly than it was to walk, like in the Army," he explained.

Flying wouldn't be part of the plan, though. Instead, Beck was trained as a firefighter. For the Air Corps, that most often entailed putting out fires on planes that crashed while attempting to land. Assigned to the 314th Bomb Wing, 69th Air Service Group, Beck would be sent to the island of Guam in the Pacific.

By this point in the war, January 1945, Guam was being used by American B-29 squadrons to launch bombing raids on mainland Japan. The island technically had been secured months earlier. But only technically. Many Japanese soldiers and snipers were still at large in the jungles, looking for easy targets.

Beck, part of a firefighter crew of nine, said he and his comrades were warned to stay out of the jungle: "Marines were still hunting Japanese and shot anything that moved." Beck never had any trouble with the Marines. But he did have one face-to-face encounter with the enemy. It happened one night as he and his crewmates were asleep in the tent they shared.

"All of a sudden I woke up," Beck said, "and I see this Japanese standing there looking at me with a knife in his hand. He was fixing to do some carving."

Beck reacted immediately, rolling off his cot and grabbing for the rifle he kept under the bed.

"By the time I come up with it, he had faded back into the jungle. He was gone."

Beck still marvels at just why he woke up at that moment. He didn't hear anything, he said. "Somebody was looking out for me, that's all I can tell you."

After Beck's arrival on Guam, it still took several weeks for Navy construction crews to build the base and airstrip where his team would be assigned. But once it was established, the bombing missions commenced. Their fire trucks stocked with CO2 and foam, firefighters had to be ready at takeoffs and landings.

It didn't happen often, but occasionally a B-29 would crash on takeoff, he said. Loaded down with firebombs and tanks of fuel, "if you lifted them too fast, the next thing you know you didn't have a plane. Just a ball of fire out there. It looked like the sun had just came up over the water. And there wasn't anything left out there to go hunt. It was all gone."

Returning planes faced their own challenges. Often they were damaged or nearly out of fuel, making landing that much trickier. Once, Beck said, a B-29 came back with one of its 500-pound bombs still stuck in the bomb doors. When the plane touched down, the bomb was jarred loose and went skidding down the runway. It didn't explode, he said. But "you never saw so many people running."

Paul Beck was an Army Air Corps firefighter on the island of Guam. COURTESY

Priority one

The incident that led to Beck's wounding and medal involved an incoming B-29. He remembers watching it touch down — it "hit too hard and bounced and landed over in the coral." The fire started immediately.

The first priority with a burning plane, Beck said, was to make sure the dozen or so airmen on board were safely out. In this case, his crew quickly determined one man was still inside. Beck and another firefighter entered the burning plane to look for him.

"We finally found him tangled up in some aluminum," he said. "By the time we got him loose — well, we had to leave an arm. He'd lost one (in the crash)."

With their help, the severely wounded man was able to walk out. Beck, who was following behind, was not so lucky. Just as he was stepping out of the plane, a fuel tank blew up. It set his clothes on fire and drenched him in 130-octane gasoline. Rolling on the ground put out the flames, but not before Beck had been burned over much of his body. It would keep him hospitalized for the next 2½ months.

It was an ordeal, he said. At the hospital, after medical personnel cut his clothes off, they "told me, 'we're going to have to clean you up.' They got a bucket of warm water and a scrub brush and went to work scrubbing on my skin."

Much of his burns were second-degree, and the "skin was peeled off, a lot of places gone." The scrubbing was the most painful experience of his life, he said. But it had to be done: They had to get all the bits of coral and debris "out of your meat."

Next, they wrapped him from head to toe in medicated bandages. He would remain wrapped for 12 days, a nurse "waiting on me hand and foot." Eight days into it, Beck said, "it smelled like I'd died. You talk about stinking."

When the bandages came off at last, the healing still had a ways to go. He had to stay "till the skin grew back. They didn't do grafts." Finally, he had healed enough and was sent back to his unit.

'God blessed you'

His time in Guam wasn't all waiting on fires to fight. When not on duty, Beck and his friends played baseball, went skeet-shooting or hunted for wild hogs. The natives there, he said, "were wonderful people to us. ... Life on Guam was good in general."

All told, Beck, who reached the rank of corporal, was on Guam for just over a year, departing in February 1946. After finishing his military service, he returned to his wife, Ann, and his job with Safeway. Soon after, at Ann's encouragement, he took advantage of the G.I. Bill and enrolled at the University of Tulsa. Earning a degree in accounting, he would go on to a long, rewarding career as an oil company accountant.

Beck likes to joke about all the pretty nurses and other girls who caught his eye during the war. But it's clear he was devoted to his wife. They wrote each other constantly during his time overseas. While he was immobilized with his burns, his crewmates took down his words for him. Later, Ann helped him put his war service in perspective, Beck said.

"Every once in a while, she'd tell me how fortunate I really was. She'd say, 'God blessed you. You should be thankful.' She was right."

The couple, who never had children, were married for 73 years.

Military firefighter Paul Beck and his crew. COURTESY

A plane burns during a firefighting exercise. COURTESY

Ann died in 2012. As for Beck, he's still enjoying life. Just three years shy of 100, he still drives, still goes to church, and every weekday morning gets together with a group of veteran friends for coffee.

As Beck looks around at the world today, and at the current generation, he doesn't like everything he sees, he said. Especially the preoccupation, as he deems it, with making money and getting ahead. His generation was more service-minded, he believes.

"We respected our country, our flag and our military," Beck said. "God has blessed me that I was able to serve my country, and I'm very glad that I did."

United by love, duty

Navy veteran Kay Berry served as an engineering officer on the USS Robert I. Paine. COURTESY

Kay and LaVonne Berry both served in the Navy

Eventually, Kay Berry would get around to noticing the rest of LaVonne Olsen. But for the moment, he was satisfied just taking in the splendor of her hair. A deep, rich auburn, "it was just beautiful," he said. "Amazing, really."

Seeing her for the first time at a ski lodge, where they were introduced by his sister, Kay wasted no time and called up LaVonne afterward. They made plans for a ski date.

A love for skiing was not unusual for young people in Colorado. But Kay and LaVonne soon discovered they had something else in common. Namely, the Navy.

LaVonne Berry was assigned to a hospital in San Diego where she helped treat sailors from the Pacific theater. COURTESY

Going to sea

Married now for 68 years, Tulsa couple Kay and LaVonne Berry have accumulated a lot of memories since they first met. They welcomed the Tulsa World to their home in June 2016 to share some from World War II.

Kay, 93, served as an officer on a destroyer escort ship in the Atlantic. LaVonne, 92, was a member of the Navy WAVES, the one-time women's branch of the Naval Reserve, and served at a naval hospital in San Diego.

Kay grew up in South Dakota, where his family had a farm. But with "the Depression, drought, dust storms and all that," they had to give up farming, he said. In 1938, they moved to Colorado, where his father worked in a mine.

Graduating from high school two years later, Kay went on to earn a degree from the University of Colorado in Boulder, and from there, already a Naval reservist, he attended midshipman school. In September 1944, he began his war service as an engineering officer on the USS Robert I. Paine, which as a destroyer escort helped guard convoys and hunt for German U-boats.

The convoys usually consisted of 50 to 60 merchants vessels, carrying supplies, arms and more across the Atlantic. The engineering officer, Kay said, "was responsible for all the machinery on ship. If something wasn't running right, they called the engineering officer."

The Paine's captain required all officers to take regular watch duty. Destroyer escorts were smaller than destroyers, Kay said, and "were notorious for making people seasick. They bobbed around like a cork. It took me about three days to get over it."

'Wanted to be a part of it'

About that same time, back in the states, new WAVES member LaVonne Olsen was preparing to report to the naval hospital in San Diego, where she was assigned to serve as a nurse's aide. Prior to joining the Navy, LaVonne was already helping in the war effort. At 18, after completing an aircraft instrument mechanic course, she had gone to work at Lowry Field in Denver, installing and repairing aircraft instruments. But military service was calling, she felt.

"It seemed like everybody was going. I just wanted to be a part of it," she said, adding that her older sister and two brothers were

World War II veteran Kay Berry served on the USS Robert I. Paine (below), a destroyer escort in the Atlantic. COURTESY

already serving.

Enlisting in the Navy WAVES (Women Accepted for Volunteer Emergency Service), LaVonne immediately felt part of something much bigger. On the trip back from training in Maryland, her train was so full of servicemen and women, she said, she rode the whole way sitting in the aisle on her suitcase.

At the hospital, LaVonne's job was to help to care for wounded men returning from service in the Pacific. Her duties ranged, she said, from giving patients their medicine to emptying bedpans and giving sponge baths.

The job hadn't been her choice. "They were shorthanded and needed people." But it turned out she enjoyed the work, she said, "helping the men get back on their feet ... helping them get through the day."

LaVonne has often thought of the men and wondered what became of them. "I was really impressed with the sacrifice they had to make for all of us."

The end of the war — with the U.S.'s atomic bombs forcing Japan to surrender — came suddenly, she said. "Just like that (it was over). And it seemed like the next day they sent me home."

Staying vigilant

With the war against Germany winding down, Kay's ship remained vigilant, dropping depth charges whenever a submerged U-boat was suspected. But the ship had no serious encounters. The closest Kay came to the enemy was a few days after the war in Europe ended, when his ship was sent out to escort eight German U-boats that wanted to surrender.

He recalls well his surprise upon seeing the vessels' crews. Instead of the war-hardened men he expected, "it seemed like they were either 16-year-old boys or 65-year-old men. (The Germans) were running out of men."

With the war in the Pacific still going on then, Kay and his crewmates weren't done. In the works was a planned invasion of mainland Japan, and for this, the Paine was converted into a radar picket ship. However, after the atomic bombs in August 1945, no invasion was necessary.

"You better believe I was glad," Kay said. As a picket ship, he added, the Paine would have been out in front of the invasion force, warning others of any enemy planes.

Right person, right time

By the time LaVonne met Kay at that ski lodge, they were like a lot of other young Americans — trying to pick up where they had left off before the war. She was back in Denver, working at Lowry Field. He had begun work at a Colorado Bureau of Mines research facility. Introduced through his sister, who had worked with her at Lowry, LaVonne met both Kay and his brother at the same time.

"Truthfully, I thought he was his brother when he called me later," LaVonne confessed with a laugh, recalling her surprise when it was Kay who showed up for their first date. But the wrong brother, she said, turned out to be "the right person at the right time. It moved kind of fast from there."

After meeting in February 1947, the couple got engaged in April, and married in September. They would raise three children together.

World War II veterans LaVonne Berry (left) and her husband, Kay Berry, pose for wedding photographs. COURTESY

Kay — who continued for 10 years with the Naval Reserve, finishing as a lieutenant junior grade — became an engineer in the oil industry. It was his job with Standard Oil Co. that eventually brought the family to Tulsa. In building a lasting marriage, the Berrys had several things going for them, they said, starting with "luck" and "compatibility."

"You have to persevere. We are perseverers," Kay added. "And you have to be able to discuss things and come to an agreement."

One thing the Berrys definitely agree on is how they feel about their war service. As Kay put it for both of them: "You didn't feel like it was any hardship. I just thought I was doing my part."

A life-saving letter

Arthur Bonifazi fought with the 94th Infantry Division in Europe

"Love, Patty."

Arthur Bonifazi can't say for sure how many times he read and re-read those words — or a variation of them — at the end of a letter. But whatever the number, it could never be enough. Thousands of miles from home, those written reminders of his sweetheart Patty Shurley's undying affection helped him remember what he was fighting for.

"She still lays claim to saving my life," Bonifazi, 91, said, recalling one letter he received while in Dusseldorf, Germany, near the end of the war in Europe. Sitting in a chair outside a building to read it, he had just finished it and gone back inside, when he heard the explosion.

It was an artillery shell. It had hit the chair where he'd just been sitting, blowing it to pieces. Today, 69 years into their marriage, she sometimes reminds him of it.

Arthur Bonifazi and Patty Shurley met at Tinker Air Force Base during World War II. COURTESY

Arthur Bonifazi is seen during his service in the Army in the European theater during World War II. COURTESY

"She says if she'd written one more line, I'd have gone with the chair," Bonifazi said with a chuckle.

Immigrant's son

A native of Dubuque, Iowa, where his father had settled after emigrating from Italy, Bonifazi was drafted into the Army Air Corps in 1943. While stationed at Fort Dix, New Jersey, he and his fellow troops often received USO passes to go to New York shows. One day, a buddy invited him to see the original "Oklahoma!" on Broadway.

But Bonifazi declined. He already had plans for an evening at the Ringling Brothers circus. Imagine his surprise, he said, when he learned the next day that he was being sent to Oklahoma. He was transferring to Tinker Air Force Base in Oklahoma City.

"I didn't know if that was punishment or what" for not going to the show, he said, laughing. If it was punishment, it worked out in Bonifazi's favor. It was at Tinker that he began dating Shurley, who worked at the base. They hadn't been together long, though, when word came that they would have to part.

Bonifazi was being transferred from the Air Corps to the Army. A year and a half after he was drafted, he was going overseas to join the fight.

"Patty wanted us to go ahead and get married," Bonifazi said. But feeling it wouldn't be fair to her, he decided against it. If he didn't come back, he didn't want her to be left a war widow. So they would settle for writing.

Shipping out for England via the Queen Mary, Bonifazi would serve with the 302nd Infantry Regiment, 94th Infantry Division, which would eventually be assigned to the 3rd Army under Gen. George S. Patton. Not long after they arrived, the 94th moved on to France in September 1944 and into the Brittany region.

A long way from giving up

Bonifazi remembers his first night in a combat zone, German flares lighting up the skies. "They loved to shoot those flares," he said. "They could see us, but we couldn't see them."

The next morning, as a patrol leader, he went to check on his men, who were huddled in their foxholes. He was in for a big surprise. Yelling to the guy on the far end, "I asked 'Who's in that hole next to you?' ... and a German soldier popped up out of it," said Bonifazi, chuckling at the memory.

The German, who had joined them sometime during the night, had no fight left in him. He just wanted to give himself up, Bonifazi said. Nazi Germany as a whole, though, was still a long way from giving up. In mid-December 1944, the German counteroffensive that would become known as the Battle of the Bulge began.

"There was so much artillery fire. I don't know how we came out of that alive," Bonifazi said. The worst part, though, was the cold. That winter was one of the worst Europe had experienced in decades.

"I was born and raised in Dubuque; that was cold to begin with," Bonifazi said. "This seemed like it was twice as cold."

Taking care of your feet was vital. Frostbite and trench foot were serious and all too common among the troops. Bonifazi remembers shivering in his foxhole, "feeling like I had to get those shoes off and try to get my feet warm." He took his shoes off, he said, and hung his socks up to dry.

If he got captured, Bonifazi recalls thinking, at least it would mean going someplace warmer. The unit was fighting throughout this time, and after the Bulge, when it resumed advancing, the opposition was still intense. Death was all around, Bonifazi said.

"You'd see one of your guys laying in the mud dead — they wouldn't even let us pick him up. They said the medics would get him."

A sample of some of the Nazi flags, armbands, patches and belt buckles Arthur Bonifazi brought back during his service in the Army. MICHAEL WYKE/Tulsa World

Among the many fallen soldiers he saw, he remembers one especially well — a guy from his company whom he knew. Bonifazi was catching a ride atop a tank when he saw the body lying off to the side. "I got his Bible off of him," he said. "I eventually brought it home. I carried it with me for a long time."

There were lighter moments, too. Once, while manning an outpost by himself, looking out across a river, Bonifazi suddenly felt a warm breath on the back of his neck. Freezing for a second, he grabbed the receiver to the outpost phone and swung it, trying to hit whoever was behind him. He was greeted by a slightly bemused "moo."

So focused on the river, he said, he hadn't noticed one of the local cows sauntering up behind him. Over the next few weeks, German forces were gradually worn down and began retreating. The 94th kept in pursuit, taking many prisoners as they went. "Near the end of the war they were glad to surrender," Bonifazi said.

Letters

Patty Shurley, who grew up in Sallisaw, started at Tinker Air Force Base after Bonifazi was already there.

"I remember somebody saying we were going to get a new girl Monday," he said. "That was Patty." It didn't take long for the new girl, who worked in the control room, to catch Bonifazi's eye. "One day," he recalled, "I got up the courage to get my friend to ask Patty if she'd be interested in going to a basketball game with me. She said, no, she was going dancing. ... But I didn't give up."

His persistence was rewarded. After he was called away to the war, their bond by then cemented, Bonifazi and Shurley wrote to each other almost daily. An attractive brunette, Shurley could've passed for one of the era's pin-up girls (she was "Miss Tinker Field" at one point). Once, when her photo appeared in a military publication, she began getting letters from all over from young servicemen.

Shurley felt it was her duty to answer them all and began corresponding regularly with some of them. Just hearing about her days, as mundane as she felt they were, seemed to lift their spirits. But her heart, along with the bulk of her spare time and stationery, still belonged to Bonifazi.

Dusseldorf

Later in March, Bonifazi's unit crossed the Rhine River. Their course would take them eventually to Dusseldorf, where they would remain for the next few weeks.

One of Bonifazi's memories from Dusseldorf was meeting for Mass one Sunday in a chapel. The chapel was connected to a hospital that had been partially destroyed by bombs. But there was enough of it left for a service. One thing was missing, though, Bonifazi said.

"The priest didn't have an altar boy — I guess all of them were in the Army." So Bonifazi stepped in. He might not have looked the part, dressed in his Army uniform, rifle on his shoulder. But afterward, he said, one of the nuns did compliment him on his Latin.

Bonifazi was still in Dusseldorf when the war in Europe ended in May 1945. Part of four campaigns with 209 days in combat, the 94th had more than distinguished itself. It would receive a Presidential Unit Citation for its contributions. He's not sure when, but Bonifazi remembers Patton coming and speaking to the division and "thanking us."

With the war over, Bonifazi's main duty was helping keep order in Dusseldorf. Priority No. 1, he said, was going house to house collecting any kinds of guns. Bonifazi kept a German Luger pistol he confiscated. But he ended up trading it to a guy in his company who had his heart set on one.

Bonifazi believes he got the better deal in return — a beautiful triple-barreled shotgun, which he boxed up and sent home for his mother to keep for him. Trading was also common with the German residents, for whom cigarettes were in big demand.

Arthur Bonifazi is shown on May 27, 1945, while occupying Germany during World War II. COURTESY

"I didn't smoke," Bonifazi said, "so it was easy for me" to trade his Army-rationed cigarettes. His best deal was a nice camera with a bellows that some Germans gave him for his cigarettes. Along with items he traded for, Bonifazi took home enough war-related memorabilia to stock a small museum. But several years ago, his home was burglarized. The most valuable items were stolen, including the shotgun. "It was a great shotgun," he said, still sorry for the loss.

Reunited

Discharged in January 1946 as a first sergeant, Bonifazi sailed for home on a Navy ship.

He'll never forget his arrival in New York and first sight of the Statue of Liberty. "They deliberately went by and then turned around, so the guys on the other side of the ship would have a chance to see it, too. It kinda made you cry," Bonifazi added, his own eyelids reddening. "After a year and half, you finally see something that you recognize."

An even better sight was waiting for him in Oklahoma. Connected only through their letters for all that time, he and Patty Shurley were reunited in the flesh. They married in Oklahoma City shortly after his return. The couple would go on to raise seven children together. Bonifazi graduated from Oklahoma A&M with a degree in mechanical engineering. He would eventually have his own firm in Tulsa.

Reflecting on his military service, he said: "People of this generation should really do all they can to keep the peace. ... I had a year and a half of good times (before going overseas). But war is really hell." He saw too many men lying dead in the muck to ever think otherwise. "When you see that," he added, "you'd think 'Who in the devil wants to start a war?'"

'You had a job to do'

Bowling saw action at Omaha Beach, the Battle of the Bulge

In an interview just before New Year's Eve 2015, Don Bowling recalled how the day used to set his teeth on edge. It wasn't that he didn't want to celebrate the new year. It was just that the noise of it all stirred the wrong kind of memories.

"The Fourth of July was the worst," said Bowling, 90. "All the fireworks — it sounded like World War II."

Quiet settings weren't all that safe, either. For years, if he listened, he could still hear the bombs and shells from the war. But eventually it all subsided.

"It took a few years but you got over it," he said.

Omaha Beach

The sixth of his parents' 10 children, Bowling grew up in the mountains of West Virginia near the town of Penoke and attend-ed high school in Beckley. It was while in high school, encouraged by a coach who was in the National Guard, that Bowling and a number of his classmates also joined the Guard. From there, in 1943, Bowling moved on to the Army.

Three of his brothers — Clarence, Glen and Ray — also served in the military during the war, but only Bowling was sent overseas to fight. Assigned to the 2nd Infantry Division, he was part of a group that, because of fears Germany might invade Iceland, trained initially to become ski troops. For that, Bowling said, they were sent to northern Michigan, where temperatures often dipped well below zero. He remembers "marching 25 miles in snowshoes, and then we skied back."

The plan soon changed, however, and Bowling and his unit were sent instead to England. There, they joined in preparations for D-Day. The invasion began on June 6, 1944, and Bowling went in two days later at Omaha Beach.

Although the fighting was not as intense as the previous two days, German artillery was still active. As he set foot on the beach, Bowling saw dead American troops scattered everywhere.

Don Bowling (back row, sixth from right) stands with his unit before deployment overseas during World War II. He served from 1943 to 1945 in the U.S. Army's 2nd Infantry Division. COURTESY

"I was scared to death. Everybody was, I think. You worried about it, but there was not much you could do."

The war, for Bowling, had officially begun. For the next few months, his days would alternate between fighting and looking for a fight.

The daily grind of infantry life "was the worst of it," he said. "Sleeping on the ground. Walking for miles and miles."

The fighting to capture German Hill 192 was fierce. But it was nothing like the battle for Brest. Brest was a key port the Allies wanted to use to bring in supplies for the invasion of Europe, and it took the Americans 46 days to take the city. The Germans were solidly entrenched. Bowling, who carried a rifle and helped out with the mortars, remembers having to climb atop buildings at Brest and move from roof to roof.

"That helped in surprising them," he said.

Finally, the city was taken. Afterward, one of the surrendering soldiers gave Bowling his pocket watch. Bowling kept it, he said, and still has it somewhere.

The more Bowling was around the Germans, the more he decided he didn't hate them.

"Probably they were just like us. Stand there and fight or get killed. ... Most of them were pretty nice people to talk to," he said. While, in general, he holds no animosity, he said he can't forget the atrocities he witnessed. He remembers coming across dead American paratroopers who had landed in the trees. The Germans had shot them as they hung there, helpless.

A job to do

As for the men he served with, Bowling has forgotten most of the names. It seemed like you didn't have much time to associate with anyone closely, he said. New faces were constantly coming in, as you joined with other units, or replacement troops arrived.

When men around you died, he said, "You had a job to do and you just had to go on. ... You couldn't let it affect you."

In December 1944, with the start of the Battle of the Bulge, as the final German counteroffensive of the war is known, the Allied advance was halted. Pushed back several miles before the tide turned, Bowling's unit was involved in fighting at Antwerp, Brussels and Liege, Belgium. The frigid conditions made everything more difficult. But Bowling had that winter training in northern Michigan to fall back on. One of the things he had been taught, he said, was to avoid the temptation to overdress, which would only make you sweat. Despite his precautions, Bowling later became seriously ill and had to be hospitalized.

"I think it was the flu. From the conditions," he said.

From Luxembourg, he was flown to England. That's where he was when a few weeks later, in May 1945, Germany surrendered.

"There was a lot of drinking and cutting up," he said of the reaction of his fellow troops.

Shortly after, he was on his way back to the states. All told, Bowling had spent a year-and-a-half overseas, receiving the Combat Infantryman's Badge and other decorations.

No desire to go back

Discharged on Nov. 23, 1945, Bowling eventually settled in Tul-sa with his wife, Betty Ann. The couple, who moved recently to Forest Hills Assisted Living in Broken Arrow, celebrated 66 years of marriage in 2015. They raised three sons and Bowling built a successful 30-year career with the office furniture company Scott Rice, doing the interior furniture design for many buildings in downtown Tulsa.

Bowling's sons, who came of age during the Vietnam era, did not serve in the military. He had made it clear that he did not want that for them, he said, due to "all the danger and everything." He spent too many years living with the nightmares to wish the experience on anyone else.

One of Bowling's sons traveled to Europe and he brought his dad some sand from Omaha Beach. That's about as close as he wants to get, Bowling said. Unlike some of his fellow veterans, he has never had the desire to revisit the places he fought.

"I just never wanted to go back," Bowling said.

A scene at Omaha Beach on June 6, 1944. U.S. ARMY

'Hell on wheels'

Tank driver served with Patton in famed 2nd Armored Division

The Germans had guns that could blow a hole right through an armored tank. Dee Burns had seen proof of it more times than he cared to recall. But still, he figured, there were worse places to be.

"I'd rather be in a tank than an infantryman out on the ground in a foxhole," the former World War II tank driver said. "It was scary at times. ... But you at least had a little protection."

To benefit from that protection, though, you had to stay inside. One time, during the Battle of the Bulge, a passenger on his tank did not — and it cost him. Burns remembers it well:

It was in a pine forest near Samree, Belgium, and the man, a colonel, wanted a better view, so he got out of the tank and went ahead on foot. A half-hour later, a major brought the bad news: The colonel had been killed by a shell.

"They told me not to look; it was pretty bad," said Burns of the

body, which soldiers brought back to the tank wrapped in a blanket. But he saw enough: "It looked like he was shot in half."

From there, Burns had to drive the colonel's body back to the command post. "I must admit, I cried during the trip," he said.

Sometimes, life in the 2nd Armored Division was everything its gung-ho nickname "Hell on Wheels" suggested. But other times, Burns said, it was just plain hell.

Fresh off the farm

Welcoming the Tulsa World to his home in 2015, Burns, 93, talked about the war and his days with the celebrated 2nd Armored.

His service began in 1942 when he was drafted. A native of Bennington in southeastern Oklahoma, where his family had a farm, Burns' trip to Tulsa to report for duty was as far from home as he had ever been, he said.

Sent to North Africa initially as a replacement soldier in April 1943, Burns was assigned there to the 2nd Armored Division. A unit that would be on the front lines for most of the war, crossing 10 countries and two continents, the men of "Hell on Wheels" were

Dee Burns drove an M5 Stuart light tank across Europe during World War II. COURTESY

proud, Burns said, believing that "nobody could touch them and that they could win the war by themselves." It was hard not to feel that way, given the swaggering confidence of their commander, Gen. George S. Patton.

Burns remembers hearing Patton give a speech right before D-Day. Close enough in the crowd to see his face clearly, Burns heard the fiery orator's famous declaration — that "we're going to rip out (the Germans') guts and use them to grease the treads of our tanks."

Patton could be intimidating, Burns said. But he was also respected, and in fighting for him, "somehow we dug a little deeper inside and pushed a lot harder."

Starting out, Burns served on a half-track crew in Africa and Sicily. But with the D-Day invasion pending, he returned to England and trained on tanks. He would drive a light tank — an M5 Stuart nicknamed "Tarbaby" — for the rest of the war.

Safe passage

Burns and his unit landed at Omaha Beach, Normandy, on June 9, 1944, three days after D-Day. Much blood had been spilled there, he said, and the sand was red with it.

Rolling through northern France with the 2nd Armored's 66th Armored Regiment, Burns was part of a tank company tied to regimental headquarters. As such, his job was to carry officers, providing them safe passage from one place to another. Unlike tanks in line companies, Burns' unit didn't directly engage in combat. But they were still in the line of fire — and in trying to dodge instead of engage, he felt their job was more dangerous.

Tough terrain and conditions complicated things. The worst, he said, was the ice and snow during the Battle of the Bulge, which made tank-driving treacherous. And sometimes, the deep snow hid horrors.

Like one field near Malmedy, Belgium, where Burns "could see arms sticking up out of the (snow)." It was the site of the Malmedy Massacre, where more than 80 American prisoners had been murdered by the Germans, and Burns had to drive across it a couple of times.

"I tried not to run over any of them. But I know I did."

Christmas 1944

Nightmarish scenes like that aren't Burns' only memories of the war. There are happier ones. Like Christmas 1944, Burns said, when the Army converted an old barn into a temporary mess hall and fixed the troops Christmas dinner. Burns and his crew were staying with a poor Belgian family nearby and shared their Christmas meal with them. The family had a little girl, and the soldiers treated her to small gifts.

While in France and Belgium, Burns also kept up a practice he'd begun back on the farm. After learning barbering while cutting his brother's and father's hair, in England he'd started cutting his fellow soldiers' hair.

"Over in France they still wanted me to cut their hair," he said. "Then the officers got to calling me; I'd have to go to their tents." His highest-ranking regular customer, he said, was Lt. Gen. John "Pee Wee" Collier.

From Belgium, the 2nd would enter Germany, engaging in more battles on its way to Berlin. Burns' first priority, he said, was still to "protect the officers we were driving for."

The 2nd was one of the first American units allowed into Berlin. While there, Burns would go into the bunker where Adolf Hitler and his wife, Eva Braun, had committed suicide just days earlier. There was still a couch at the scene with blood on it, he said.

Losses and gains

Burns made a trip back to Europe a few years ago, visiting many of the sites where he once fought. One special stop was Belgium's Henri-Chapelle American Cemetery. There, Burns would pause to pay his respects at the grave of Col. C.J. Mansfield. Former commander of the 66th Armored Regiment, Mansfield was the officer who had been killed when he walked away from Burns' tank.

"It was sad," Burns said, reflecting on the fate of a commander he admired. Unlike others he drove for — who would've "throwed your butt right out of the tank" for the smallest infraction — Mansfield "was a very caring man."

For Burns, the visit to Europe was a time to reflect on everything he lost in the war. Youth and innocence had been early

Dee Burns: Tank driver

With the 2nd Armored, the Bennington native transported officers from one place to another.

ENGLAND

HOLLAND

Rhine River

GERMANY

Brussels

Tournai

Maastricht

BELGIUM

Celles

M5 Stuart Light Tank
Dimensions: 14.44 x 7.35 x 8.92 feet
Total weight: 16.5 tons (33,070 lbs)
Crew: 4 (Commander, driver, gunner, loader)
Speed: 36 mph - road; 18 mph - off-road
Range: 99 miles at medium speed
Production (M5/M5A1 combined): 8,884

Carentan

Elbeuf

Seine River

Caumont

Paris

Domfront

FRANCE

STEVEN RECKINGER/Tulsa World

Dee Burns (left) and a buddy pose in Germany in 1945. Burns served in the 2nd Armored Division. COURTESY

casualties. The military "was such a different life than being on the farm," he said. "You were taught a lot, and you learned a lot on your own ... to keep from getting killed."

For all Burns lost, though, he also gained things. Like a new-found faith in God. It started before he shipped out, prompted by a chaplain who gave him a small pocket Bible. Burns kept it with him throughout the war and still has it, a prized keepsake he would never part with.

His fledgling faith grew, and later in his life Burns was called to volunteer. He became well known for his church mission and disaster-relief work, and for building houses for Tulsa's Habitat for Humanity. For his work in the community, he was recognized in 2000 with one of Blue Cross Blue Shield of Oklahoma's Ageless Heroes awards.

A couple of years ago, Burns decided to write down his war experiences. With a family member's help, they were compiled into a book — "Bennington to Berlin and Back with a Man Named Dee."

Burns is proud of having served with the 2nd Armored Division. But sometimes, he said, the myth overshadowed reality.

"I sometimes think it was forgotten that we were just a group of men, bound together by a war and a tank," Burns wrote in his book. "It was men in those tanks, men firing the artillery, men charging in the infantry — men that fought, bled and died."

Brothers in arms

Pilot, POW was the youngest of five brothers who served

They had all gone in different directions when the war started. But now that it was over, Bill Caldwell's first "band of brothers" could finally be one unit again.

"We all had wild stories to tell," said Caldwell of the first time he and his four siblings — each of them battle-hardened veterans — were together after World War II.

During the war "all of us got the daylights scared out of us," he said. "Well, except for Wayne (the oldest)," he added, laughing. "He said he had a good time."

For his part, Caldwell, the youngest, was just happy to be there. As a B-17 pilot who had been shot

down and held as a prisoner of war, he could appreciate more than anyone how such reunions are not guaranteed.

Had to 'fudge' on his age

Caldwell, now 93 and the last survivor of five Oklahoma brothers who served during WWII, talked in 2015 about war and family at his apartment at Burgundy Place senior living community in Tulsa.

Growing up in Durant, Oklahoma, Caldwell began his military service in 1936 with the National Guard. He had to "fudge" on his age to join, he said; he was only 14. But he was motivated because his brothers had served. Plus, "I liked the idea of getting $1 a week," he said.

Caldwell stayed in the Guard more than three years while continuing school, only leaving, he said, because of a football scholarship offer from the University of Oklahoma. But with the U.S. entry into the war in 1941, Caldwell, who by then had

Bill Caldwell poses in uniform during a visit back home during his service in World War II. COURTESY

moved on to Marquette University, felt strongly that duty called him to serve again.

Opting against infantry — "I'd been a ground-pounder long enough" — he joined the Army Air Corps. He graduated as the outstanding cadet in his class in May 1944. From there, Caldwell was assigned to the 8th Air Force, 452nd Bomb Group, based in Deopham Green, England. That November, he began flying missions.

Trouble en route

Caldwell remembers the impression his first bombing run — to Hamburg, Germany — made. The flak was heavy, but they flew so far above it that it never touched them.

"So we went back home thinking this was going to be a walk in the park."

While it wouldn't be quite that easy, Caldwell did manage to avoid any serious problems. At least, until his 22nd and final mission. Set for March 19, 1945, "they told us the night before it would be the longest flight a B-17 had made, and with the biggest bomb load. If we didn't think we could make it back, we were to land in Brussels."

Anticipating a little fun in the Belgian capital after the job was done, Caldwell's crewmates — "a bunch of spirited young fellows" — stocked up on chocolates, perfume and silk stockings. "But it didn't work out," Caldwell said.

The next day, en route to their target in Zwickau, Germany, Caldwell's B-17 was intercepted by two German Messerschmitt Me 262 jet fighters. The jets' vapor trails coming into view first, the B-17 took three direct hits before the crew even knew what was happening, Caldwell said. One of them was deadly, taking out their ball-turret gunner. The other hits set two inboard engines on fire.

Caldwell quickly realized the plane was doomed, but they still managed to drop their bombs. Then, he said, I ordered "all guys out." He followed them in the last parachute.

Help from a friend

Free-falling through the air from a high altitude, Caldwell said, is "like pre-op in the hospital — you just drift off to sleep." But this descent would be anything but restful.

Deploying his chute, Caldwell was "just floating along, big, fat and happy," he said, when a German fighter plane appeared and started circling him. He was looking for a "little target practice,"

Caldwell said.

Before the German could shoot Caldwell out of the air, help arrived. An American P-47 fighter zoomed in — "close enough I could see his face" — and ran the German off. He then circled back, Caldwell said, and gave him a salute.

"I never saw him again. But I sure felt better seeing him."

'Scared to death'

Caldwell landed safely, as did six of his crew's 10 members. But they and several other downed airmen were quickly rounded up by the Germans. After coming down about 20 miles north of Dresden, the new prisoners were taken to a nearby village, where it looked at first like their confinement would be short.

Four German soldiers had them all stand facing a wall, Caldwell said. Then, from behind, they could hear the soldiers "start tripping the bolts on their rifles." Sure they were about to be executed by firing squad, he braced himself. But after a few tense moments, they were told to turn back around.

The experience had "scared us to death," Caldwell said. "I think that's all they wanted to do."

Five stars

During the war years, no one who passed by the Caldwell family home could miss it — the service flag in the front window with five blue stars on it.

Mamie Caldwell was the only mother in Durant with five sons serving in the war. The flag would hang in the window until they all came home.

"She was a sweet little woman," Bill Caldwell said of his mother. "And she was so proud she couldn't contain herself; she loved to talk about her boys."

Having five sons facing danger abroad didn't seem to faze her, townsfolk noted.

"A lot of mothers won't ever go see their boys play football — not her," Caldwell added. As far as the war was concerned, she felt her sons "were doing what they need to do, what they were supposed to do."

Bill Caldwell: B-17 pilot

The Durant native was shot down over Germany and spent six weeks as a POW.

Hamburg

Berlin

Shot down March 19, 1945

Buchenwald

Weimar

Rhine River

Dresden

Zwickau

Nuremberg

Stalag VII-A liberated April 29, 1945

Moosburg

Munich

STEVEN RECKINGER/Tulsa World

The fighting Caldwell brothers

The five Caldwell brothers (oldest to youngest) and their World War II service records:

• Wayne Caldwell, Navy construction battalion, chief petty officer, 1943-45, Pacific. He died in 2000.

• George Caldwell, Army field artillery, captain, 1942-45, Europe. He received a Bronze Star and four Purple Hearts. He died in 2004.

• James Caldwell, Army Air Corps, technical sergeant, 1942-45, Pacific. He died in 2008.

• Floyd Caldwell, Army medical unit, sergeant, 1940-45, Europe. He died in 2012.

• Bill Caldwell, Army Air Corps, lieutenant, 1942-45, Europe.

The five Caldwell brothers and their father appear in a family photo outside their home.

COURTESY

If anything could shake Mamie Caldwell's resolve, though, it was what arrived in the mail one day in 1945. It was a letter from the war department telling her that her youngest son, Bill, was missing in action.

'A string of ol' boys'

From the time they were captured, Caldwell and his fellow prisoners would march hundreds of miles, he said — "just a string of ol' boys walking along."

They stopped at various places. Weimar. Nuremberg. Munich. But never for long, he said. They passed by Buchenwald concentration camp, and even a Hitler Youth camp, filled with goose-stepping boys in uniform.

Eventually, though, the POWs' trek ended. They would spend their imprisonment at Stalag VII-A, a prison camp near Moosburg, Germany.

Patton arrives

Caldwell came to view the German soldiers and civilians "in a different light than before the war."

Down through history it has often been the "vocal minority" that starts wars, Caldwell said, adding that "I bet 90 percent (of Germans) didn't want that war." Even at the prison camp, "the only thing they were really derelict on was food. Most of us were never beaten or punished."

Caldwell's stay at Stalag VII-A would be brief. Once they began to hear the guns, "we knew our guys were getting close." Liberation finally came on April 29, 1945.

Caldwell remembers the moment vividly. They were standing in the camp yard, he said, when the front gate swung open and Gen. George S. Patton himself — "on the back of a jeep, looking like he

was King Tut" — rolled in. The POWs flocked around.

"We were close enough," Caldwell said, "to see his ruddy complexion, his pearl-handled pistols."

But the general didn't acknowledge the POWs at all. Patton reportedly took a dim view, Caldwell said, of soldiers who "allowed" themselves to be taken prisoner. Still, he added, a gesture or something would've been nice.

'How close we came'

After the war, Caldwell came home, married Clare Hoard — "the most beautiful woman I'd ever seen" — and eventually went to work in Tulsa for New York Life Insurance, where he would stay for 53 years. He and Clare raised three children together. Interrupted only briefly when he was called up for Korea, they have been together for 68 years.

Caldwell is one of only two members of his B-17 crew still living. The other, Ed Howard, the plane's radio operator, is a close buddy and the two stay in touch.

Caldwell's memory remains strong. But if it ever needs any prodding, he has a few mementos to help. They include his decorations — three Air Medals, and another recognizing his time as a POW. Most special to him, though, is his mother's service flag. It hangs in his apartment in a frame, right next to his dog tag, the five blue stars still intact.

As the last surviving Caldwell brother — his brother, Floyd, died in 2012 — he's proud to be the flag's caretaker. Caldwell hopes the significance of his family's stars and all the other stars like them representing all the men and women who have served will not be forgotten, and that future generations will "be conscious and grateful and thankful" for their freedoms. They need to understand, he added, "how close we came (to losing them)."

BILL CLARK   NAVY 1943-45

Serving to the end

Veteran volunteered with honor guard for military funerals

Even after some 330 military funerals, Bill Clark's reaction to hearing taps hasn't changed.

"When it plays, there's always a lump in your throat," the 92-year-old Tulsa World War II veteran said in a 2015 interview. "I force myself to concentrate, though. I want to make sure I get everything right and at the right time."

As a member of American Legion Post 1's volunteer honor guard, Clark participated in funerals and veteran's parades regularly for 16 years. For much of that time, he was in charge of the rifle guard. Although Clark officially retired from the duty in 2010, a dwindling number of guard members means he still steps in as needed. So, make that 330 funerals and counting.

Clark got the call just a few weeks earlier, in fact: for the rites of Bob Hunt, a fellow former Post 1 honor guardsman who died in January 2015.

"I do it," Clark said, "because these men want it. ... It's important to them."

Aboard the Ward

Clark's own war experience began in 1943. Kissing goodbye his high-school sweetheart, Mary, the Drumright resident left to begin his service to the Navy. He was assigned to the USS J. Richard Ward, a destroyer escort in the Atlantic, where he would serve as a radar man.

Like other escorts, the Ward's main job was helping protect convoys from German U-boats. By the time Clark joined, the enemy subs were sinking dozens of Allied merchant ships a month and with them precious cargoes of arms, supplies and food.

During Clark's tenure, the Ward accompanied convoys across the Atlantic and back three times before later joining in U-boat hunts. By then, the escorts had helped make the sea lanes safer, and the

Bill Clark (second from left) poses during World War II with three other Okies he knew while growing up. COURTESY

The USS J. Richard Ward DE 243 escorted convoys to and from Europe across the Atlantic Ocean. COURTESY

Ward never engaged any U-boats. Still, Clark said, the possibility of death loomed over you, always just one torpedo away.

But as he and his shipmates manned their stations in the pitch-black darkness — it was too risky to allow lights at night — he kept his mind on other things. Like his Mary.

"Whenever I watched that radarscope, watched it going round and around and around, all I could think of was that beautiful blonde. ... I hoped she was waiting for me."

After the war, Clark enjoyed the community of other veterans who had served on ships like his. Today, there's one former destroyer escort left afloat, the USS Slater of Albany, N.Y., which doubles as a museum. Clark, who was involved with the group responsible for saving it, got to ride on it a few years ago.

"There was a big celebration when she came out of drydock, helicopters flying over. When we (sailed) by West Point, they fired their guns." Discovering that their guns, too, would still fire, he and his shipmates responded in kind, Clark said, his eyes flickering to life at the memory.

"We fired them all the way back to Albany."

The least he could do

After his discharge in December 1945 as a petty officer first class, Clark and Mary got married. Settling in Tulsa, they would raise twin sons together, while Clark, a mechanical engineer, worked for various companies, including North American Aviation on the historic Apollo 11 project. The Clarks enjoyed 67 years together before Mary's death in 2013.

After retiring, Clark stayed busy. A lifelong golfer, he's proud to have recorded five holes-in-one. But his most lasting legacy, he hopes, will come from what he did for veterans.

In addition to his Legion activities in Tulsa, Clark was a charter member of the group that helped create the National World War II Memorial in Washington, D.C., and was on hand for its dedication in 2004. He also led the effort to start Oklahoma's Honor Flights program, which flies veterans to Washington to see the memorial.

It's the least he could do, he says, to ensure that those who didn't make it home won't be forgotten. Clark's voice cracks when he talks about them, eyes tearing up: "400,000 (Americans) killed — that's a lot of people. Men and women. ... War is not good. It's just horrible. Any way you look at it."

One every 90 seconds

Clark is grateful to have been one of those who did make it home. But no one knows better than the longtime honor guardsman that

Bill Clark (right) poses with his eventual brother-in-law in 1944, during their service in the U.S. Navy. COURTESY

the generation's days are numbered.

"They say we're losing one every 90 seconds," Clark said of the rate at which WWII veterans are dying. Many of the funerals he's appeared at were for veterans of that war, said Clark, who has kept careful records. And a fair number were men he knew.

In the guard's early days, Clark recalls, his buddy, the late Bob Hunt, would pore over each day's newspaper obituary page, looking for funerals that might want a military honor guard. But the word gradually got out.

"Soon people were calling us all the time," he said, adding that occasionally they would even serve at two funerals in a day.

Clark, who turned 93 in April 2015, keeps looking ahead, unfazed by old age. He watches his calendar for the days he will fly his flag on his porch and makes plans to be involved at this year's parades.

"The best part are the kids," he said. "They love to wave their flags."

Still, when Clark's own date with an honor guard comes, he will be ready, he said.

"I've already got all of that arranged," he added. "It's going to be a Navy guard."

Danger down below

Sailor served aboard the USS Piranha as quartermaster

About 300 feet was as deep as John Cockrum's submarine had been approved to go in tests. But in the field, sometimes the limits had to be pushed.

"It was the deepest I can ever recall us going," Cockrum said, describing a 550-foot descent his sub once made. It happened during an attack, and it put a lot of water between them and the enemy ships.

But even then, Cockrum said, they were far from comfortable.

"It would be quiet for 30 minutes, then it would start again," said Cockrum, who was 19 at the time. When enduring a depth-charge attack on a sub, he said, "you just sit there and take it; you can't do anything about it."

Rocked by explosions, sometimes near, sometimes far-

ther away, the vessel would "undergo violent shaking. Lights blink. A valve might start leaking water."

This time, continuing off and on for more than eight hours, it was worse than usual. At one point, the captain had the pharmacist's mate go from one end of the sub to the other, Cockrum said, "passing out a little glass of brandy to each and every one of us."

"That was my first taste of brandy," he added. It didn't register then. But now he thinks his captain "probably thought we weren't going to come back."

Aboard the USS Piranha

Long since retired from Sapulpa Public Schools where he finished as assistant superintendent, John Cockrum, 89, talked in 2015 to the Tulsa World about World War II and his service on the Navy submarine USS Piranha.

Earning a total of five battle stars, including for Iwo Jima and Okinawa, the Piranha was part of a Navy submarine force that was vital to winning the war in the Pacific. It was a dangerous job, Cockrum said. Sailors

The submarine USS Piranha is seen alongside a sub tender ship in the Pacific. COURTESY

John Cockrum: Quartermaster

The Claremore native joined the Navy at the age of 17. He was assigned to the USS Piranha, a submarine that received a total of five battle stars, including Iwo Jima and Okinawa, during its run in the Pacific.

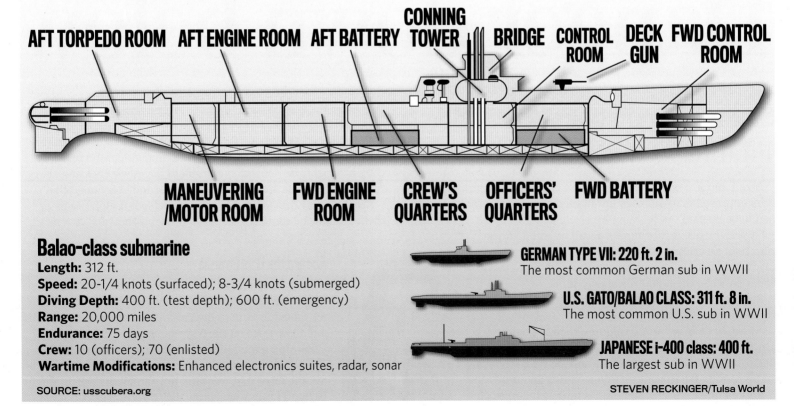

AFT TORPEDO ROOM AFT ENGINE ROOM AFT BATTERY CONNING TOWER BRIDGE CONTROL ROOM DECK GUN FWD CONTROL ROOM

MANEUVERING/MOTOR ROOM FWD ENGINE ROOM CREW'S QUARTERS OFFICERS' QUARTERS FWD BATTERY

Balao-class submarine
Length: 312 ft.
Speed: 20-1/4 knots (surfaced); 8-3/4 knots (submerged)
Diving Depth: 400 ft. (test depth); 600 ft. (emergency)
Range: 20,000 miles
Endurance: 75 days
Crew: 10 (officers); 70 (enlisted)
Wartime Modifications: Enhanced electronics suites, radar, sonar

GERMAN TYPE VII: 220 ft. 2 in.
The most common German sub in WWII

U.S. GATO/BALAO CLASS: 311 ft. 8 in.
The most common U.S. sub in WWII

JAPANESE i-400 class: 400 ft.
The largest sub in WWII

SOURCE: usscubera.org

STEVEN RECKINGER/Tulsa World

might survive a ship being sunk, but surviving a sinking sub was rare.

Facing danger was one reason "submarine sailors were kind of cocky," Cockrum said. Laughing, he added: "I wouldn't say 'kind of' — we were."

A Claremore native, Cockrum was in his junior year at Claremore High School when Pearl Harbor was attacked in December 1941. Later, as seniors, he and four of his classmates — anticipating they would be drafted — agreed to join the Navy together. For Cockrum, though, there was a snag: Too young at age 17, he needed a parent's permission to enlist. And his mother wouldn't give it.

"I told her it was the thing to do, that I had to go over there and win the war," said Cockrum, who was an only child. "But she was just dead set against it."

Finally, he succeeded in getting his father to sign.

"I graduated on a Tuesday night," Cockrum said, "and Friday we were on our way to San Diego" for boot camp.

In the Navy, Cockrum would choose submarines because "it sounded kind of neat." He trained, and eventually, in November 1944, was assigned to the Piranha in the Pacific.

'Doing some good'

A Balao-class submarine with a crew of about 70, the Piranha had already seen its share of war. Cockrum was named quartermaster and kept the submarine's log and other records, tracking changes in course, speed, etc.

When submerged, he said, the sub operated at a depth of about 60 feet. When it surfaced, he pitched in frequently on lookout duty, scanning the waves through a pair of binoculars.

Armed with torpedoes and deck guns, the Piranha would sink a total of 14 enemy vessels during the war. Cockrum joined the sub in time for about half of those, he said. The kills included warships and merchant marine vessels. In addition, the Piranha severely damaged many others.

Cockrum remembers the feeling — watching through the sub's periscope as another enemy vessel went down — that "we were doing some good, helping defeat the Japanese."

"We tried to sink every ship we saw. That was our mission. And we were pretty good at it."

To do that, of course, meant trying not to get sunk in the process. Ships carried depth charges — explosives released to detonate under water. Dodging depth charges remains Cockrum's most vivid memory from the war.

When under attack or one was imminent, the sub would go into "silent running" mode, he said. "(We would) turn off everything except for emergency lights. ... You lie on the bottom (of the sea) and be as quiet as you can, and hope they wouldn't pick you up on their sonar."

Living in tight confines and under those conditions took its toll. During breaks off ship, submarine men gambled heavily, Cockrum said. And even though they were paid more than other sailors — sub sailors drew hazard pay, 50 percent of their base salary — many burned through it fast.

"I saw a lot of money change hands," he said, adding that sub men, knowing they might not live long, often had a "devil-may-care" attitude.

Cockrum sent most of his pay home.

"But I did play some cards," he said.

The crew of the submarine USS Piranha with John Cockrum (standing in the fifth row from the front and marked with a small "x") is photographed in May 1945. Cockrum served on the submarine during World War II in the Pacific. COURTESY

A life in education

Balao-class submarines like the Piranha — and including the USS Batfish, which is now preserved as a museum in Muskogee — acquitted themselves well during the war.

While helping thin out the Japanese Navy, they were also credited with almost totally destroying the Japanese merchant fleet.

Cockrum came home after doing his part. He liked the Navy, he said, but "it made me realize I needed to get an education." Taking advantage of the G.I. Bill, he would earn his bachelor's degree from Northeastern State University in Tahlequah and a master's degree from the University of Tulsa.

Cockrum's career in education would span nearly 40 years, 28 of that in Sapulpa. He would go from teacher and coach to principal and eventually assistant superintendent.

He and his wife, Carolyn — three years behind him in Claremore schools — celebrated their 68th anniversary in November. They met while he was in the service and married afterward, raising one daughter together.

A different war

Through the years, Cockrum spoke often to groups about patriotism and military service — an opportunity he always relished.

As a high school principal, too, he tried to impress on his students "that someday it might fall on them to make sacrifices (like his generation) and defend the country."

Just how prophetic his words would be, though, did not occur to him at the time. He still remembers them well — eight young men from Sapulpa, just boys really, "brought back in those black boxes" from Vietnam. They were among a number of the principal's onetime students who served in the war.

A couple of years ago — while visiting Washington through Oklahoma's Honor Flights program — Cockrum wanted to find those students' names on the nation's Vietnam Veterans Memorial.

"But I couldn't handle it," he said, voice breaking. "I had to get back on the bus." Although from a different era and war, Cockrum imagines he and those boys were much the same at 17.

"When you're that age, I guess you think you're bulletproof. When I went in, there wasn't a doubt in my mind I would (survive to) go back to Claremore."

Cockrum and the four classmates he'd joined the Navy with lost track of each other until after the war. But all of them came home, where they got together to catch up and share stories. Cockrum said he is now the only survivor of the five.

"When you're 17, you don't know anything. You think you do," he said.

The Navy "was a good thing for me. I gained a lot of maturity. ... I'm proud of my Navy service, and I'm especially proud I was a submarine sailor."

Saved by a bomb

The 17-year-old was on USS West Virginia at Pearl Harbor

With the sailors' gifts having to be sent by ship, Arles Cole knew there was no time to waste. He needed to get his Christmas shopping done.

So on Dec. 6, 1941, upon arriving back at Pearl Harbor, Hawaii, the 17-year-old went ashore to shop in Honolulu. As he picked out gifts for his family, at one shop a picture of a Hawaiian bird caught his eye. He bought one each for his oldest sister and grandmother. And when the owner offered to mail them for him, he took her up on it.

Later, he would be glad he did: The pictures would be the only two of his presents to make it home. The others, which he took back with him, would go down with his ship, the USS West Virginia, the next day during the Japanese attack. When Cole got home

years later, long after Pearl Harbor and the war that followed, he saw the bird picture again.

"It was colorful and beautiful," he said. "At least I thought it was beautiful. Nobody else in the world thought it was."

Eventually, the one that had belonged to his late grandmother found a place outside Cole's own door. It would still be there, he said. If somebody hadn't stolen it.

There will be no stealing his memories, though, Cole added. Time and age have tried and failed. And at age 91 — and as one of Tulsa's last survivors of "the date that will live in infamy" — Cole has dedicated himself to making sure no one else forgets, either.

Destiny

Cole joined the Navy in 1941. But long before that, destiny, it seemed, had marked him for war. The second of three sons born to a Porum farm family, Cole got his name from his father, a World War I veteran who had fond memories of Arles, France, a city he had visited during the first war. (Cole's name is pronounced differently, though: "Ar-liss.")

At 16, Cole almost joined the Army. He had tagged along with his father and older brother, Jay, who was enlisting, when the recruiter in Muskogee made him an offer. He took one look at Cole, who was bigger and stronger than his brother, and said to their father: "I'll take him, too, if you'll say he's 18."

But his father wouldn't lie for him. So while Cole was willing, he would have to wait. A year later, in 1941, the opportunity came again — a Navy program, dubbed the "Kiddie Cruise," which would allow him to join early. This time, Cole seized it.

After basic training, Cole opted for navigation school. From there, he was given his choice of ships. He chose the battleship USS West Virginia.

The ship, home to more than 1,400 men, was stationed at Pearl Harbor, Hawaii, where it was helping guard against possible Japanese attack. Consequently, it spent most of its time practicing for battle.

"I was such a green kid from the farm, but I knew my battle stations," Cole said. He wouldn't have long to wait to put that to the test.

'Something was wrong on Ford Island'

Cole remembers the attack and events leading up to it vividly. The night before, after he'd returned to his ship from Christmas shopping, he went to sleep in what had become his usual spot: on a pallet on the chart table in the pilot's house.

The next morning, Dec. 7, he woke just before 8 a.m. He walked out on the wing of the navigation bridge, from which he could see the men on the deck below.

"I'm up there, stretching my arms, waking up, thinking about Sunday," he said. "All of a sudden, I see black smoke. Something was wrong on Ford Island."

The island was nearby in the center of the harbor, and it took only seconds, Cole said, to realize "it was the Japanese attacking." As alarm spread among the sailors, the urgent announcement followed, calling everyone to their battle stations.

"We had trained for this — to get to our battle stations as fast as possible," Cole said.

His assigned spot was in central station, from which the ship could be steered if something happened to the bridge. He had four decks to descend to reach it. Riding the handrails of the ladders down, he got as far as the third deck. That's where he was when the first torpedoes hit.

Hearing the explosions, Cole looked down the passageway ahead. There, he saw "two big gushers of water coming in the side of the ship."

It was the last thing he saw: "It went black. The lights went out. It was totally dark." He tried to go back up the way he came, but the

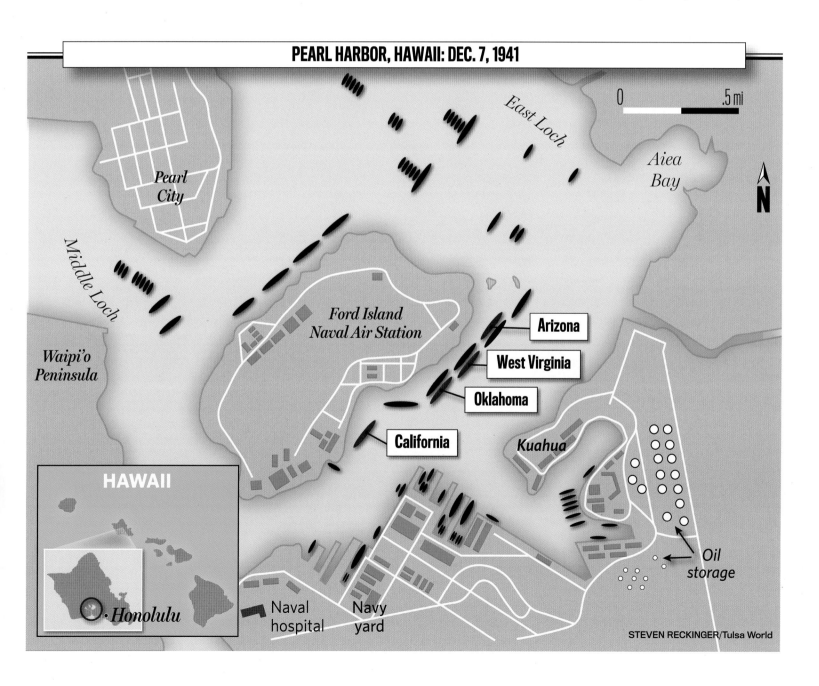

PEARL HARBOR, HAWAII: DEC. 7, 1941

East Loch

Aiea Bay

0 .5 mi

N

Pearl City

Middle Loch

Waipi'o Peninsula

Ford Island Naval Air Station

Arizona

West Virginia

Oklahoma

California

Kuahua

Oil storage

HAWAII

Honolulu

Naval hospital

Navy yard

STEVEN RECKINGER/Tulsa World

The destroyer USS Prichett is the ship on which Arles Cole served following sinking of the USS West Virginia at Pearl Harbor.   COURTESY

hatch had been sealed off.

Deliverance from above

Looking back now, Cole can only guess why he didn't panic at being effectively trapped. Possibly it was his upbringing.

"I was dad's tough kid. ... farm boy from Porum, Oklahoma. ... I was tough and I thought fast and I burned energy real fast." Wasting no time, he looked around in the darkness. Ahead of him, he could just make out a dim light and made for it. It was coming, Cole discovered, from a hole in the ceiling. A Japanese armor-piercing bomb had crashed through the ship's main deck. Thankfully, it was a dud and had not exploded. But the hole it made gave Cole his way out.

On his climb upward, he ran across a compartment with other sailors still in it, many of them wounded. He picked up one who was lying on his back.

"I'm strong but I didn't know I was that strong," he said of carrying the 240-pound man. "To me it was a miracle that I was able to."

By the time he got the man to safety on the main deck, Cole was exhausted. But not so exhausted, he said, that he didn't notice something was missing.

"I realized the flag wasn't flying. I ran to the lockers and got the biggest American flag I could lay my hands on." Then he returned and raised the flag.

The first day of WWII

Just under two hours after it began, the Japanese attack on Pearl Harbor was over.

The West Virginia, hit by seven torpedoes and two aerial bombs, stayed afloat for a few more hours, as Cole and others tried to fight the fires aboard it. But eventually the order was given to abandon the battleship. Cole was taken to Ford Island with other sailors who had lost their ships. He slept that night on the concrete seating of an amphitheater. He remembers waking up there the next morning.

"I'm laying there and I look east," he said, toward the home he didn't know if he would ever see again. "Then I looked the other way, west — where the Japanese came from. That was the first day of World War II for me."

More than 2,400 Americans died at Pearl Harbor, with another 1,282 wounded. Cole's West Virginia lost 70 men. It was one of four battleships sunk, along with the Arizona, California and Oklahoma.

Cole chokes up talking about the Arizona, which accounted for almost half the total killed — 1,177 men. The ship was hit by four armor-piercing bombs.

"If the ones that hit (the Arizona) did that," Cole said, "then why I didn't get hurt, I don't know."

'Everything at sea'

A few weeks after the attack, the West Virginia was salvaged from the sea floor and repaired. It returned to service in the Pacific. By then, Cole and the other survivors had been transferred to other vessels. For the next four years, he didn't see much time off ship.

"Week after week, month after month, we were at sea," Cole said. "Fueled at sea. Supplied at sea. Did everything at sea."

After a year-and-a-half on a mine sweeper, Cole, in early 1944, was transferred to the destroyer USS Prichett, where he spent the rest of the war. From its decks, in 1945, he fought in the Battle of Okinawa, where, as he puts it, "all hell broke loose."

The worst of it, he said, was the kamikaze pilots "zooming at us." Of the four destroyer escorts in his group, only the Prichett survived. Cole and his ship was still afloat a few weeks later when the big announcement came.

"We had dropped the atomic bombs," he said. "Katie bar the door — the war was over."

Cole came home shortly after that. He was still just 21 years old.

Doing the Lord's work

The war was a formative experience for Cole.

"It made a man, a strong man, out of me. A veteran — proud to serve my country, serve my veteran friends."

In serving his fellow veterans, he's devoted much of his later life to volunteering.

"I'm a strong believer in the Lord," Cole said, adding that looking out for veterans is just part of doing the Lord's work. Cole also perceives a divine mandate in his efforts to keep the story of Pearl Harbor alive.

Through Tulsa's Pearl Harbor survivors group, he helped get a section of U.S. 169 renamed Pearl Harbor Expressway. He also helped compile the stories of area survivors into a book for schools. Cole has returned to Pearl Harbor five times over the years. He's planning, Lord willing, a sixth and final trip — for the 75th anniversary commemoration in 2016.

One more time, he said, he wants to pay his respects to those who died at the place where it all happened.

Many of the sailors killed on the West Virginia had been trapped below decks, a fate Cole might well have shared. But somehow that dud bomb fell right where he needed it to.

"That escape hatch saved my life," he said.

"I was given a very special gift, to be able to stay alive," Cole added, unable to control his tears. "And here I am — still going."

And still taking every opportunity he gets to tell the story.

"I'm going to keep telling it," he said.

Supplying troops

Coley served with the Merchant Marine in the Atlantic, Pacific

Jim Coley's grandmother wasn't big on tearful farewells.

But while she didn't say much when he was leaving for the war, her words couldn't hide her concern.

"She said, 'So — you're going over all that water?'" Coley recalled recently. "I said, 'Yes, ma'am.' Then she said, 'Reckon you'll ever come back?' I said, 'Yes, ma'am. I'm coming back.'"

That, he added, was all that would be said about it. But then, his grandmother knew him well enough not to try to change his mind. "My grandma always said I was hard-headed," Coley said. "But I believed what I believed, and I'd stand up for what I believe. That part has never changed."

Coley, 93, welcomed the Tulsa World to his home in Bixby in 2015 to talk about World War II and his experience with the U.S. Merchant Marine.

A native of Meadville, Mississippi, Coley needed that hard-headedness, he said, just to get in the war. Almost blind in one eye from a cataract, Coley, 19 at the time, was rejected when he tried to join the military after the U.S. entered the conflict.

But that didn't stop him. Working as a deck hand on a dredge boat, he had seen the big merchant ships on the Mississippi River. "I thought, 'If I can't get in the Army, I'll do that.'"

It wasn't quite that simple, though. The first time Coley tried, the Merchant Marine turned him down, as well. But he tried again in May 1943, and this time he was accepted.

A fleet of civilian-owned vessels that during war doubled as an auxiliary of the Navy, the U.S. Merchant Marine was already playing a critical role in WWII, carrying troops, supplies and equipment around the globe in support of the Allies. "Somebody had to get the supplies to the boys out there in the jungles," Coley said. Otherwise, "they'd a been in big trouble."

With that role, though, came plenty of trouble for merchant sailors. The Merchant Marine would suffer a greater percentage of war-related deaths than any other U.S. service during WWII. Targeted because of the vital cargo they carried, the ships had to be alert.

"Many times there were enemy subs in the area," said Coley, who served in both the Atlantic and Pacific. "Our escorts would warn us and we would change course and run zigzags ... We never got hit directly." In Manila Harbor in the Philippines, "we had orders not to let a floating box hit our ship — it could be a mine they'd rigged. If we saw one we were supposed to shoot it."

'Keeping the gravy hot'

Coley's first voyage, after finishing his training in New York, was on an oil tanker bound for the British Isles. The ship carried, among other war necessities, 21 P-47 Thunderbolt airplanes.

Traveling so far from home was not easy for Coley. He left behind a wife, Pauline, and a child. "You was pulled," he said. "But everybody else was going and you certainly didn't want to stay. I wanted to do what I could." His second child was born during a later voyage — "I got the notice when I was going through the Panama Canal."

Most of Coley's time on Merchant Marine vessels would be spent in the galley. Starting as a "mess man," serving at tables for the ship's gun crew, he eventually worked his way up to second cook and baker, and then chief cook. "I kept the gravy hot," he said, laughing. In a way, he added, "pleasing that crew with the cooking" was the hardest part of the war for him.

After his first voyage, Coley would soon set sail again, this time on a different oil tanker. That trip, up and down the west coast of South America, lasted 10 months. His third voyage followed. This one, bound for the South Pacific and the fight against Japan, would give the cook his most bitter taste of war.

Human toll

A small cargo ship carrying ammunition and TNT, Coley's vessel would be one of the first allowed into Manila Harbor in February 1945 during the fight to recapture the city.

It was a scene he'll never forget. Five Japanese ships, he said, had been partially sunk. The harbor wasn't deep enough for them to go under, so there they remained, lifeless and half-submerged. And floating around them in the water, everywhere Coley looked, were dead men.

"Regardless of whether it was the enemy or whoever it was — (seeing the dead) made you feel worse than anything," he said. "No matter how tough you are, there's a tender place in you for that."

Coley said sailors at Manila were advised to sleep on land in foxholes, not on their ships. There were incidents where the Japanese scaled anchor chains in the dark and stabbed men on board. "But I never left my ship," he said. "I went aboard that ship in December 1944 and it was June before I put my foot on land. ... If I was going (to leave), it would be because the ship was going down."

Coley was still in Manila in August when Japan surrendered, ending the war. From there, his ship sailed to Australia and then back to Manila. He would arrive back in the states in October 1945.

Veterans at last

The performance of the Merchant Marine drew high praise, including from President Roosevelt. The general sentiment was "if it hadn't been for us we couldn't have won the war," Coley noted proudly.

And yet, merchant mariners who served in WWII would not be recognized as veterans for decades. They were finally granted status in 1988, thanks to a federal court ruling.

Coley says it never bothered him that he wasn't counted a vet. "We paid our own expenses. Paid our own way home. I never knew any of us who grumbled. We did it because it was our duty to do it. ... They were some tough ol' boys in the Merchant Marines."

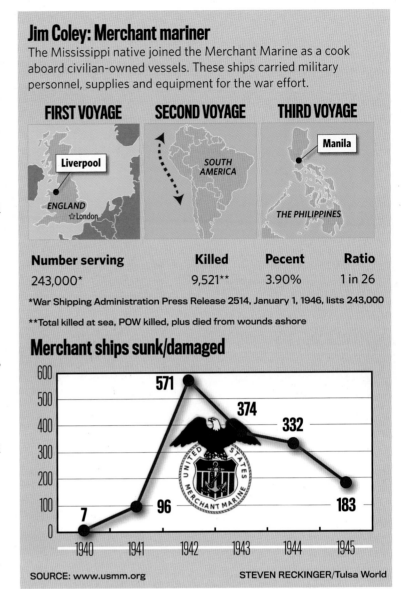

Jim Coley: Merchant mariner

The Mississippi native joined the Merchant Marine as a cook aboard civilian-owned vessels. These ships carried military personnel, supplies and equipment for the war effort.

FIRST VOYAGE — Liverpool, ENGLAND, ☆London

SECOND VOYAGE — SOUTH AMERICA

THIRD VOYAGE — Manila, THE PHILIPPINES

Number serving	Killed	Pecent	Ratio
243,000*	9,521**	3.90%	1 in 26

*War Shipping Administration Press Release 2514, January 1, 1946, lists 243,000

**Total killed at sea, POW killed, plus died from wounds ashore

Merchant ships sunk/damaged

(chart, values by year)
1940: 7
1941: 96
1942: 571
1943: 374
1944: 332
1945: 183

SOURCE: www.usmm.org   STEVEN RECKINGER/Tulsa World

Tough — but not invulnerable. In recent years, Coley has come to appreciate his veteran's benefits, he said, as he's dealt with a number of health problems, including a triple bypass.

'Got no complaints'

After the Merchant Marine, Coley would make a career in the oil industry. He worked for various drilling operations, including 21 years off-shore for Chevron. After many years in Louisiana, he moved to the Tulsa area in 1981. He continued working in the oil industry until 2007.

"The Lord has blessed me tremendously," Coley said, looking back on it all. "I've got no complaints about my life. I've left a lot of happy tracks."

His "no complaints" stance even extends to the hurricane. In 1969, Coley was living in Buras, Louisiana, when Hurricane Camille — one of the most devastating storms in recorded history — struck the coast. Coley lost everything, he said — "except the clothes I had on."

Even when events have conspired to take things away, though, Coley has gained in other areas.

Like perspective. Among the many words of wisdom he could offer, in fact, are some he'd like to say to his country.

"If the enemy can get us to fighting among ourselves and destroying each other, they can sit back and laugh," Coley said. "Let's don't fight each other over something that doesn't really amount to nothing."

Bringing 'em home

Bomber crew chief Lew Dillon had right tools for the job

Right before climbing aboard for their next mission, the pilot and crew members of A-20 No. 9 paused to hand something to Lew Dillon.

"It was their billfolds," said Dillon, who was No. 9's crew chief. "They'd give them to me, and say 'If I don't come back, it's yours.' I remember holding them in my hands as they took off."

As the man in charge of maintaining the plane, Dillon did his part to make sure they did come back. Once they were in the air, though, it was out of his hands, he knew. After a mission was over, "when the airplanes started coming back, you were always apprehensive," he said, adding that you never knew for sure if yours would be among them.

But No. 9 always turned up. Over four years and more than 100 missions, possibly as many as 150, the bomber returned every time, and remarkably never lost a crew member. "Some were wounded. ... Sometimes (the plane) had a lot of holes in it," Dillon said. "(But) thank the Lord they always (made it)."

If he wanted, Dillon — who served in North Africa and later Italy with the 47th Bomb Group, 84th Squadron — could take his share of the credit for his plane making it back. "I never turned an airplane loose that I wouldn't put myself on," he said.

But instead he defers to the pilots. "They were the real heroes. They were the best. I admired them so much."

Cry 'Havoc'

Dillon, 94, grew up on a small dirt farm outside of Union, Iowa. After graduating from high school in Union, he worked for his father on the farm for a while and then at a grocery store. But he got tired of it, he said.

So in January 1941 — almost a full year before Pearl Harbor and the U.S. entry into World War II — he joined the Army Air Corps. At three weeks shy of 19, the required age at the time, he had to have his parents sign for him, he said.

Planes from the 47th Bombardment Group, in which World War II veteran Lew Dillon served, fly during a mission. COURTESY/Mark O'Boyle, 47thbombgroup.org

Shortly after enlisting, Dillon got his first introduction to Tulsa. It would change his life forever.

Sent to train at Spartan School of Aeronautics, he met Vernal Moran while in town. It was during an outing at The Wheel roller-skating rink at Mohawk Park, he recalled. "She went skating right by me. I walked over and tapped her on the shoulder and went skating with her."

Vernal was 15 at the time and forbidden by her father to date. But by the time Dillon shipped out, after stops in Fresno, California, and Oklahoma City, the two were a definite item. Dillon hated to leave her. But, he said, "I signed up and was a member of the Armed Forces, and I was to go wherever they sent me."

Where they sent him, after a short stay in England, was North Africa, where the fight was on against the German Afrika Korps and Field Marshal Erwin Rommel. Assigned to the 12th Air Force, the A-20 squadrons of the 47th were there to support U.S. and British ground forces.

Unlike larger bombers, the A-20 Havoc light bombers had small crews of three or four — a pilot, bombardier and gunners — and typically operated at much lower altitudes. Often, they flew single-ship missions, and with no escort of fighters to protect them. Flying low, Dillon said, the planes tried to "lay their eggs" (drop their bombs) to where they would slide in underneath an enemy tank, to get at the "soft spot."

Often, this brought the aircraft dangerously close to the ground. Once, No. 9 came back from a mission with a phone line draped around a wing. On another occasion, Dillon said, the returning pilot asked him to check the propeller because "he was sure he had hit a German (soldier) in the head."

With crews changing over time, Dillon got to know several pilots of No. 9. Their relationship, he said, was one of mutual respect. "The pilots knew their lives depended on us. And my life depended on them — by keeping the enemy at a distance from our base."

The skill it took to land planes in the desert of Tunisia only made Dillon admire the pilots more. "On some fields there were no runways at all — just sod or sand."

Members of the 47th Bombardment Group, in which World War II veteran Lew Dillon served. COURTESY/Mark O'Boyle, www.47thbombgroup.org.

American ingenuity

Assigned to the same plane, Dillon said: "It was almost like it was a person. You thought you understood it. It only put out what you put into it."

Challenges to the job included the harsh setting — "sands of the desert ruined a lot of engines" — and a lack of supplies and equipment. With the latter, "American ingenuity" could overcome a lot, Dillon said. The tin from cans of Spam, for example, worked well for patching flak and bullet holes in the planes.

Bases frequently had to endure air raids, sometimes two or three times a day. "Anybody who claims they weren't afraid during a raid is a liar," Dillon said, recalling how German planes swooped in, strafing and bombing as they went.

The 47th Bombardment Group dealt destruction to the enemy during World War II. COURTESY/Mark O'Boyle, 47thbombgroup.org.

A-20 attack bomber No. 9 is the plane that 47th Bomb Group crew chief Lew Dillon worked on during the war. COURTESY/Mark O'Boyle, www.47thbombgroup.org.

Lew Dillon: Crew chief

The Iowa native was assigned to the care and maintenance of A-20 No. 9, a light attack bomber, in North Africa.

Battle of Kasserine Pass
February 19–24, 1943

	Allies:	Axis:
Strength	30,000	22,000
Casualties (including Sidi Bou Zid)	10,000 (6,500 Americans)	2,000
	183 tanks	34 tanks

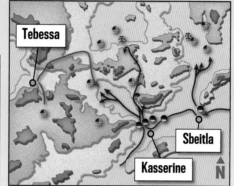

Axis line of defense
Allied movements
Axis reinforcements

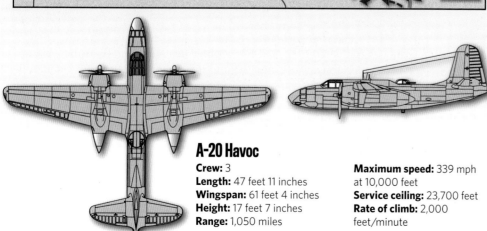

A-20 Havoc

Crew: 3
Length: 47 feet 11 inches
Wingspan: 61 feet 4 inches
Height: 17 feet 7 inches
Range: 1,050 miles

Maximum speed: 339 mph at 10,000 feet
Service ceiling: 23,700 feet
Rate of climb: 2,000 feet/minute

STEVEN RECKINGER/Tulsa World

He remembers his first raid well. Jumping in a foxhole a few feet from his plane as the firing began, Dillon climbed out afterward to find a large hole underneath his plane — a bomb had hit and slid up under it. "It was a dud. If it hadn't been, it would have blown my plane up and possibly me, too." It was one of many examples, he said, of how "the Lord was with me."

The Battle of Kasserine Pass in Tunisia in mid-February 1943 — the Americans' first major engagement with the more battle-hardened Germans — would go down as one of the nation's worst military defeats ever.

But for Dillon and the 47th, it was to be their finest hour. On Feb. 22, though short on men and supplies, the group flew 11 missions, attacking the German armored columns and keeping them from breaking through American lines.

No sooner had the planes returned from each mission, it seemed, than they had to take off again, said Dillon, who was stationed at Youks-les-Bains. The air crews worked around the clock. "We had a lot of servicing to do" on No. 9 that day, Dillon said. For its performance at Kasserine Pass, the 47th Bomb Group was awarded a Distinguished Unit Citation.

'Never wanted to see another airplane'

Lew and Vernal wrote each other just about every day while he was away. Two weeks after he got home in 1945, they married. They raised four children together. The couple celebrated their 70th anniversary July 15, 2015.

At first, when he left the service, he "never wanted to see another airplane again," Dillon said. But that feeling wouldn't last. He went on to a 32-year career with American Airlines, including as an aircraft mechanic and instructor.

Later on, he reunited with many of his fellow 47th Bomb Group veterans. Dillon attended group reunions annually — 20 in all through the last one in 2002. "It was getting too hard for the members to travel," he said of the decision to discontinue it.

One place Dillon still travels frequently — if only in his mind — is the North Africa American Cemetery in Carthage, Tunisia. Unlike other cemeteries home to American war dead, he said, "a lot of people don't know about it."

When he thinks about the men buried there — Americans who died in the North African Campaign — Dillon gets emotional. "The ones that gave everything are my superheroes," he said. "Next, are those who gave body parts — were wounded. Third is anybody who has worn or is wearing the uniform and has not disgraced it. ... Those are heroes."

Images of Iwo Jima

Lloyd Dinsmore fought with a Marine amtank crew

The best part of leaving Iwo Jima? For Lloyd Dinsmore, it had to be the shower.

As Dinsmore and his fellow Marines climbed aboard the ship that would take them to Hawaii, they were offered a choice, he said: "What did we want first — a hot breakfast or a hot shower." It was an easy choice, he said. Over the previous four weeks on the island, there had been no bathing or showers. He made it count, he added, letting the hot water run over his face and body for about 45 minutes. It would take multiple showers, he said, to fully wash the black sludge from the island's volcanic ash out of his hair.

Dinsmore would be disappointed, though, if he thought he could ever wash Iwo Jima out of his head. More than 70 years later, at age 93, he still lives with the horrifying images.

Amphibious tanks

Dinsmore welcomed the Tulsa World to his home in 2016 to talk about his experiences serving with a Marine Corps tank crew in the Pacific war.

The youngest of eight children, he grew up in Missouri, where he graduated from Galt High School in 1940. From there, he went to work on a cattle ranch. But in 1943, at age 20, the draft would call him away. Kissing his sweetheart, Lois Colter, goodbye at Union Station in Kansas City, Dinsmore caught a train west to begin his service with the Marines. With his two brothers quite a bit older, he would be the only one of the Dinsmore siblings to serve in World War II.

In San Diego, Dinsmore was assigned to the 2nd Armored Amphibian Battalion. It was a recently formed unit, and boasted a new kind of tank that had not yet been used in combat — an amphibious tank, or "amtank" as it was often called. Designed to travel on land and water, the tanks could be transported to within several thousand yards of an island and released, making them useful in leading invasions.

Dinsmore was one of two ammunition handlers on his seven-member crew. It was his job to assemble the tank's 75 mm shells, which came in two pieces, and then pass them to the loader to be fired at the target.

By the time Dinsmore arrived on Saipan in September 1944, the tanks had already seen their first action on the island in June, clearing the way for Marine infantry landing behind them. "The battle was pretty well over," he said, "but there were still a lot of Japanese soldiers. They had taken to the high hills on the island ... and would make night raids."

Saipan represented several firsts for Dinsmore, not only his initial fighting experience but his first loss of a comrade, as well. The latter happened about 2 o'clock one morning, he said. "Caught unawares" by a Japanese air raid, the base sounded its warning sirens a little late.

Before Dinsmore and his crewmates could make it to their foxholes, one of the Japanese planes found them. "We got caught in this open space — where jungle had been cleared to make a softball field." The plane had been hit and was going to crash — but it was still able to fire its guns. "We hit the deck," Dinsmore said.

That undoubtedly saved most of them, he added. But one Marine, John Bistline, was not so lucky.

"It happened so fast. ... He had been standing right next to me," Dinsmore said of his crewmate. Hit by gunfire, Bistline died at the scene, Dinsmore said, cradled in the arms of another crew member.

'26 days and 27 nights'

The invasion of Iwo Jima began in February 1945. After Saipan, it was the next stop for Dinsmore and the 2nd Battalion. The job of the amtanks would be to accompany the 4th and 5th Marine Divisions, and lead the way onto the island.

An "8-square-mile hunk of sand and rock" whose most distinguishing characteristic was its black beaches — the sand is volcanic ash — Iwo Jima would demand everything of Dinsmore and his crew for the next 26 days and 27 nights. "We fought our way from one end of the island to the other," he said.

It didn't start smoothly. As they moved in for their initial landing, the advancing amtanks hit a wall of volcanic ash at the water's edge that they could not get past.

For Dinsmore's tank, the situation was even worse. The clutch overheated and went out. "The tank wouldn't move," he said, adding that just sitting there made them "a prime target for enemy guns — and they had an array of them." Forced to abandon the tank with enemy fire exploding all around, the crew dug in on the beach. After 45 minutes, time for the clutch to cool, they got back in the tank and retreated back out to sea with the others.

That's where Dinsmore spent the night — afloat with his crew in their tank. They had quite a view, he said, as the Navy ships and the Japanese on the island continuously fired on each other. "It went on all night. ... It was like a thousand Fourth of Julys," he said.

The next day, a Navy construction battalion cleared away the ash wall, and Dinsmore's and the other tanks were able to make a successful landing.

Tank warfare

From their station in the belly of the 26-foot-long tank, "it was a pretty scary-type operation," Dinsmore said of being an ammunition handler. "You never knew when this thing was going to take a round from an enemy." A direct hit and everyone inside could be burned alive.

At the same time, being inside a tank "gave us some protection

Amphibious tanks at the battle of Iwo Jima. COURTESY

Lloyd Dinsmore said mail was often delayed. He said he once received a delivery of 110 letters. MATT BARNARD/ Tulsa World

that regular foot Marines didn't have. Fortunately, we never took a direct hit. It was just a blessing that we didn't."

Another blessing, Dinsmore said, was the sight of the American flag when Marines raised it on top of Mount Suribachi. The subject of the famous photo by Associated Press photographer Joe Rosenthal — who was there to snap it as it happened — it was an inspiring moment, Dinsmore said.

Unbeknownst to many, there were actually two flags. The photo was of the second flag raised — much larger than the one it replaced. Dinsmore saw both events. Fighting at the base of the mountain, his tank was "approximately 500 feet below where these guys were" who raised the flag.

It triggered an ecstatic chorus, he said. Between the ships in the harbor and Marines on shore "everyone was shouting — it sounded like OU had just scored a touchdown," Dinsmore said. "All of us were like 'Gee, this fight's already over.' But it wasn't."

In later years, seeing Rosenthal's Pulitzer Prize-winning photo would give Dinsmore a feeling of "extreme pride." At the time, we didn't understand the impact that it (the image) had on the nation as a whole."

After the taking of Suribachi, there was still plenty of fighting left to do. And that meant more dying. "We saw men killed in many different ways," Dinsmore noted grimly.

One incident he didn't witness — but which, strangely, still plays over and over in his mind as if he did — involved another young Marine. "He had been attacked (hand to hand) by two Japanese soldiers. He cried out 'Mom, mom, they're killing me!' " Dinsmore pauses as he recounts this. Eyes reddening, he has to change the subject.

Troops in combat could not receive regular mail from home, and so it often piled up. Once, Dinsmore received 110 letters at one time. That's what happens, he said, when you have a girlfriend, parents and seven older siblings writing to you. "I sorted them by author," he said. "Took me several weeks to read them all." He read Lois' first, of course, he said with a smile.

Almost four weeks after Dinsmore's unit arrived on Iwo Jima, the island was mostly secured and the unit's work was done. From there, he and the others sailed back to Maui to rest up for the next mission.

That was supposed to be the invasion of mainland Japan, as Dinsmore later learned. But the atomic bombs dropped on Hiroshima and Nagasaki in August 1945 convinced Japan to surrender. Suddenly, invasion was no longer necessary.

When the news of the first bomb broke, Dinsmore was still on Maui — mere hours, he said, from shipping out for Japan. "We were elated," he said. "The fact that this whole mess was probably going to be drawing to a close. As bad as those A-bombs were, they actually saved a lot of lives. There would've been untold lives lost — Japanese civilians, American military — in an invasion."

Back at home

After the war, Dinsmore went on to a career with the federal government, most of it with the Department of Labor. The family lived in Kansas City and then Houston, before moving to Tulsa in 1982. Dinsmore and his wife, Lois — who celebrated their 70th anniversary in June 2016 — raised a son and daughter. Of their five grandchildren, two have gone on to distinguished careers in the Navy.

Active with veterans groups in Tulsa, including the Marine Corps League and All Veterans of Tulsa, Dinsmore has spoken publicly many times about his experiences, including for programs about Iwo Jima at the Circle Cinema. Over the years, Dinsmore kept in touch with his fellow crew members. Until age made travel difficult, the group got together for regular reunions.

As for reuniting with Iwo Jima, Dinsmore probably won't ever get closer than the small vial of sand he has from the island. A gift from someone a few years ago, the tiny black pellets remind him of the island and all who fought there, answering their country's call. "I am honored to have been a small part of a job that needed to be done," Dinsmore said.

The canteen and knife were used by World War II veteran Lloyd Dinsmore. MATT BARNARD/Tulsa World

JAY AND WINIFRED DUDLEY ARMY AIR CORPS 1943-45

In love and war

The Dudleys volunteered for the Army Air Corps

Jay Dudley during his service in the Army Air Corps during World War II.

From her command post at the clinic's information desk, Winifred Dudley has watched it unfold time after time.

"Our waiting room (is) not like other doctors' waiting rooms," the volunteer said of Tulsa Veterans Clinic. Instead of sitting quietly or thumbing through magazines, she said, patients want to engage. "They ask each other, 'Where were you?' — 'What did you do?' ... Vets are a close-knit group."

An Army veteran in her own right, Dudley, 93, has asked those questions plenty of times herself.

And she's answered them.

But when she does, her stories are never just about her. Among the countless things Dudley has in common with her husband, Jay — starting with a hometown and a high school alma mater — they also share a war.

Winifred Dudley appears in a military portrait made during her service.

Two grades ahead

The quieter of the two, and content to let his wife do most of the talking, Jay Dudley, 95, sometimes gets talked into things.

For instance, when the Tulsa World visited their apartment in 2015 for an interview, the two were wearing their uniforms — Winifred Dudley's idea. A regular at veterans events, she still dons her uniform frequently, whereas, with Jay, "it took an act of Congress to get him into his," she confided.

Jay and Winifred — or "Freddie," as friends and family call her — hail from the small town of Westville in Adair County. Their mothers had been best friends growing up, so they knew each other as children. But Jay was two grades ahead in school, and their relationship wouldn't become more than friendship until after World War II.

For Jay, his part in the war began in 1942. He decided to volunteer, figuring he was about to be drafted, and chose the Army Air Corps. He was trained as an aircraft mechanic and assigned to the 387th Bomb Group, which was sent to England in June 1943.

As chief mechanic, Jay was supposed to be strictly ground crew, repairing and maintaining the unit's B-26 Marauders. But he said he did a little bit of everything. He even went on a few flights, he said, adding with a laugh, "when I was pretty sure they weren't going into too hot a spot."

'You remember it'

During his time overseas, Jay, who attained the rank of sergeant, served in France, Belgium, Holland and Germany, including the Battle of the Bulge.

He wasn't involved directly in fighting, he said, but he didn't come away unscathed, either. Once, while working on a B-26, his assistants accidentally dropped the plane's landing gear on him. "It landed right on my back," he said. "And it weighs about 800 pounds." He's undergone four back surgeries related to the injury over the years.

There are images Jay would just as soon forget, too, but can't. Such as the water off the English coast, red-tinged with blood after D-Day, and the concentration camps in Germany. The camps had already been liberated, he said, but he could still smell bodies burning.

Winifred Dudley (right) with other WAACS in training during her service in the Women's Army Air Corps during World War II. COURTESY

Jay Dudley works on a B-26 during his service in the Army Air Corps during World War II. COURTESY

"Something as bad as that was, you remember it."

He remembers some of the former occupants, too, "underfed and in terrible shape, almost dead. I was an Air Force guy. It was not my job to see that kind of stuff. It just happened to be where I was."

'Go for it!'

While Jay was serving in Europe, Winifred Whelchel was doing her part back in the States.

She started in 1943 as a civilian, working the graveyard shift at Douglas Aircraft in Tulsa, where she helped assemble B-24 bombers. While there, she learned that the military was taking women. That interested her, she said, so she talked to her father.

"I said 'What do you think about it?' " Her dad, who regretted missing his chance to serve in World War I, didn't mince words.

"Go for it!" he said.

Considering her options, Winifred chose the Women's Army Air Corps (WAAC). She joined in June 1943 and was sent for basic training to Fort Oglethorpe, Georgia. Assigned to the 3rd and later 5th Ferrying Groups of Air Transport Command, she served at eight bases around the country over the next two years; her longest stint was in Dallas.

Her duties ran the gamut, she said. With air transport, she helped load and unload the planes, which carried everything from mail and supplies to blood plasma. Once she was even a chaplain's assistant. This still brings a chuckle, even after 70 years: "I'm a Baptist," she said, "and I was a Catholic chaplain's assistant." Later, with a mobile separation center, she helped discharge troops at bases.

Military life served her well, Winifred said, and every generation could stand to experience it. "In the military you learned to obey and follow orders, discipline. You learned to get by with nothing — to sit on a foot locker because you didn't have a chair.

"I matured pretty quick. And I'm very glad I did it."

Marriage or Okinawa

By the time the war ended in August 1945, Jay and Winifred still had no clue what the future held for them. But come November, it suddenly got a lot clearer and fast.

Still in the Army, Winifred had come home to Westville to attend her grandfather's funeral. While there, she ran into Jay downtown. He was out of the service by then. That chance meeting, Jay said, led to an invitation to have a soda at the drugstore.

"And doggone it," he adds, "if I didn't marry her."

Up to that point, Winifred's plan had been to return to the Army. She was due to ship out for Okinawa, where she would've spent the next two years.

But instead, on Dec. 4, 1945, she exchanged Army khaki for a white wedding dress. The whirlwind courtship, encouraged by both sets of parents, had taken only three weeks.

"It was either get married or go to Okinawa," Winifred said, laughing.

Gratitude

These days, Jay is taking things slower, age and declining health catching up with him. But Winifred is still very much on the go. After eight years, she remains a popular volunteer at the VA clinic, where she works every Tuesday. She's also involved with Oklahoma Honor Flights. She calls herself a "recruiter" and has been responsible for no small number of veterans going on the trips.

Winifred, whose eyesight is becoming a problem, is also active with a Tulsa group for blind and visually impaired veterans.

All of this is volunteer work. She does get a $5.99 meal voucher for every shift at the clinic, but she usually gives that away to a veteran who can't afford a meal.

For the last 25 years, ever since moving to Tulsa, Winifred also has participated in the annual Tulsa Veterans Day Parade. "I walked

Jay Dudley (left) stands with a buddy in front of a B-26 during his service in the Army Air Corps. COURTESY

Winifred Dudley (standing right) poses with other WAACS in the Women's Army Air Corps during World War II. COURTESY

every one until last year's," she notes proudly. "They made me ride in that one."

A recent back injury — she was shocked to learn she had breaks in multiple places — has slowed her a little. "The doctor can't figure out how I did it," she said, adding that she's on the mend, doing exercises to help.

It would take much more than any of her current ailments, though, to make her feel sorry for herself, Winifred said. "I thank the Lord I'm doing as good as I am. (At the VA,) I see people come in with no arms or legs, in wheelchairs. I'm just real thankful."

Built to endure

"It feels like it's going to last," Jay joked, when the subject turned to his and Winifred's marriage. The couple celebrated 70 years together in December 2015.

Not bad for a three-week courtship.

After tying the knot, the Dudleys went on to raise four children, living in Bentonville, Arkansas; Cave Springs; and other places where Jay worked as a high school principal. They settled in Tulsa 25 years ago to be closer to family.

There are many ingredients, the Dudleys say, to building a marriage that lasts. But one is most important.

"Put God at the head of your life," Winifred said. "You can survive everything."

"Absolutely," Jay concurred.

Serving to heal

Mary Glass cared for GIs as an Army nurse in the Pacific

Being a patient was not what Mary Glass had signed up for.

But for one week, at least — with a raging typhoon making it impossible to disembark at Okinawa — that's what the Army nurse would feel like.

"I was seasick the whole time," Glass said.

Of course, the storm did eventually pass. By the time the landing craft dropped her off in the island surf, Glass again was feeling fit. Which was a good thing. Because on Okinawa — though Japan had surrendered a couple of weeks earlier — there was still plenty of nursing to be done.

A lieutenant in the Army Nurse Corps during World War II, Glass, 92, revisited those days in a 2015 interview with the Tulsa World.

Working at a hospital made up of a series of tents, Glass was as-

signed to general care duties. It included feeding and bathing ailing troops, and taking them on walks, she said. "The ones we got pretty much had all of their battle scars fixed," she added, noting that her hospital didn't receive the more critically wounded men.

Still, it was the hardest part of her war experience, "seeing those patients really sick or hurt," she said, and knowing that "some would go back home and never be the same."

Seemed like the thing to do

A native of Cherry Tree, Pennsylvania, Glass, formerly Mary Jane Sechler, was 20 and fresh out of nursing school when she joined the Army Nurse Corps. It just seemed like the thing to do, she said. Of the approximately 25 graduates in her 1943 class, all of them were signing up, too.

Glass wasn't the only one in her family to take part in the war effort. She had a brother who joined the Army as well; he went on to serve in Italy.

And although she didn't know it yet, her future husband was doing his part. Gene Glass of Tulsa was the officer in charge when

Mary Glass, an Army nurse during the end of World War II in the Pacific Theater, had rifle training during her service. COURTESY

she was training at an Army rifle range in Aberdeen, Maryland. They later began dating and would marry, Gene bringing Mary back to Tulsa with him.

But before all of that could happen, there was a war to win.

For her part, Glass was bound for the Pacific. She would go on to spend several months at Army medical facilities in Honolulu, Hawaii. From there, aboard the hospital ship USS Repose, she sailed on to Okinawa, arriving in September 1945. Just weeks earlier,

Okinawa had been the site of what would go down as the Pacific's bloodiest battle, as Allied forces had eventually won out over the Japanese.

'There wasn't anything to talk about'

Glass' children and grandchildren say they were surprised to learn of her wartime service. She never mentioned it, and was in her 80s before they found out. "There wasn't anything to talk

about," Glass said, explaining her silence with a shrug of her frail shoulders. "We just cared for our patients and did our duties."

Her military experience wasn't all work. When not on duty, Glass told the World, she and her fellow nurses tried to have a good time. "But parties were never too big because there weren't many men around," she said, laughing. "It was pretty much all females."

With the end of the war, Glass looked forward to coming home and the chance to "have a normal life again."

After a war, though, some things are never the same. It changes you, she said — in some ways, even for the better:

"You look at a lot of things differently. You're kinder. You show more sympathy. You appreciate things more."

"B" Company, 1st Battalion, moves up to reinforce "A" Company on Okinawa. NATIONAL ARCHIVES

WORTH GROSS   NAVY 1942-47

Treating the troops

Navy surgeon led medics in Pacific campaign

His days of hunting bigger game are behind him. But don't think for a second that Worth Gross is ready to put away his guns.

"I still go duck hunting," the Tulsan, 99, observed cheerfully. And while he has scaled it back, Gross' hobby still occupies a big place in his life. Evidence of it is everywhere in his home — from the mounted animal heads on the walls to the Kodiak bear rug on the floor. The latter — large furry head still attached — "is from a hunt in Alaska," he said.

As fond as Gross is of his guns, though, there have been times when he left the shooting to others. Long since retired from his career as an orthopedic surgeon, Gross, the oldest member of the Tulsa County Medical Society, talked to the Tulsa World in 2015 about his service in World War II as a Navy surgeon.

The casualties mount

Attached to the 1st Marine Division to treat troops in combat zones, Gross was in charge of a team of six medics during the war. Traveling from island to island, setting up first aid stations as they went, they patched up whomever they could. But "our No. 1 priority," he said, "was to get (the seriously wounded) evacuated."

As such, Gross said his title of "surgeon" was a little misleading: "It was not real surgery. Just enough to get them to where they could be transferred to better facilities ... the hospital ships in the fleet."

If not careful, the medics themselves could join the ranks of the wounded. Gross and his team were often under heavy gun and mortar fire after disembarking and looking for a place to set up. In fact, one of his men was killed before the team set foot on its first island. He was hit while in the back of the landing craft and disappeared over the side.

"We didn't see him again," Gross said.

The first one there

Gross grew up in Lindsay in Garvin County, Oklahoma. The son of an old-time country doctor, Gross knew from an early age that he, too, wanted to pursue a career in medicine. He graduated from Oklahoma Military Academy in Claremore in 1935 and went on to earn his undergraduate degree at the University of Oklahoma.

Gross was close to finishing medical school at Northwestern University in Chicago when world events almost caused him to drop out. The reason: the attack on Pearl Harbor, Dec. 7, 1941.

"I was at the Navy yard in Chicago at 8 o'clock the next morning — I was the first one there," said Gross, whose mind was set on joining up. Navy officials, though, told him to finish school first. Lacking only a few months, Gross did as he was advised. He even got married in the interim. But after graduating, he followed through and joined the Navy.

After a yearlong internship at the U.S. Naval Hospital in San Diego, he shipped out for the war in the Pacific, where he was attached to the 1st Marine Division, 1st Amphibian Tractor Battalion. Guadalcanal had already been secured by the time Gross arrived for a short stay.

But at upcoming destinations, like Papua New Guinea, Peleliu and Okinawa, he arrived in time for the worst of the fighting. Okinawa was the last stop. He was there about a month, operating an aid station in the battalion area. The island of Pavuvu served as home to the division between campaigns.

Doing what he could

It was a sight that still haunts Gross' dreams. At an island where he'd just arrived, "I was walking down the beach trying to find my headquarters," he recalled, "when this Marine staggered out of the woods — walked right into me. I could see he was holding his face with his hands."

Recounting what he saw next stirs old emotions Gross must fight to choke back. "His jaw," he said, "had been completely shot off. There was nothing (connecting to) his trachea. ... He couldn't talk or anything." Gross helped the man get to where he could be evacuated. A lot of the time, that was all you could do, he said.

Gross says he respected the Japanese — "I tell you, they were a tough bunch of cookies. ... They fought like the devil." But it was nothing compared to the level of respect he had for his American comrades.

Gross might have been a Navy man, but the special bond he feels with the Marines is real. And he couldn't be prouder of those he served with. Many of them were barely 18 at the time, much younger than Gross, who was married and already had a couple of college degrees.

"They were very young," he said. "They had nothing but training. But they sure were good at it." He tried his best for them, he said. "I did everything that I thought I could do properly for a Marine under any circumstances."

The call home

Gross' arrival back in the states in August 1945 coincided with a big announcement: the news of Japan's surrender. The war was finally over.

Stepping off the ship in San Diego on Aug. 15, V-J Day, the first thing Gross wanted to do was call his wife, Charlotte, in Chicago. But the nearest row of phones was occupied from end to end — "as you might imagine, with a bunch of guys just back from overseas."

So Gross took a walk. He hadn't gone too far into the city when he spied a telephone booth. "It was empty," he said, eyes widening as if he still can't believe it. The next thing Gross knew, he was talking to Charlotte. It was the first time he had heard her voice since

Dr. Worth Gross was a Navy surgeon in the Pacific Theater during World War II. COURTESY

he shipped out two years earlier.

"I can't describe" what it felt like, he said. The couple would soon be reunited. In 2015, Worth and Charlotte Gross had been married 73 years. Charlotte, 98, is the younger by a few months.

Making his mark

Other than a recurring case of malaria that struck again after he came home, Gross suffered few ill effects from the war. He remained in the Navy for two more years, rising to the rank of lieutenant senior grade.

Settling in Tulsa in the 1950s, he first made his mark working with polio patients before going on to specialize in spinal procedures. He was president of the Tulsa County Medical Society (1961) and named doctor of the year in 1984.

He was honored in 2015 as Oklahoma Military Academy's oldest living alumnus at the former school's annual reunion. Gross might not go hunting for bear anymore. But he's still very much a straight shooter. His advice to future generations?

"Be the best you can be. If you can't, get the hell out of it."

'Very glad to land'

Navy pilot flew bombing raids on Japanese ships

Leo Haas made one attempt at keeping a diary during the war. But after his first entry, he put away his pen.

"It was bad enough to be fighting — I didn't want to write about it," said Haas, who still has his old diary, most of its discolored pages blank. It would be a mistake, though, for anyone to assume he was lacking for material.

The lone diary entry itself, penned in a uniform, rightward-slant-ing cursive, is filled with intrigue, even describing a new "secret weapon" his unit was getting. Indeed — as the pilot of a Privateer patrol bomber in the Pacific Theater, heading out every third day for another death-defying run on the enemy's big ships — Haas could have written volumes.

'Almost suicidal'

Haas, 91, recipient of a Distinguished Flying Cross and other medals during World War II, welcomed the Tulsa World to his home in 2015 to talk about his service with Navy Bombing Squadron VPB-109. A land-based bomber unit featuring Privateers — a modified Navy version of the Army Air Corps' B-24 Liberator — Squadron 109 flew out of the Philippines, and eventually Iwo Jima and Okinawa, moving closer to Japan as the war progressed.

"Our job," said Haas, "was to find big ships and to go in and strafe them and bomb them." The task was "almost suicidal," he added. Unlike the bombers in Europe, which flew primarily at high altitudes, squadron pilots were trained to fly very low, almost hugging the water's surface as they made their attack run.

"We were told that if you were that low," Haas said, "you were too low for the ship's guns to hit you. But that wasn't the case."

Closing in on a target ship, Haas would take the plane up again, and at 200 or so feet — bombs away. Then it was back down to the water's surface to make their getaway. Over 12 months of flying missions every three days, Haas and his crew sank about 17 ships, and damaged countless others.

As a result, he wasn't too disappointed he never got to try out the "secret weapon" he wrote about. That weapon, the Navy's "Bat," was a radio-controlled glider that carried a 1,000-pound bomb. The first of its kind used by U.S. forces in the war, planes equipped with it carried one on each wing.

But Haas and his crew did more than enough damage with their bombs, which they weren't shy about dropping. Haas named one of his planes, "The Blind Bomber."

"I guess that meant we'd drop bombs anywhere," he said, chuckling.

Two against 20

One time in particular, Haas was sure he was going to die. Consequently, he said, "I decided to fight to the death." That was how it began — the air battle that would earn him a story in his hometown newspaper, the Tulsa Daily World.

On May 17, 1945, Haas' plane and another were returning to their base when they crossed paths with a group of around 20 Japanese fighters. Faced with no alternative, Haas braced himself for a fight. The odds weren't good: Not only were they heavily outnumbered, fighters were much faster than bombers. But, sticking tightly together, Haas' plane and its companion would more than acquit themselves.

"We dropped right down over the water, as close as we could, to keep them from going under us."

Over the next 20 minutes, enduring both phosphorus bombs and a hail of bullets, the Americans were able to stay airborne while shooting down three of the enemy planes.

"I'm not going to say they were whipped," Haas said, adding that the remaining Japanese planes left after that. "But I guess they had had enough. They had their own base to get back to."

Both Privateers took a beating: Haas' was shot up, and though no one was seriously injured, one or two crewmen were nicked. Their commander told them later it was amazing they survived.

One of the Japanese planes that got away is now at the Pensacola Navy Air Museum in Florida. Haas visited a few years ago at the invitation of the museum director. The aircraft still had "some of our bullet holes in it," he said.

Navy pilot Leo Haas (back row, third from left) poses with the crew of his Privateer patrol bomber during his service with the Navy in the Pacific Theater during World War II. COURTESY

Flying missions every three days for over a year, Privateer patrol pilot Leo Haas and his crew sank about 17 Japanese ships, and damaged many others. COURTESY

Too young to join

As a senior at Holy Family High School in Tulsa, Haas would've deferred graduation if he'd had his way. The day after the Pearl Harbor attack on Dec. 7, 1941, he told his parents he was joining the Marines. Haas was underage, though, at 17, and needed their permission. But when he saw his mother crying, he decided not to press the matter.

Instead, he finished high school and accepted a football scholarship to the University of Tulsa. There, Haas found himself backing up TU legend-in-the-making Glenn Dobbs at tailback. "I knew I wasn't going to play," he said, laughing. "So I decided to join the Navy." Nine months later, Haas had his pilot's wings.

'Not indispensable'

Haas, who attained the rank of lieutenant junior grade, credits the Navy with wising him up.

"I was pretty young when I went in, and I thought I could do about anything," he said. "(But) things happen that let you know you are not indispensable."

Or invincible, either. That might have been the hardest lesson. You were reminded of it, Haas said, every time "you would come back from your flight and ask about somebody and they weren't there." Of the 200 members the squadron started with, 48 would be killed in action. A squadron was a tight-knit group, Haas said, and he knew all of them. He remembers attending funerals for buddies on Okinawa and Iwo Jima.

"I just thank God that he let me get back. ... You really always thought you'd be fine. But in the back of your mind you knew

something could go wrong. You were always very glad to land."

Just being on the ground, though, didn't mean you could be completely at ease. Kamikaze attacks, especially toward the end of the war, sometimes were directed at bases, including Haas' on Okinawa. But one day, just like that, it all stopped — the bombing runs, the attacks. Everything. For one of their final flights together, Haas and other 109-ers escorted the planes of Japanese dignitaries to Okinawa for the official surrender.

Writing it down

Haas and his late wife, Vivian, who died in 2010, were married for 66 years. They met as students at Holy Family. While Haas was overseas during the war — his favorite photo of Vivian never far from him — she worked at Douglas Aircraft in Tulsa.

They married in 1944, before Haas' last tour of duty, and raised four children together. Haas eventually made up for his brief tenure as a diarist. In 2008, he sat down and wrote a short memoir for his family. Chronicling his war experiences, Haas enjoyed reflecting on his beloved Squadron 109.

"Can you imagine the unspoken affection we have for each other," Haas wrote, "an affection that allowed men to offer their lives for each other without hesitation and I suppose without understanding. I will always remember them as my brothers."

The surviving members of 109 have held reunions annually for many years, including more than once in Tulsa. Of the seven or so members left now, he is the only surviving pilot.

"I flew with brave guys," Haas told the World. "They were fun to be around. I was very proud to be a member of the 109 squadron."

The PB4Y-2 Privateer patrol bomber, a Navy reconfiguration of the B-24 Liberator bomber, was flown by pilot Leo Haas during his service with the Navy during World War II. COURTESY

American in Paris

Minnie Hampton was an Army teletype operator in Europe

As her ship pulled away, putting more distance between her and the only home she'd ever known in Oklahoma, Minnie Hampton couldn't help admiring how smooth the water was in New York Harbor. At the same time, though, she knew surfaces could be deceiving. Her own calm exterior, for example, was hiding plenty underneath.

Watching the Statue of Liberty as it "just kept getting smaller and smaller," Hampton felt something "welling up inside of me. It was like pride (mixed with), a little bit of being scared and anxious."

It was the same, probably, for most of the young Women's Army Corps volunteers on board. Most had come from just as far away, and from similar backgrounds. As for Hampton — Minnie Myers at the time — she had worked at different jobs around her hometown of Enid after high school before deciding, at age 21, to volunteer. That was October 1944.

Minnie Hampton served with the WACs during World War II. COURTESY

Minnie Hampton (left) clowns around with buddies during gas-mask training while in service with the WACs during World War II. COURTESY

Three of her brothers — Walter, Alvin and Raymond — were already serving in the war by then, she said — two in the Army and one in the Marines. Their example was probably part of why she joined, she said. But it was also a case of a small-town girl's wanderlust.

"I guess I was just tired of staying at home and wanted to see some country," said Hampton, now 92, reflecting on it in a 2015 interview at her home in Broken Arrow.

After basic training, she would be trained as a teletype operator, going on to serve with American forces in Europe. Before Europe, though, came the ship ride over, and the first of the strange new worlds she would find herself experiencing. Crossing the Atlantic was itself an adventure.

"They told us to be quiet because there were mines everywhere," she said. Sometimes you could see them in the water — "they called them 'tin cans,' but they were really barrels."

The ship never hit one. But you heard them explode once in a while, she said, from someone shooting them from the deck. "That was really scary."

Hampton's ship would land at Le Havre, France. From there, they moved on to Paris, which had been liberated from the Germans a few weeks earlier. Hampton was assigned to the 3341st Signal Service Battalion. It was the first activated women's battalion in the Army, and included telephone and teletype operators, radio operators, cryptographers, draftsmen, typists, clerks and message center couriers.

According to Army records, the 3341st eventually reached a peak strength in Europe of 738 enlisted women and 28 officers. In Paris, where Hampton would be stationed for several months, the women were part of what was billed as "the largest message center in the world outside of Washington, D.C."

Hampton's unit operated out of a former German blockhouse, which boasted 10-foot-thick walls of reinforced concrete.

"There were no windows in the building," Hampton recalled. "We worked in a room with no way out. Unless somebody unlocked the door."

The center exchanged upward of 1,000 messages a day with the War Department alone. Of the 50,000 messages handled each week, about 95 percent were radio-teletype and teletype.

Still a war going on

While in Paris, Hampton and other servicewomen were put up at the Hotel Bradford. For a young girl who'd never really been outside Oklahoma, Paris was the stuff of dreams. When she wasn't working, Hampton enjoyed the city with her friends.

She would try champagne for the first time there, and remembers going up in the Eiffel Tower as high as it went. There were plenty of reminders, though, that there was still a war going on, she said.

Like the wounded soldiers she would see on the streets, hobbling by on crutches. And because of the threat of bombings, Hampton said, "they'd have blackouts at night and everything would be shut down. No lights (in the hotel)."

Although she never witnessed the fighting firsthand, she saw the damage it left behind. In parts of France, and in Germany after the war, there were "just piles and piles of rubbish. Some of the places would be fenced off. I guess we never forget how terrible it was."

Hampton was still in Paris when the war in Europe ended in May 1945. The news of Germany's surrender sent everyone pouring into the streets, she said.

"We were singing and dancing, just really celebrating. ... Everybody was your friend and buddy. A lot of people were drinking and carrying on," she added. "But we (she and her friends) didn't do all of that. We were just so happy it was all over."

An honor to serve

Because she didn't smoke, Hampton would often trade cigarettes for items she'd rather have. Like nylons, or cashews and candy. Nylons were prized, she said, and "made you feel good and look good." And she has good memories of "sitting on my bunk eating cashews all night long."

Hampton considered staying in the military. "I just wasn't through seeing what all there was to see," she explained, adding that as a bonus, had she stayed, she would've been promoted to staff sergeant.

But after two years, she missed her family. So in August 1946 she took her discharge and returned to Enid. Shortly after, she would meet her future husband, John Hampton, who was also in the Army and would serve in Korea.

Hampton is proud of the two years she served in the Army. She still has her service hat.

"I wish now I had saved my uniforms," she said. "I think I would've tried them on to see if they still fit."

In spirit at least, Hampton has never been out of uniform. Three of her children — two daughters and a son — would follow their parents' example, growing up to serve in the military. Hampton said she encouraged her children to do it, teaching them "it was an honor to serve your country."

Men and women with military backgrounds have a certain pride in the way they walk and carry themselves, she said. "You can always tell when somebody has served their country."

Work to be done

Patriotism led Estelle Harrington to join WAVES

Estelle Harrington thought she had her mind made up: After reviewing the options, she was going with the Marine Corps.

"The Lady Marines had such cute hats," she said.

But the Navy, it turned out, had something going for it, too. Namely, a stronger sales pitch. After a visit to a recruiting office on San Francisco's Market Street, Harrington, then 21, ended up enlisting with that branch of service instead.

"There were two retired old Navy men there," she said. "And they must've done a good job — they signed both of us up."

The "us" included Harrington's younger sister, Nita. That was a surprise, Harrington added. Nita, who was 20, never had any intention of entering military service; she had just been out for a stroll with her sister.

"(Nita) said she'd wait outside for me" at the recruiting office,

Harrington said. "I said no, come in and sit down." The recruiters soon had them both hooked. "To this day, she blamed me" for her joining the military, Harrington said, laughing.

Doing her part

A resident of Tulsa's University Village retirement community, Estelle Harrington, still perky and good-humored at 93, talked to the Tulsa World in 2015 about her service with the Navy WAVES — Women Accepted for Volunteer Emergency Service — during World War II.

Harrington, who was Estelle Flambard at the time, said it wasn't long after the U.S. entered the war that she began seeing the ads for women in service. And being patriotic, she wanted to do her part. Harrington and her sister joined the WAVES on Nov. 18, 1943. The women were natives of Berkeley, California, and fellow graduates of Alhambra High School in nearby Martinez.

After basic training at Hunter College in New York and yeoman training at then-Oklahoma A&M in Stillwater, Harrington was sent to Utah and Nita to Nevada. Harrington would spend the rest of her service stationed in Clearfield, Utah, where she worked at a Naval base and supply depot.

Established in July 1942 as a division of the U.S. Naval Reserve, the WAVES corps was still relatively new. And in Clearfield, they still did not have any barracks on base when Harrington first arrived. Until they were built, she said, the women stayed in Army barracks in another town, "riding a rickety old bus" to Clearfield every day. Later, WAVES barracks were erected on site, "and we finally had a place of our own."

As a Yeoman 2nd class, Harrington's work was mostly clerical. She handled "confidential and secret" mail, she said, and even had her own jeep and personal driver.

Benefits of service

The military experience broadened her horizons, Harrington said. "I met women from all over the country," she said. Among them were her two best gal pals, Dottie and Ruth, while there.

When off duty, she said, her friends liked to go to Ogden to drink beer and have fun. But Harrington seldom went along. "I did my best to stay out of trouble," she said.

Harrington's service would also bring her future husband into her life — a young petty officer from Detroit, Michigan, named Charles Harrington. However, their first meeting — while waiting in line at the base PX — did not exactly hint at a harmonious future.

Charles, who was standing behind her, "said something to me, and I didn't like what he said," Harrington recalled, laughing. "I wasn't very nice to him. I pulled rank: I said, 'Who do you think you're talking to?' He was third class. I was second."

Meeting later under different circumstances, though, the two hit it off. Harrington had gone out with a few other servicemen before Charles, including an Air Force captain.

"WAVES were not to date officers. But we did anyway," she said. But after she met Charles, that was it. They married after she left the service in 1946 and together they raised eight children.

Her base had other interesting people on it, too, Harrington said. At one end was an area where German prisoners of war were kept. It was off limits, but a couple of the POWs worked at a base shoe repair shop. Harrington also remembers a Greek cook. He loved the WAVES, she said, and used to make them doughnuts.

Helping the war effort

Harrington, who has lived in Tulsa since 1968, is still active. Besides her daily exercises, she loves crossword puzzles. She cuts them out of the paper, she said, keeping a stack of them at hand, always ready to go. Harrington's time with the WAVES is something she thinks back on fondly.

"I was glad I'd gone. I enjoyed it." She added, "It seems terrible enjoying war. A lady said to me once, 'Well, it sounds like the war was fun for you.' I guess in a way it was — it was something different. But the main reason I joined was I was patriotic," said Harrington, who had two younger brothers who later served in Korea.

"I wanted to do what I could to help the war (effort). You do your job, that was it. ... And the work that we did had to be done."

Estelle Harrington said she joined the Navy WAVES in 1943 because she wanted to do her part for the war effort. COURTESY

The liberator

Olin Hawkins served in both WWII and Korea

Still uncertain about what they were going to find inside the Nazi compound, Olin Hawkins was preparing to open the gates when one of his men spoke up in alarm.

"He said to me 'blank blank, sergeant'" — I'm not using God's name in vain — "'look at this!' " What Hawkins saw next would set the tone for all that followed. Looking where the soldier was gesturing, off to the side of the compound, Hawkins observed a set of railroad tracks and "seven or eight, maybe 10" boxcars.

"It was a sight to behold," he said, adding that the doors were open, so they could see the dead bodies inside each car — heaps and heaps of them. Hawkins walked over for a closer inspection. But after the first couple of cars, he said, he'd seen all he needed to. He led his men back to the gates, ready to enter the camp itself.

Hawkins doesn't remember when on that day — April 29, 1945

— he first heard the name "Dachau." But with the boxcars he had effectively had his introduction. And he has never forgotten the name since.

Rare breed

"Men could grow to love combat, and I have to say I did. I was part of a rare breed," Olin Hawkins, a veteran of World War II and Korea, told the Tulsa World during a 2016 interview.

Hawkins — a former Sand Springs resident who lives at The Gardens Nursing Center in Sapulpa — made a career of the military, retiring as an Army major after more than 20 years. He started as an enlisted man, but was promoted by commission to officer.

The journey, he said, began in north-central Kansas, where he was born. Hawkins was 7 years old when the family — which included his two sisters and a brother — lost its farm and moved into town, where his father would work at various jobs. Hawkins went to high school, where he starred in track and other sports, and after graduating, attended college for a year.

After Pearl Harbor, Hawkins went into Salina, Kansas, intent on joining the Marines. But he couldn't pass the eye test. He then tried the Navy, but was turned away for the same reason.

"So I said, 'Just go ahead and draft me, then.'"

The Army soon obliged. On Oct. 26, 1942, Hawkins, 21 at the time, was drafted. After reporting to Oklahoma to train at Camp Gruber, he shipped out for Europe with the 42nd Infantry Division, arriving in Marseilles, France, in December 1944. He started as a squad commander before later being given charge of a platoon, and experienced his first combat at Gansheim, Germany.

"I was scared," he said, "but I didn't let it control me."

A fighting platoon

Hawkins, 94, clearly enjoys telling his stories. Voice raspy but raring to go, at times he's barely able to contain his enthusiasm, as though the words — getting in too big a rush as they march out — keep running into each other from behind.

Like the good infantry commander he still is, though, Hawkins is able to restore order to the formation and make his points. As a commander, Hawkins said, he was never afraid to defy the conventional wisdom. Such as the rule that "when the firing started, you were supposed to hit the ground." That only made you an easier target, Hawkins observed, and so his rule was "fire and advance and keep going."

On his first combat patrol as a platoon sergeant in February 1945, he again started out by doing things his way. "All patrols went out at 5 a.m. ordinarily. But I said no, we're going out at 8 a.m. Because (the Germans) expected us at 5 a.m. They didn't expect us at 8 a.m. And I was right. We caught them in their bunkers, sleeping or eating."

Hawkins and his platoon of about 25 men would engage and kill 46 German soldiers on that first patrol, earning Hawkins a Bronze Star. Only one of his men was wounded, hit in the leg. From there, over the next few weeks, the fighting would keep coming, as units of the 42nd fought off counterattacks and captured towns.

Hawkins says most of the time he had the lead platoon. That, in part, was why he didn't have a lot of casualties, he said.

"Most of the time, the Germans wouldn't fire on the lead platoon. They wanted the main body so they'd let it pass through."

Even 70 years removed, Hawkins can't say enough good things about his men. "That was a fighting platoon — they were fighters. Aggressive people. ... I don't think I could've had a better platoon."

Even those who were not natural fighters quickly proved their mettle. Hawkins said his assistant squad leader — who later became a preacher — had confessed to him earlier that he didn't know "whether I can kill anybody."

"I said, 'Mister ... I want to know real quick whether you can or not.'"

On that first combat patrol, the man took out a German officer at a machine gunner post, undoubtedly saving lives. Hawkins was satisfied. "He can kill," he remembers thinking.

At the gates of Hell

Leading up to their arrival at Dachau, Hawkins said, they had heard "not a single word" about the Nazis' concentration camps or the mass extermination of the Jews.

"Somebody up at division headquarters may have known. But we didn't know anything," he said.

The morning of April 29, 1945, began like most before it: with Hawkins and his platoon moving down the road on foot. Before long, however, Army trucks came along and loaded them up. Hawkins recalls the ride that followed as they zoomed right by

Olin Hawkins helped liberate Dachau (seen here in 2015) in April 1945. **TIM CHAMBERLIN/Tulsa World**

Olin Hawkins helped liberate Dachau concentration camp in 1945. TIM CHAMBERLIN/Tulsa World

German outposts along the route without stopping to fight. And that's how it was, he said, that "we came to the edge of Dachau — as I know it now."

A group of about 50 German SS troopers stopped them there, and a firefight ensued with Hawkins' platoon.

"We ran them up a dead end. And that was all she wrote for them SS troopers," he said. "We fired mortars, shooting rifles into them, everything. ... Killed them all. They didn't surrender." There would be no more resistance from there, he said.

Looking around, Hawkins spied "a compound over to my left." A large facility of many buildings, it was surrounded by a fence, with a canal out front and a little wooden bridge across it. Hawkins remembers lamenting the lack of cover as they approached the compound's gates.

"I was thinking that if they shoot at us, there's no place to hide," he said. He quickly forgot that concern, though, when he saw the boxcars. Between all the cars, Hawkins estimates, there were several hundred dead bodies — prisoners en route to Dachau who had died of starvation or exposure and had been just left to rot.

Later, Hawkins would learn that one man had been found alive among the bodies — one survivor out of the hundreds. Many years later, the man came to one of Hawkins' division reunions to express his gratitude.

'I was there'

The boxcars prepared them, at least, for all that came after. Entering Dachau camp itself, Hawkins "saw these piles of dead bodies, like you throw cordwood on a pile. Just piles of them. Their legs weren't any bigger around than a bone. All it was was just a bone and skin, no meat to speak of."

The prisoners still alive — all of them men; women were kept at a different camp — were in bad shape, too. But it didn't stop them from celebrating.

"They were just tickled to death," Hawkins said. "They were waving their arms, real happy. They knew we were the Allies."

Shortly after, the Dachau camp commandant officially surrendered to American forces. For the prisoners' own good, Hawkins said, they attempted to keep them in the camp while waiting for Army medics to arrive. "But some got out and started roaming the countryside."

Hawkins and his platoon spent the rest of that day and the night at Dachau. Confronted with such horrific images, somehow he wasn't fazed, he said.

"I don't remember what was going through my mind. It didn't bother me, I know that. It didn't seem to bother any men in the platoon. I guess we'd already seen enough that something like that didn't bother us."

Hawkins' status as an eyewitness to the Holocaust is something he takes seriously. "A lot of stories came out about Dachau, a lot not necessarily true. I was there. I saw it."

Together with the 45th Infantry Division, which had approached from another direction, the 42nd was credited with liberating Dachau and its estimated 35,000 surviving prisoners. From there, Hawkins' unit went on to Munich and then into Austria. That's where they would be when the war in Europe ended.

Ideal for the Army

After his discharge in October 1945, Hawkins returned home. However, he re-enlisted in January 1947. He would go on to serve 20 years in the Army, including service in Korea, and encountered much more of the fighting he had developed a taste for.

Between WWII and Korea, Hawkins was part of eight major campaigns, three in the first conflict, five in the latter. Somehow in all of that, despite several "bullet holes in my jacket," he was never wounded, he said.

Also coming through in one piece was his psyche. He would never suffer from nightmares, something he chalks up to his upbringing. Growing up in the Depression era, Hawkins said he knew nothing but hard times, hard work and hard winters — winters he had to endure without any kind of coat, and with holes in the soles of his shoes. Also, he said, he fought a lot as a boy.

"We were always fighting to see who was the best man. We went to dances just to get in a fight. It was a tough generation," he added. "All of us came from that. I think it made me ideal for the Army." Ideal for the combat infantry in particular.

"The combat infantryman lives in a hole in the ground — a foxhole — 24 hours a day, seven days a week," Hawkins said. "The only thing between him and the enemy is the front side of his rifle. And he is the only man that actually comes into contact with the enemy ... face to face. You better believe I'm proud to be a combat infantryman."

Proud enough, he added, that he chose the same role in both his wars.

"When the Korean War broke out, I volunteered to go. I could've stayed at Fort Dix, New Jersey. But I went to Korea. I must be a little touched in the head," he said, laughing.

'Flying the Hump'

Pilot Kelly Haynes carried supplies over the Himalayas

It was at an all-base assembly, just before he shipped out for India, that Kelly Haynes finally got a hint about what was coming his way.

"The chaplain asked if there were any pilots there," he recalled, "and he asked us to stand. He then proceeded to say (to the audience), 'We ought to think very carefully about these guys. Because only half of them will be coming back.'"

The revelation caught Haynes off guard — and, frankly, made him a little angry. How, he wondered, could the chaplain be so thoughtlessly blunt? But it was better, Haynes guessed, than not knowing anything.

From the time he'd arrived in Greensboro, North Carolina, "our orders had been very secretive," said Haynes, a native of Cleveland, Ohio. "We received a lot of lectures. But we were never told where

we were going or what we would be doing." Ultimately, he would have to go all the way to India before he learned his role in full.

As a transport pilot with the Army's 10th Air Force, Haynes would be carrying supplies in the fight against the Japanese, including over the Himalayas, the world's tallest mountain chain, to China. "Flying the Hump," as those missions were called, was probably what the chaplain had been referring to.

Because of all the planes that had crashed there, the route had picked up another, more ominous name as well. The Aluminum Trail.

Miss Dot

The revelation from the chaplain that many would not be coming back hit him hard, Haynes, 92, told the Tulsa World in a 2015 interview at his home. It wasn't because danger bothered him personally. Rather, it was the timing.

He had met "Miss Dot" by then, he said. And suddenly, the future mattered a whole lot more. At the mention of "Miss Dot" — as he calls his wife, Dorothy, of nearly 70 years — Haynes chokes up. The two had met on a blind date in Greensboro, her hometown, shortly after he reported for duty to the Army overseas replacement depot there.

"If things had been different," Haynes says, struggling to control his emotions, "I'd of asked her to marry me then. But we both agreed it would be a bad deal."

After all, he was headed for God-knows-where, and very well might not survive. Dot did give him a photo, though. He kept it close by — in his flight log — for the rest of his service.

When Haynes had joined the Army Air Corps in January 1943, transport aircraft were not what he'd had in mind. He "wanted very badly," he said, to fly P-51 Mustang fighters. But instead he was assigned to multi-engine aircraft and for most of his service would fly C-46s and C-47s.

Most of that service would be in the war's China-Burma-India theater. Arriving in early 1945, a member of the 443rd Troop Carrier Group, he would begin flying transports out of Ledo, India, to Burma.

"We got there just in time to run the (Japanese) out" of Burma, he said. Carrying ammunition, fuel and supplies, "our mission was to supply the front. Although there was not a front per se — just pockets."

The Hump

After Burma, Haynes was transferred to Dinjan, India — from where the missions to China over the Himalayas were being flown. Thankfully, by the time Haynes arrived, aircraft improvements had greatly cut down on the number of crashes.

Still, he said, flying the "Hump" of the Himalayas — "or Rockpile, as it was referred to" — was nothing to take lightly. Over the next

Kelly Haynes served as a pilot in the Army Air Corps, flying planes over "The Hump" in the China-Burma theater during World War II. This is his notebook, with notations of routes and other information from that time of his service.
MICHAEL WYKE/Tulsa World

few months, Haynes flew more than 80 missions over the Hump, primarily carrying drums of gasoline. Flights were about four hours each way. And weather, he said, could make the experience "very hairy."

"There was no consideration for the weather. You were going to go when scheduled," he said. With no weather radar at the time, "you could inadvertently fly into a thunderstorm. Then you were in for a ride."

Often during flights, he added, you would see "little blue lightnings" of St. Elmo's Fire flickering on the windshield. Flying the Hump successfully boiled down more than anything to your engines, Haynes said.

"You needed two running engines," he said. Engine failure of any kind could be deadly, he added, and was the leading cause of crashes. Earlier C-46 models had a problem with this.

'Mail-order' bride

Through it all, Haynes said, he "never thought about not making it out." Or not making it back to Miss Dot. During the war, the two kept in touch through letters. Later in his service, having decided he was probably going to survive, Haynes even proposed by mail.

After she wrote him back, accepting, he mailed her an engagement ring, too. Buying it at a shop in Calcutta, "I cut two slits in a piece of cardboard and put the ring in that, then dropped it in the mail." The actual marrying, though, would have to be done in person. The ceremony was held after Haynes' return — Jan. 23, 1946.

Work still to do

V-J Day — Aug. 14, 1945 — still stands out clearly in Haynes' mind.

"I was descending to land at Dinjan on a clear night," he said, "and you could see tracers all over the place. I called the tower: 'What's going on? Looks like a war zone.'"

The tower: "Haven't you heard? The Japanese have given up." The tracer rounds were being fired by celebrating troops.

Although the war was over, Haynes and fellow transport pilots still had work to do. They would continue flying their theater, including carrying troops for the Chinese. Just because Haynes had survived the Hump didn't mean he was in the clear.

In fact, in November 1945, he came closer to dying than at any time while in the air. He and his unit had set up quarters in the hangar of a former Japanese base, he said, when one day, without warning, an adjacent bomb storage facility exploded. Haynes said about 40 people were killed. He had been sitting in a hangar corner, when suddenly, he said, he found himself "floating backwards in the air." Somehow, he was uninjured. An advance survey party had found the bombs earlier and recommended their removal, Haynes said. But tragically, it had not been done.

'Never had to kill'

Haynes received a number of decorations for his service, including a Distinguished Flying Cross and two Air Medals. Coming home to Ohio, he took advantage of the G.I. Bill to earn an aeronautical engineering degree from Ohio State University.

He would go to work for American Airlines, the job that brought him to Tulsa, and raise a family with Dot. The couple, who would celebrate their 70th anniversary in January 2016, are still active. And still very much an item — although a date now, they say, is more likely to consist of a road trip to Porter to pick peaches.

Although he once dreamed of flying fighters in the skies over Europe, Haynes says he's grateful things worked out like they did. Flying transports meant he "never had to kill anyone." Of the ways the war changed him, he added, most of it was for the good.

"It made me a better person. More thoughtful. More serious. More dedicated. I served with an awful lot of good people."

'Hard to watch'

Kamikaze attack sank Alvis Holloway's ship near Okinawa

Alvis Holloway wasn't sure how long he'd been unconscious. But piecing things together, he knew it couldn't have been too long. The wound to his head was too fresh.

"I was bleeding real bad," Holloway said. To make things worse, he added, he was all alone.

"I was the only one down there (on the ship's bottom deck). It was then I realized we'd been hit. And that I needed to get out of there."

Now 93, Holloway, a Sand Springs resident, talked to the Tulsa World in 2015 about his time as a machinist on the destroyer USS William D. Porter during World War II. The Porter operated in both the Atlantic and Pacific war zones, participating in several battles before being sunk near Okinawa.

The possibility that his ship might sink was the furthest thing from Holloway's mind, though, when he came to. Blood streaming

from his head wound, he made his way to the top deck, he said. And there he learned what had knocked him senseless: A Japanese kamikaze plane.

The suicide pilot had missed hitting the Porter directly, going over the starboard side. But there the plane had exploded.

"It had ripped a seam (in the ship)," Holloway said. "We couldn't pump the water out as fast as it was coming in."

In the Navy

Working in a Tulsa machine shop after graduating from Central High School in 1940, Holloway sensed the inevitable after the Pearl Harbor attack in December 1941.

"I figured I was going to be in it," he said of the war. So, not wanting to be drafted into the Army — "I didn't want to be laying in the mud" — Holloway volunteered for the Navy.

It was a decision he says he would never regret.

Making the same decision later were two of Holloway's younger brothers, who joined him in the Navy. The sons of a Baptist minister, a lot of prayers were said on behalf of the Holloway brothers by members of their father's church, Hale Baptist, while they were away at war.

Alvis Holloway was assigned to the USS Porter, where as a machinist, he would work deep in the belly of the ship. Among his many duties, he checked and maintained the pumps.

"If they wanted more steam," he said, "we would give it to them."

One of the Porter's first assignments, in November 1943, would also be one of its most memorable — although, noted Holloway, he and his crew mates would just as soon forget it. Helping escort a convoy carrying President Franklin D. Roosevelt to a war conference overseas, the Porter accidentally fired a live torpedo at the president's ship, the USS Iowa. The Porter broke radio silence to warn the Iowa, and fortunately the vessel changed course, leaving the torpedo to detonate in its wake.

"You think it wasn't hectic when that went off," Holloway said. "The captain was really upset. ... And the first thing we heard, we had been quarantined."

Concerned that it might have been an assassination attempt, officials placed the Porter's captain and entire crew under arrest, a U.S. Navy first. Thankfully, the incident was quickly ruled an accident: A torpedoman had neglected to remove the torpedo's primer, enabling it to fire.

Kamikaze attack

From the Atlantic, the Porter would go on to spend nine frigid months in the Aleutian islands — patrolling for enemy subs and shelling Japanese islands — before sailing to the Pacific. There, the ship would serve in the Philippines and at Okinawa, racking up four battle stars, and shooting down a number of enemy planes.

Okinawa would spell the end of the line for the Porter, though.

Holloway remembers it well: June 10, 1945. Coming off watch at midnight, he had just dozed off in his bunk when, suddenly, an alert sounded, calling everyone to their battle stations. But before Holloway could react, he said, everything went black. Something hit the ship, sending his bunk toppling over into the lockers. When he came to, he was lying in the floor bleeding from his head.

The crew would try its best to save the vessel after the kamikaze plane exploded, but to no avail. A couple of hours after the attack, the order to abandon ship went out. Twelve minutes later, the Porter was gone. Amazingly, although 61 men were injured, everyone on board was evacuated safely, and no lives were lost.

From the decks of a neighboring vessel, Holloway would look on as the USS Porter — his home for 2½ years — slipped beneath the waves.

"It was hard to watch," he said.

Holloway's injuries — his back was hurt in addition to his head wound — would send him to a hospital in Saipan and earn him a Purple Heart. He was home on leave a few weeks later when Japan surrendered and the war was over.

Unsinkable spirit

After finishing his service, Holloway married and raised a family, working many years for Ajax Die Casting in Broken Arrow. His wife, Blanche, died in 2013; the couple was married for 66 years.

"I saw some bad stuff I guess," Holloway said of his military service. "But I enjoyed the actual sea. And I made a lot of friends. I liked the Navy. I'm not sorry for my experience."

Holloway kept in touch with his buddies and was a regular at reunions through the years. In 2012, he participated in the Oklahoma Honor Flights program, traveling to Washington, D.C., to see the nation's WWII Memorial.

Holloway remembers the war era as a time of neighbor helping neighbor, and he regrets how society has changed.

"People used to help each other. ... You knew everyone in your neighborhood, you sat on your front porch with them. Now people don't even know their neighbors."

The USS William D. Porter, a Fletcher class destroyer, was sunk after an attack by a Japanese kamikaze plane. COURTESY

Luck on his side

Meeting Pope Pius XII was a high point of time in Rome

Just what the pope was saying to him, Ralph Jones couldn't tell exactly. The heavy accent made his English hard to understand. But the gesture communicated plenty.

Handing Jones and each of his fellow GIs a missal and a rosary, "he said, 'hold these up and I'll bless them for you,' " Jones recalled. It was a moment that still, 70 years after the fact, is amazing to him.

A working-class boy from the south side of Chicago talking to Pope Pius XII — who would've ever imagined it? It happened, Jones said, during World War II. Stationed in Rome as a military police officer, he had been standing in St. Peter's Square one day when members of the pope's personal Swiss Guard walked up.

"They said 'the Pope would like to see some of you guys,' " Jones recalled. "So about 20 of us went in." The half-hour they spent with the pope remains one of Jones' favorite memories.

Even though, "I'm Methodist now," he said, the rosary and missal are treasured objects. He still has them, framed and hanging over his bed — mementos of a different time and place, not only for him, but for the world.

A Chicago boy in Africa

If you didn't know he was from Chicago, Jones' distinctive accent tips his hand pretty quickly. He was born and raised in the Windy City, and continued to call it home until the 1980s, when he moved to Tulsa to be near family. Still real to Jones are the issues that all Chicagoans take seriously. Like the age-old "Cubs or White Sox?" question.

"I'm a Sox man," Jones said, and when acknowledging the Cubs' success, can do so only grudgingly. You might as well be talking about Allies vs. Axis. Which, it turns out, is another subject that's very real to him.

Jones, who was drafted into the Army in 1942, served in Africa and Europe during the war.

The Tulsa World sat down with him in 2015 at Legend Assisted Living community in Tulsa to talk about his wartime experiences.

Jones was assigned to an independent unit that provided military police officers and guards. As a Louisiana-based unit of the National Guard, the bulk of the 156th Infantry Regiment's soldiers were from that state, and a number of them spoke their region's French dialect. This made the unit invaluable, Jones said, and often dictated where they were deployed. Initially, that would be Algeria in North Africa, still a French territory at the time.

There, on the sandy edge of the Sahara Desert, Jones helped man a stockade that had been erected to hold German and Italian prisoners of war. They quickly learned how to tell them apart:

"The Germans played soccer in the daytime and the Italians sang opera at night," Jones said, laughing.

His duties while there included processing new arrivals and emptying their pockets before locking them up. He also guarded the stockade and led groups of prisoners on work details.

When in Rome

From Africa, Jones moved on to Naples, Italy, then to Anzio, before arriving in Rome on June 4, 1944. The German Army had just vacated the city, making his unit, assigned to serve as MPs, some of the first American troops to enter the Eternal City.

As Jones likes to joke, they would have been bigger news if not for other events. The D-Day invasion of Normandy started two days later — June 6 — trumping just about any other headline in the world. Getting to Rome first had its advantages, Jones said: His first night there he stayed in the elegant Excelsior Hotel.

"But the brass showed up the next day. They got the Excelsior. ... The next night I was sleeping in a pup tent."

One of his first encounters with a Roman, he said, also happened shortly after he arrived. It was about 4 a.m., and he was walking along when an Italian woman approached him and made a shocking proposal.

She said, "I'll sleep with you if you'll kill my husband." Jones immediately refused. "Two weeks later I see her again — walking down the street with a major."

Among his duties in Rome, Jones and his fellow MPs were given the addresses of known Fascists and other wanted civilians, and sent to round them up. To hold them, a prison camp had been set up in the city center, surrounded by barbed-wire fences. The arrests, Jones said, were mostly uneventful. The suspects would proclaim their innocence but then go along quietly.

Jones would remain in Rome for about three months. He remembers it fondly, most of all his meeting the pope.

From Rome, it was goodbye to Italy and on to Marseilles, France.

Jones remembers the journey well: "All night long the German airplanes were dropping flares, trying to find our convoy. But they never did."

Jones was stationed in Marseilles about a year, again serving as an MP.

Sipping Ike's wine

One assignment during Jones' time in France was especially memorable: guard duty at a chateau during a meeting between Gen. Dwight Eisenhower and Army Chief of Staff George Marshall. Jones doesn't remember the exact time or place, but records show the two leaders met secretly Jan. 28, 1945, at Chateau Valmont near Marseilles.

"Eisenhower — he was very pleasant, smiling, just walked right in. I don't recall him saying anything," said Jones, who was stationed with a partner at the doors to the meeting room.

With Jones' stories, there's usually an additional angle that he seems almost embarrassed to tell. This one is no exception. From his station outside the room, Jones could see into the nearby kitchen,

Ralph Jones' discharge papers are shown along with a portrait of Pope Pius XII and a rosary blessed and given to him by the pontiff during an audience at the invitation of the pope. MICHAEL WYKE/Tulsa World

where some bottles of wine had been set out for the generals.

"I left my post," he said, a mischievous smile breaking out, "and I had a glass of wine." He hoped Eisenhower wouldn't hold it against him.

"I always had a great impression of (Eisenhower)," he said.

A constant refrain for him during the war was "Thank the Louisiana guys and Eisenhower."

As other groups moved out to fight, "Ike would say 'Leave that unit behind — they can talk French.' "

The usefulness of the French speakers kept his unit out of combat, and, Jones believes, probably saved his life. There were other times as well when fortune seemed to intervene on his behalf.

From Marseilles, Jones' unit was poised to join the fighting in Germany. But the Germans surrendered and the war in Europe ended.

Next, they shipped out for the Philippines to train for a planned invasion of Japan.

"Our convoy got halfway across the Atlantic," Jones said, "and the captain comes out and says the war is over. All in all I was very lucky."

A brighter future

Jones' luck didn't end there. Once, during his service when he was hospitalized for complications from malaria, he read a book on poker. After he was released, he took up the game. By the time of his discharge, he had piled up $5,000, all of it won off his fellow soldiers.

"Like most dumb guys I bought a car with it," Jones said.

Back home in Chicago, he started working as a draftsman. He would go on to a long career as an electrician for the city of Chicago.

Having seen the worst of the Depression — his father was out of work for three years — Jones was proud of the prosperous nation that emerged from the war. More than ever before, people "were able to go to college and become very successful."

A lot of his fellow troops used the G.I. Bill to go to college. He was happy to see many of them do well.

"I think that's true of a lot of the World War II guys," they did better after the war than they or their families had before it, Jones said.

Jones didn't seek higher education. But he said he had a good career that he enjoyed and it laid a foundation for his family.

"All four of my children went to college," he said proudly.

Perilous rescue

King fought with the 103rd Infantry, received a Silver Star

"We're missing one. Who'll go back?"

They were words that no one ever wanted to hear. But as usual, when volunteers were wanted, Erwin King didn't have to be asked twice.

Just back from a nighttime scouting mission to the German side of the river, he and his comrades had failed to notice at first — caught up in a firefight in the darkness — that they had lost one of their number. A return trip would be extra dangerous. But King didn't hesitate when it was proposed: "I said 'I'll go,'" he recalled.

Recrossing the river, it took him and two other volunteers about half an hour, he said, to locate the man. The situation didn't look good.

"Half his scalp was blown off. You could see his brain pulsing," King said, as he held up his fist, clenching and unclenching it, to illustrate.

To get the wounded soldier back, he said, he and the others put him in the raft. Then they swam alongside, pushing it across the icy river. This part, he added, had to be done under heavy machine-gun fire from the Germans, who by then had seen them.

For the effort, King would later be awarded a Silver Star medal. He shrugs off the honor, though. His real reward, he said, was knowing he did some good. He saw the man a few weeks later. Other than a metal plate in his head, King said, he'd "healed up."

'Controlled fear'

"Hemingway said that courage is 'controlled fear.' I firmly believe that," King, 92, said in a 2016 interview, recalling his time as a rifle-man with the 103rd Infantry Division in World War II.

"Every battle it was the same thing. You were scared to death — don't let anyone tell you otherwise. You were scared sick. Scared so bad you couldn't think. You had to learn to control your fear. And that took several battles."

For King, that conditioning process began after arriving in southern France. He and his unit officially entered combat on Nov. 11, 1944. Part of the effort to take the town of St. Dies, they were given a rude introduction, King said. Before they even got into the battle, "one of our own got killed by friendly fire." For him and many of the men, it was their first dead body.

"We all looked at him," King said. "Shot in the throat, blood all over him. Most of us threw up."

Over the next few months, the unit would cover more than 500 miles on foot, fighting as they went. Making matters worse, winter set in quickly and they soon had to battle the elements as well. It was under those icy conditions, near Merzweiler, Germany, that they had to mount the rescue mission for which King got his medal.

The swim back was the worst part, he said. The water was so cold, when they got out "we couldn't walk. We could only crawl. We couldn't feel anything. You felt like you were just shoulders and arms."

The cold hampered other efforts as well. For example, there was no digging fox holes, King said. The ground was so hard, they had to blast out holes with cordite.

World War II veteran Erwin King holds the Silver Star he received for rescuing an injured soldier. MATT BARNARD/Tulsa World

'A big red flash'

One thing King doesn't doubt about his war experience is that he had a divine hand on him: "I think God spared me. Why I'm here — had to be God."

A perfect example, he said, was March 15, 1945. He remembers running through an orchard "under a tremendous artillery barrage," he said, "when the next thing I knew I was blown 8 feet in the air."

A shell had hit at his feet, burrowed into the soft dirt and exploded underneath him.

"The ground had just been plowed," he said.

Twice more as King ran, shells would hit the loose dirt close to his feet and blow him skyward. The last time was the worst.

"I saw this big red flash," he said. "I thought 'this is it.' I thought I was seeing my own death."

He has no memory of what happened next, just that he was running and someone tackled him. It was a couple of his fellow soldiers.

"They said, 'You can stop running,'" King recalled. "Most of my clothes had been blown off. My skin was black from the powder. I didn't know where I was." But he was OK. In fact, in spite of being nearly blown to bits three times, he didn't have a scratch, he added.

"They gave me new clothes," he said. "But the next day it was back to war. They don't give you long to rest."

He found out later that the barrage had been friendly fire.

'Cannon fodder'

King lives with his wife, Alice, in the same house they moved into in 1957. Both from El Paso, Texas, they grew up on different sides of town, and attended schools that were fierce rivals in football. They met later in the college library, where she was working. King said he would check out books just for the chance to talk to her.

As a student at what's now the University of Texas at El Paso, King joined the Army Specialized Training Program, which had been started to develop more troops with technical training. But the program was shut down later in the war and most of the students were sent to infantry units to fight.

"It was getting bad over there," he said, "and they needed cannon fodder."

Speaking of himself and his fellow soldiers in such terms, King said, is just part of the fatalistic outlook you inevitably developed in the war.

"We had a philosophy — 'We're going to die before we get out of here.' Your chances of living through all those battles was about zero.

"Dog meat — that's what we called ourselves."

Still, he added, you didn't want to tempt death. When new replacement troops arrived, because they were inexperienced and undertrained "you didn't want anything to do with them," King said.

"Often they had rushed through training to get them there."

And, anyway, he added, they'd probably be dead in a few days.

"You didn't even want to know them. It's terrible, I know," he said, shaking his head. For similar reasons, King didn't want anything to do with leadership either. Later, when made a squad leader in charge of eight men, he initially protested.

"I said no, that I didn't want to send men to their deaths. But they said 'you're in the Army.' Which meant I didn't have a choice. That was the end of that."

What was probably King's closest personal brush with death actually didn't involve fighting. For six weeks, King suffered from a case of dysentery, and tried to go about his duties despite severe diarrhea and bleeding. Eventually so weak he could hardly stand, he had to be hospitalized.

"They told me I was going to die," he said. "That was the worst day of my whole 92 years."

Given a new experimental drug, King, while waiting to see the results, tried to prepare himself to die. Fearing that he'd be separated from his dog tags and go unidentified, he made a small ring out of aluminum and engraved it with his initials, "EEK." He then put it on his little finger.

King still has his dog tags and the ring. In the end, thankfully, the drug worked and he didn't need either. By the time he recovered, he said, he'd lost 25 to 30 pounds off his already wiry frame.

World War II veteran Erwin King (right) stands with his squad mates in Germany. COURTESY

'Don't treat it cheap'

King's memory is still good. In some ways, too good.

Among the many things from the war that he'd like to forget are the cries at night — the ones you'd hear on the front lines sometimes while trying to go to sleep.

"Out in no man's land, you'd hear them, dying men trapped out there," he said. "Sometimes ours, sometimes Germans. They weren't screaming, they were shrieking. You ever heard a man shriek? They were shrieking, crying for their mothers. They wanted their mothers real bad."

The worst part, he added, was "there was nothing you could do about it. You couldn't go out there. You'd die if you tried." So you just lay there, listening, he said. "And you'd think 'Oh I wish they'd die.' Because you knew that was the best thing for them."

For three years after he got home, King suffered from frequent night sweats.

"After the war, during the occupation, you could drink it away," he said. "At home, my wife nursed me through it."

King and Alice got married four months after his return. He went on to complete a degree in geology. The couple, who raised five children together, moved to Tulsa in 1951 when he got on with Sinclair Oil. After years of not talking about the war, King eventually found relief by opening up.

"I waited 50 years," he said. "I didn't want to hear about the war, talk about it. But they (fellow veterans) told me it would help me, so I agreed. They were right."

He went on to speak publicly about his experiences, and has appeared at a number of schools and churches. Included in the topics you might hear King talk about these days is a warning.

Erwin King rests against a fence in Germany. COURTESY

"People say this is America, and that (what happened in the war) can't happen here ... They think it can't happen to them. But it can! People need to understand," he said. Moreover, King added, people shouldn't take America for granted.

"Don't treat it cheap. ... Get up and vote. And stand up when they play the national anthem."

War from the sky

Kinzer helped bomb Germany with an 8th Air Force B-17

Feb. 15, 1945, was Roland Kinzer's 19th birthday. But while there were no candles to mark it, there would be plenty of fire.

Not quite a year since he had joined the service, Kinzer and the rest of his B-17 crew mates participated in a devastating series of air raids on Dresden, Germany, which burned much of the city to the ground. From his position as tail gunner, Kinzer had a good view out of the rear of the plane. However, with so much smoke covering the ground below, there was little to see. What couldn't be obscured, though, was the significance of the raid and the others that Kinzer would be part of.

With the war in Europe now in its final phase, the Allies were turning up the heat on Hitler's Germany. For the Nazis, just two options remained: surrender unconditionally or feel the full force of the Allies' wrath.

Ranch life

Kinzer, who flew 28 combat missions over Germany between February and May 1945, was a member of the 381st Bomb Group, 8th Air Force. It was a brief interlude in what otherwise would be a life of open pastures.

Kinzer, 90, who lives in Jenks, is a former rancher who for years ran a family cattle and hay operation near Morris.

The son of a ranch manager, he learned about ranch life early on, he said. With his father's work, the family moved around a lot. Kinzer grew up in Texas and Iowa, and while still a senior in an Iowa high school, he enlisted in the Army Air Corps.

After graduating in May 1943, he reported for training, hoping to become a pilot. But pilots weren't needed at that point. So Kinzer chose to go to gunnery school, he said. Training as a gunner on a B-17, Kinzer was initially slated to become a gunnery instructor. It offered better pay and a far easier ride, Kinzer said, "but I said 'no.' I didn't want to do that."

While his request was sorted out, Kinzer wound up being

Roland Kinzer holds a shadowbox filled with medals and other mementos of his wartime service. MATT BARNARD/Tulsa World

separated from his gunnery training group. They shipped out for England, where they were assigned to the 15th Air Force. When he finally arrived two weeks behind them, in December 1944, he was assigned to the 8th Air Force.

"Everybody thought the war would be over by December," said Kinzer. But the Battle of the Bulge — a German counteroffensive that lasted several weeks from December 1944 to January 1945 — "just prolonged it."

Kinzer's first mission was on Feb. 3, 1945. A massive effort involving 1,000 B-17 bombers, the air raid, one of the biggest of the war, zeroed in on Berlin — Hitler's capital and the very heart of the German Reich. Specifically aimed at the city's government district, Kinzer's plane's target in the raid was the Reichstag building, seat of the German Parliament.

The idea that Hitler himself was down there somewhere was motivation, Kinzer said. His crew would have liked nothing better than to drop a bomb right in the Fuhrer's lap. One group after another — 36 planes to a group — the Americans released their bombs. What their bombs hit, Kinzer and his crew had no idea. Because of the heavy smoke on the ground, you never knew for sure, he said.

The raid brought no resistance from enemy aircraft, but the flak from the ground was heavy. The 381st lost 26 planes. It was far costlier, though, for Berlin. The raid leveled a large portion of the city and left 2,500 dead.

Dresden

Pummeling Germany from on high, the American and British air forces often teamed up, the former bombing during the day, the latter at night. By that time, with the German air force largely neutralized, the main threat for bomber crews was flak fired from enemy anti-aircraft guns on the ground.

"Flak would go right through the aluminum (of the plane)," Kinzer said. It began from the time they crossed into continental airspace.

"The Germans had this flak battery on the Dutch coast," Kinzer said. "We called him the 'One-eyed Dutchman.' He welcomed us to Europe."

Luckily, Kinzer's planes didn't lose any crew members during their missions.

Just two weeks after his debut raid — and coinciding with his 19th birthday — Kinzer was part of another mission for the history books. The air assault on Dresden consisted of four raids between Feb. 13-15, 1945. During that time, British and American bombers combined to drop nearly 4,000 tons of bombs and incendiary devices on the city.

Kinzer's crew's mission to Dresden was supposed to be on Feb. 14. But as happened sometimes, he said, it went awry. The squadron's lead navigator "got lost and we went clear into Czechoslovakia."

"(But) when you miss your target, you look for a 'target of opportunity,'" he added. So they dropped their bombs on German-occupied Brux instead.

The next day, they tried Dresden again. They were successful this time — though by then it seemed like overkill. The city was already decimated, Kinzer said, and still ablaze from British bombs of the night before. All told, the three days of bombings and the resulting

A fleet of B-17 bombers is shown being outfitted on a tarmac in Tulsa. COURTESY

firestorm would destroy more than 1,600 acres, and kill up to an estimated 25,000 people.

Later, the Dresden bombings came under widespread criticism, with questions raised as to whether they were justified.

"There was a lot of talk about it after the war," Kinzer said. "It was a beautiful town. We sure did a lot of damage."

Bombing Dresden had questionable strategic value, Kinzer admitted.

"We shouldn't ever have gone down there. It came down from headquarters. We were told to go, and we had to go."

Even so, he didn't feel too sorry for the Germans.

"We were mad at them and what they were doing," Kinzer said. "They were the enemy. They were doing it to everyone else."

Mission prep

Over his three months of aerial action, Kinzer — based at Ridgewell Airfield in Essex, England — flew two to three missions weekly, racking up 213 total combat hours.

On the days they were called to fly, Kinzer and his crew rose at 3 a.m.

"We got real eggs those days," he said. "The others were served powdered eggs."

Mission preparations took time. Weather permitting, crews usually flew out about 8 or 9 a.m. Kinzer and his crew alternated between several aircraft — B-17s with names like L.A. City Limits, Pair of Queens and Tinker Toy Too. Bombers usually flew above 20,000 feet, an altitude at which temperatures were well below zero.

On one mission, said Kinzer, who like his crew mates wore a heated suit, the temperature on board hit 60 below.

"The navigator said to us 'the thermometer just goes to minus 50. And it's well below that.'"

Missions to Germany were always several-hour affairs. One flight — at nine hours 30 minutes — was almost too long: Kinzer remembers the pilot, as they were crossing back over the English Channel, calling everyone to the nose of the plane.

"He said we were out of fuel and were going to have to ditch. In that deep water."

Just then, Kinzer looked out.

"I said 'Wait a minute! I think I see the white cliffs!'"

He was right: Just ahead of them lay the coast of England. They were able to find a nearby airfield for an emergency landing, Kinzer said, but "our fuel was exhausted. The engines quit as we were landing. They had to come out and tow us off the field, out of the way of the other planes."

When the war in Europe ended on May 7, Kinzer happened to be in London on a 48-hour pass. "Oh that was something. The crowds. Everybody was doing a lot of drinking."

The only problem with the Germans surrendering, Kinzer said, was "I was hoping to get in a few more missions."

At 28 missions, he was a few shy of the 35 required of a bomber crewman at the time. And with the war in the Pacific still raging, he feared he would be sent there next.

Japan surrenders

From England, Kinzer was reassigned to a replacement depot in California. But that's as close as he would get to going to the Pacific. He still remembers where he was when he found out the war was finally over.

Enjoying a few days of leave in San Francisco, "I

Roland Kinzer (top row, third from left) stands with his crew. COURTESY

B-17 bombers flying in Europe. COURTESY

was driving across the Golden Gate Bridge," Kinzer recalled, "when the radio said the Japanese had surrendered."

Back in Oklahoma, Kinzer, who finished military service with the rank of staff sergeant, took advantage of the G.I. Bill and attended what was then Oklahoma A&M. He got a degree in animal husbandry, and became a rancher.

He married his wife, Barbara, in 1950. They raised three children together. The Kinzers were married for 64 years up until Barbara's death in October 2015.

Kinzer still has a strong sense of camaraderie for fellow 8th Air Force veterans. There were enough in Tulsa at one time that they had their own group, he said. But their numbers have dwindled. Kinzer knows of just a handful now.

The nightmares Kinzer suffered after he first got home from the war eventually went away. Now, he thinks back on it mostly with pride for having served.

"It was quite an experience for an 18-year-old kid," he said. "I was glad I got to do it. I'm glad I didn't stay behind and be a gunnery instructor."

'Walking on flak'

The radio operator and gunner flew in a B-26 Marauder

Half a world away, on what would be his first day of real warfare, John Kirkland suddenly found himself reminded of home. Tulsa, it turned out, was not as far away as he'd imagined.

For his first mission, Kirkland, a radio operator and gunner on a B-26 Marauder, was surprised to learn he would be aiding a National Guard unit that included many soldiers from his area.

"A lot of my friends, no doubt," he said.

Effectively trapped by the Germans in Anzio, Italy, the Oklahoma-based 45th Infantry Division needed a little help. Called out in response, Kirkland would fly two missions with his squadron that day. And thanks to support like that, the 45th eventually would be able to break out and from there advance toward Rome.

The day's missions would also give Kirkland a pretty good idea of what was to come. The Tulsan still remembers his first taste of

it — flying at "13,000 feet with flak all around us."

With 51 more missions in front of him, his war experience was just beginning.

Ahead of the draft

Back in Tulsa three years earlier, the war had been weighing on Kirkland's mind. Although the U.S. was not in it yet, it was looking more and more inevitable. He was working for Stanolind Oil Co. at the time, doing aerial photography.

"When we started getting drafted," said Kirkland, who turned 21 that summer of 1941, "a whole bunch of us went ahead and joined the (Oklahoma National Guard's 125th Observation Squadron)," which was stationed at Municipal Airport in Tulsa.

Kirkland's experience shooting pictures from the air earned him the same role with the 125th, and he moved on to Fort Sill, where he took aerial photos of field artillery training. All of that changed soon, though.

On the first weekend of December 1941, Kirkland jumped in his powder blue 1936 Ford with some friends and headed back to Tulsa.

That's where they would be when, after a night of fun and dancing, the news broke about Pearl Harbor. They were called back to Fort Sill immediately.

With the U.S. entry into the war, Kirkland was sent to radio school and then gunnery school. From there, he was transferred to Barksdale Field in Louisiana for flight training.

"That was where I got my first sight of a B-26 Marauder medium bomber," he said.

It would also be his first sight of aerial tragedies. During his time at Barksdale, training accidents would claim the lives of many young pilots and crewmen. In some notes of his own, he recorded 31 men died in his first 31 days of training.

The main problem, Kirkland said, was that they were being taught to fly in extra-tight formations, with eight or nine planes taking off at the same time. With so small a margin for error, many of the novice pilots crashed.

The Italian campaign

Kirkland made it through, though, and in early 1944 found himself headed overseas to the war. Assigned to the 441st Bomb Squadron, 320th Bomb Group, he would be stationed at Sardinia and later Corsica, flying missions in support of operations in Italy.

After those first two missions to help out the 45th, the unit would spend the next few weeks bombing enemy installations around Rome and then seaports north up the Italian coast. The bomber formations flew with an accompaniment of fighters, usually P-47s.

Kirkland sat behind the pilot, operating the radio, until they got into combat. Then he would go back and take over the plane's waist guns.

John Kirkland served as an aerial photographer before his service in the Army Air Corps in Europe. COURTESY

John Kirkland (standing in background) cleans mess kits with his unit in Abilene, Texas, while in the Air National Guard before his service in the Army Air Corps in Europe from 1941 to 1945. COURTESY

"I had the tail gunner behind me and the turret gunner above me."

For a time, they bombed exclusively in Italy's Po Valley, including in and around Brenner Pass in the Alps.

"The Germans were bringing trains down every night," Kirkland said. "We'd knock the bridge out every night. Every morning they'd patch up the bridge and come back through again."

The Brenner Pass missions were intense and fiercely resisted, he said.

"A lot of boys got shot down, a lot of them shot up. ... Nearly every day, we got jumped by (enemy) fighters, anti-aircraft fire from the ground. We used a whole lot of evasive maneuvers."

He's still thankful for "that good ol' B-26. A fast-maneuvering medium bomber with big engines. It could change altitudes and maneuver better (than previous bombers)."

Not that they usually had a choice, but Kirkland preferred facing enemy fighters to flak. In a Tulsa World article from 1944, Kirkland talked about it:

Whenever someone said the word "bandits," which meant enemy fighters had been sighted, every man would snap to attention as if jabbed by a pin, he said. "When flak comes up, you're just stuck and have to sweat it out. But when fighters jump you, you know they're alive and you've got a chance to do something about it."

More than 70 years later, his opinion hasn't changed. He recalls at least two flights where the anti-aircraft fire from below was so heavy "we were walking on flak."

It was unnerving, he added, to "look out and see 30 bursts of flak all at one time ... and no place to go to walk home."

Advance training

In his mid-20s, Kirkland was older than many of his fellow airmen, who in a lot of cases were still in their teens. He also had some previous experiences that served him well.

Back during the era when funeral homes provided emergency ambulance service, Kirkland had driven an ambulance for Harold Bailey Funeral Home in Tulsa.

The job "matured me to a point I was able to help others (in difficult circumstances), where other young kids just fell apart," he said. "I did very well with hard knocks."

From Italy, Kirkland and the 320th would eventually move on to Dijon, France. But first they had a part to play in the D-Day invasion. It was June 6, 1944, which also happened to be his 24th birthday. Kirkland flew two missions that day, bombing the German beach defenses to soften them up for the invading ground forces.

"We did our job very well. We were very well prepared."

For its service during the war, the 320th would be recognized. Among its honors were a Presidential Unit Citation and the French Croix de Guerre with Palm.

Kirkland received a few decorations of his own, including a Purple Heart and five Air Medals.

'Pretty darn lucky'

Another keepsake from Kirkland's war days, his leather bomber jacket, is still in pretty good shape. Best of all, he can still wear it.

Accolades, on the other hand, are not a comfortable fit. Kirkland has never sought them. Still, he enjoyed the attention when Home Builders Association of Greater Tulsa singled him out for special recognition. Kirkland, a retired investment banker and life member of HBA, was guest of honor in 2015 at HBA's military appreciation event.

In recent years, Kirkland has become a student of history and the war. He knows how fortunate he was. Kirkland's planes took a lot of hits, but he always made it home.

"The crews I flew with were pretty darn lucky," he said.

John Kirkland makes snowballs between missions in Dijon, France, during his service in the Army Air Corps in Europe from 1941 to 1945. COURTESY

He shared in the all-around good luck. The incident for which he got a Purple Heart easily could've been worse. It was during a mission, and he was leaning over at his station when a piece of shrapnel hit him. It went up under his flak helmet and into the back of his neck.

"It scared the crew more than it did me," Kirkland said, adding that it turned out to not be serious.

Kirkland dwells less on his and his crewmates' luck, though, than on the fates of those whose luck ran out. Which keeps him coming back to his training days.

"The thing I think most of these days," he said, "is Barksdale and those poor people whose kids were lost there trying to fly a plane. That tore me up more than anything else. All we lost before we ever went overseas."

To the men he served with, the younger ones in particular, Kirkland can say only, "God bless 'em all."

LARRY LANTOW   ARMY 1942-46

Surviving the odds

Tank unit commander was lone survivor of three brothers

Whenever one of his men was killed in action, it was Larry Lantow's job to write to their families. But unlike many things done over and over, he said, it never got easier.

"I hated it," added Lantow, who commanded a tank company during World War II. The family "always wanted to know how he died. You might not want to tell them — he might've had his head blown off. (He) might've burned up in a tank."

But if writing the letters was hard, it didn't compare at all, Lantow knew, to receiving one.

Still fighting the war in Europe, he was not there when his parents got theirs — two letters, roughly six months apart. The news that Bob Lantow and then Norman Lantow — Larry's younger brothers — had been killed in action would rock not only the family

About Oklahoma Military Academy

Larry Lantow, who was named a Distinguished Alumnus in 2012, was a 1938 graduate of Oklahoma Military Academy and continues to serve on the board of the OMA Alumni Association.

During its years of operation, 1919 to 1971, more than 10,000 students attended OMA, on the site of what is now Rogers State University in Claremore.

With such a high percentage of its graduates going on to serve in the military, OMA became known as the "West Point of the Southwest."

Lantow was one of more than 1,000 of the school's graduates to serve during World War II; 68 of them were killed in action during that war.

RSU maintains an OMA Museum on its campus. Also, a memorial at RSU honors those graduates who died in WWII and other wars.

but the entire community of Claremore.

For Larry, the idea he might lose not one but both of his brothers to the war "never occurred to me. But I knew it was possible."

Lantow, now 98 and living in Tulsa, talked to the Tulsa World in 2015 about his war experiences and the unimaginable sacrifice his family had to make.

"I was sad about it," he said. "But that's what soldiers do — get killed."

Determined to spare the family any more losses, in December 1944 more than 600 Claremore residents signed a petition to have Larry brought home.

The Army complied. Although he didn't ask for it, Lantow said, he remains grateful.

After returning from the war, he would go on to raise a family and enjoy a long career with Tulsa's Hope Lumber and Supply.

In November 2016, a project to honor all four Lantow brothers, including Larry's late younger brother Bill, a Korea veteran, was finished and dedicated at Claremore High School's Lantow Field. The field — which was previously named in honor of Bob and Norman — is now home to four granite monuments, one for each of the brothers.

Tank commander

A Claremore native and oldest of seven siblings, Larry Lantow went to Claremore High for a year before moving on to Oklahoma Military Academy, where he graduated in 1938.

He was drafted into the Army in 1942.

Lantow might not have become a paratrooper like his brothers, both members of the Army's 101st Airborne Division, but his military service never lacked for action.

Arriving in France on Sept. 13, 1944, he took over as a replacement officer for a tank company — Company H of the 3rd Battalion, 3rd Armored Division. Over his next three months, he would lead his men in a number of firefights with German tanks across France, Belgium and eventually Germany. Everywhere he turned, he said, devastation greeted him.

France "was a mess, all shot up."

So, too, was Belgium. In Mons, he said, the residents even lined their dead children along the streets to "show what war had done to them."

As a tank commander, Lantow's biggest fear, he said, were the German "88s." Originally developed to shoot down aircraft, the 88 mm artillery guns were converted for anti-tank warfare to devastating effect, and Lantow lost many men and tanks to them.

Before he was done, Lantow would also receive a distinction for valor, a Bronze Star. It was awarded for his actions near Samree, Belgium, when he safely led a patrol into German territory, somehow avoiding an ambush.

War kept the Lantow brothers too busy to keep track of each other. But while, to his regret, he never had the chance to see Bob, Larry did have one last meeting with Norman that still gnaws at

him. Recovering from being shot and briefly captured, Norman, seven years younger than Larry, took a train to meet him in Bath, England, and they spent a day together.

"When he left, we shook hands, and he turned around and never looked back," Lantow said. "I don't know whether he was crying or what."

A few weeks later, Norman would be dead, killed by a mortar on Nov. 11, 1944.

A reluctant departure

On Dec. 28, 1944, Lantow, who by then knew of Norman's death, was called to division headquarters. Unaware as to why, he was surprised when they told him: He was going home.

"They said, 'We got orders from the president. ... You're leaving (tomorrow) morning,' " Lantow recalled. Informed that it was because his family had lost two sons already, he didn't exactly leap at the news.

"Frankly, I asked them if I had a choice. I didn't want to leave my unit. It seems strange, but you're like family. ... I hated leaving my unit."

But no choice was given. Within a few weeks, Lantow, by then a captain, was back in the states, serving as an Army instructor at Fort Knox, Kentucky. It was only later that Lantow learned what precipitated his return: the community of Claremore's petition.

Back to Normandy

The day his family found out, unthinkably, that it had lost a second son, Lantow was half a world away in Europe. But his youngest sister told him about it later.

About 10 at the time, she was riding her bike back from school when she saw cars at their house and ladies carrying casseroles inside. Immediately, Lantow said, his sister knew.

"Another brother had died — and she couldn't deal with that," he added, so she continued to ride around the neighborhood, not wanting to go home.

In 1999, to pay his respects to his fallen brothers, Lantow traveled back to France. It would be the first time he'd visited the graves.

"My parents couldn't bring themselves to bring the bodies home — it was too emotional for them," he said, adding that his mother and father never fully recovered from the deaths.

Bob and Norman are buried with other WWII troops in the Normandy American Cemetery, which overlooks Omaha Beach. Their graves, marked by white crosses, are side by side.

"I'm proud of them for serving their country," Lantow said, adding that like him, his brothers just wanted to "protect the folks at home."

He added that it easily "could've been the other way around" — him dying and them coming home. But he's never dwelt on that possibility.

"What happened, happened," Lantow said. "You have to let it go."

Risky business

Pilot ferried aircraft with poor radio contact and no autopilot

Flying solo — often for thousands of miles at a time, and with no autopilot — was bad enough. But the worst part, Neill MacKay said, was knowing that if his plane went down, he was completely on his own.

There would be no rescue.

"I might be flying at night 600 miles out over the Atlantic," he said, "and I knew 'If I'm down, I'm fish bait.' It was just me and the airplane and the ocean."

Or if not the ocean, then the wilds of Africa or some other god-forsaken place. For such occasions, should one arise, MacKay had been issued a .45-caliber pistol to protect himself. But it was small comfort. "This big .45 on my hip ... I didn't even know how to cock (it)," MacKay laughed. "Thank heaven I never had to use it. I probably would've shot my foot off."

When you were a ferry pilot, those kinds of concerns were just part of the job, he said.

Assigned to become one of the Army Air Corps' first ferry pilots during World War II — delivering war planes, one at a time, to American forces or their allies all over the world — MacKay knew going in it wouldn't be easy. "It was really dangerous flying in those days," MacKay told the Tulsa World.

"It would've been a bit different if we'd had a good radio system. We had radio, but not very good. And in the places we were going, we were flying virgin routes and there was nobody to talk to (by radio)." Consequently, if something went wrong, there was no one to help.

"No communications. ... Nobody to call."

The roughneck life

For MacKay, a retired Air Force colonel and former U.S. air attaché to Chile, World War II helped him make a change in career direction. Right out of high school, he had gone to work as a rough-neck in the oilfields of Corpus Christi, Texas, where he grew up. "It was a horrible job," he said, but he stuck with it for several years.

MacKay could see the war coming, even though the U.S. had not entered it yet. At age 23, he decided to join the Air Corps and become a pilot. Lacking the two years of college required to enter flight school, he took a three-day equivalency exam given once a year. Of the 125 who took it with him, he was one of only three who passed, he said.

Beginning flight school in June 1941, MacKay would discover on his first flight, which lasted just about an hour, that he had a knack for it. As a youth, MacKay had been an avid sailboat racer, and apparently it had preconditioned him for flying, he said.

On his final approach of that first flight "I saw we were drifting a little bit," and was able to correct for it. His instructor was impressed.

MacKay said his sailboat background would continue to help him as he developed as a pilot.

When MacKay graduated in January 1942 as a second lieutenant, the U.S. had entered the war just over a month earlier.

That timing would help determine his course. With so many other young airmen already sent overseas to fight, there was a pressing need to ferry aircraft.

MacKay drew the assignment. Following brief training, he was sent to Morrison Field in West Palm Beach, Florida, home of the recently formed Air Corps Ferrying Command.

Maps and compasses

MacKay's first mission would set the pattern for what he could expect. He recalled the exchange: "The commander called me in and he said, 'I want you to ferry an airplane.'"

"Where to, sir?" MacKay replied.

"To Panama."

"Panama? Where's that? I haven't been out of Texas."

"That's all right. I'll give you some maps."

That's how it would go with most of MacKay's ferrying flights: no navigational aids, just maps, to guide him, and no prior experience with the plane. In fact, for most of his flights, he was handed the plane's instruction manual just before take-off. Even if it was a plane he'd never heard of, he said, "It was always 'Oh, you can read the book.'"

Neill MacKay pauses in Istres, France, with his B-24, during his service in the Army Air Corps, ferrying different kinds of airplanes all over the world.
COURTESY

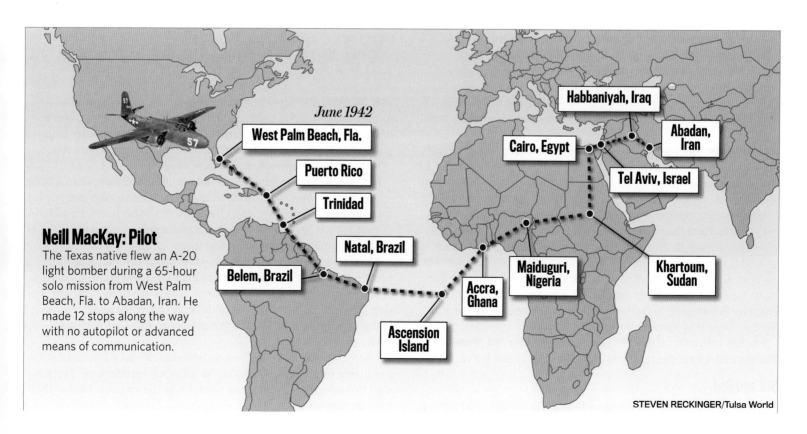

June 1942

Habbaniyah, Iraq

West Palm Beach, Fla.

Abadan, Iran

Cairo, Egypt

Puerto Rico

Tel Aviv, Israel

Trinidad

Natal, Brazil

Neill MacKay: Pilot
The Texas native flew an A-20 light bomber during a 65-hour solo mission from West Palm Beach, Fla. to Abadan, Iran. He made 12 stops along the way with no autopilot or advanced means of communication.

Belem, Brazil

Maiduguri, Nigeria

Khartoum, Sudan

Accra, Ghana

Ascension Island

STEVEN RECKINGER/Tulsa World

But while none of this was ideal, MacKay was game.

For that first mission — on which, unlike most future ones, he had a co-pilot — everything went well. There was some controversy, though. Flying an LB-40, a predecessor of the B-24 bomber, MacKay decided after crossing into the Canal Zone to "have some fun" with three P-40 fighters that greeted them. He took off and left them, he said.

"The base commander there chewed me out so badly," MacKay added, "I haven't forgotten it to this day. 'You could've been shot down.' It was a lesson I remembered for the rest of my life."

An assignment that followed in late June 1942 would be an even greater test — to ferry an A-20 light bomber, to Abadan, Iran. From there, he was told, the Russians would take it to use in their fight with the Germans.

"This one was solo," MacKay said. "No navigational aids. Just me and the airplane and a compass and hoping I'd find the airstrip."

It was a grueling flight: about 65 hours and 12 stops to refuel. And with no autopilot system, MacKay had to hold the wheel the entire time in the air. One stop — tiny Ascension Island in the middle of the Atlantic — would've been especially easy to miss, leaving him lost at sea.

But MacKay pulled it off, along with the rest of his stops, making a successful delivery to Iran.

Not for all the money in the world

"I realized when I was assigned to these missions they were not safe. But I didn't realize how dangerous," MacKay said of his time as a ferry pilot. The problem of communications can't be overstated, he said. "It's hard for anyone today to grasp just how primitive communications were," he said.

Later, after MacKay was no longer ferrying, Morrison Field even resorted to pigeons. "Nobody knows that," he said, laughing. "But it's true. We had an officer called a 'pigeoneer' who kept a flock of pigeons. When they ferried a plane, they'd put a pigeon in it." If the plane went down, the pigeon — which wore a tag denoting the plane and time of departure — would return to the base, he said.

"That way," MacKay added, "we'd know something had happened and could send out searchers."

But at the time he was ferrying, the pigeons hadn't been introduced yet, so MacKay didn't even have that to fall back on. Summing up the experience of ferrying planes, he said, "If I was asked to do it today, I wouldn't do it for all the money in the world."

After a while, MacKay was made operations officer at Morrison, and instead of ferrying planes he tested them as they arrived from the factory. "If everything worked, I'd sign off on it," he said. Between his ferrying and testing, MacKay would pilot almost 50 different planes — bombers, fighters, transports, just about every kind imaginable — over a six-year period.

Later in the war, MacKay was transferred to Europe to serve with Air Transport Command in France. During the Battle of the Bulge he would be commander of an air base near Marseilles that helped supply the front. "I never did get in combat, thank goodness," he said.

Among other highlights of his flying days, MacKay, during different stints in Palm Beach, was a personal pilot to two commanding generals, Edward H. Alexander and Haywood Hansell, flying each around his Caribbean command area. From there, after the war, his posts would include executive officer to Under Secretary of the Air Force Roswell Gilpatric; air attaché to Chile, working out of the U.S. Embassy in Santiago; and chief of plans and programs for the U.S. Nuclear Detection System.

MacKay retired from the Air Force in 1964. After "23 years, six months and a day," the time was right, he said, to call it a career.

Grit and God

The walls of MacKay's study are a Who's Who of faces and aircraft.

Neill MacKay stands at Morrison Field in Florida in 1942, during his service in the Army Air Corps. COURTESY

Included among the people are images of his late son, Jeff MacKay, a career actor who had a recurring role on Magnum P.I. There are also photos of Robert Redford (MacKay's cousin), Jimmy Stewart (a close family friend) and statesmen and dignitaries whom he had the opportunity to meet through his career.

MacKay went on to have some entertainment experience of his own. It was at the invitation of his friend Harold Stuart, who founded KVOO television, that MacKay moved to Tulsa after retiring from the military. He served as KVOO chief executive officer for eight years.

MacKay has collected a few honors as well. Most recently, in 2011, Tulsa Air & Space Museum named him a "Hometown Hero."

But perhaps the accomplishment he's most proud of is his education. While in the Air Force, taking advantage of an opportunity to have his education paid for, he earned bachelor's and master's degrees, the latter a master's in business administration. He completed each in two years, taking more than 20 hours a semester.

It took "grit" to manage it, MacKay said.

But by that time in his life, he had accumulated more than a little.

The war, for one, had "matured me tremendously. You can't imagine how much." And don't discount the importance, he added, of that old job back in the oilfields. Roughnecking prepared MacKay for just about everything life could throw at him.

That included the war, where he discovered he "was much more prepared than the guys right out of high school who had no experience in tough living. (Roughnecking) helped me to make tough decisions, including in the air in difficult circumstances."

But more than grit, MacKay ultimately credits God for his success.

There's no way he could have survived his aerial adventures without divine intervention, he said. "In all of my experiences," MacKay said, "I know that God was my pilot. I was the co-pilot. I know that he took care of me."

ARMY 1944-46

Seeing justice done

Vet was a guard at prison where war criminals were hanged

One second they were there, the next they were gone.

That's how fast condemned inmates would drop from sight — whenever the trap door opened on the Landsberg Prison gallows.

But even if Herbert McClure couldn't see them, he knew they were still there. "You could hear it when they hit the end of the rope," he said. "Just a thump."

Over his two days of standing guard at the hangings of convicted Nazi war criminals, McClure would hear that thump 28 times.

"It was 14 a day, if I remember correctly," he said.

Coming several months after World War II had ended, McClure's brief stint as a prison guard would be his last official military assignment. The Army figured he could help out at the prison, he said, while awaiting his return to the states.

"It's not something I would have volunteered for," said McClure,

Medals adorn World War II veteran Herbert McClure's jacket.
MATT BARNARD/Tulsa World

who before the fighting ended was on an infantry mortar crew. "But we were ordered to do it. In the Army you don't get a choice."

In a way, though, it was a fitting way to finish his service. Not many of McClure's fellow soldiers would have the opportunity to see justice done firsthand.

'I told her I might not come home'

Visit Herb McClure at his Tulsa home — which he shares with his wife of 70 years, Bonnie — and you can't help but notice all the beautiful wood furniture.

"I made all but one of them," said McClure, who owned and operated his own furniture business, during a 2016 interview.

Holding up his now brown hands, he wiggled his fingers to show that after 60-plus years of working with sharp instruments, all are still intact.

And they should stay that way. Earlier that year, at long last, McClure, 92, agreed to retire his tools for good. His eyesight is failing, he said, and his family thought it best.

McClure's earliest work experience was on his grandparents' Depression-era dairy farm, near Neodesha, Kansas, where he grew up. He started working there at 11, and by age 14, was able to buy his first car — a used Ford Model A.

It cost him $15. The investment paid off better than McClure could've imagined. Soon after, he started picking up Bonnie Gentry, who lived down the road from him, for school.

From those rides, a relationship took root. The pair began dating, and later, when McClure was drafted into the Army, they even talked about marriage. "But I told her I might not come home," he said. "And I didn't want to leave her a war widow."

So Bonnie agreed to wait for him. While McClure was gone, she took a job in a factory helping to make 60mm mortar shells for the war — "the same kind of shells," he said, "that I would be using."

McClure officially enlisted on Aug. 26, 1944. A friend of his from school, Bob Estes, joined at the same time. The two served in the same unit through the end of the war. "Ordinarily, they didn't keep men from the same town together," McClure said. "I guess they weren't paying close attention."

Assigned to the 90th Infantry Division (357th Battalion), known as the "Tough 'Ombres," the pair reported for boot camp at Camp Roberts, California. It was supposed to last 17 weeks, McClure said. "But our division had suffered so many casualties. They needed us real bad."

So after just 12 weeks of training, he and the other replacement troops shipped out. Next stop, the European Theater.

All in a day's fighting

They caught up with the 90th in Belgium.

By then, it was early January 1945 and the Battle of the Bulge was winding down. But not so the winter weather. With the region enduring its worst winter in 100 years, the new arrivals' first combat experiences were complicated by snow and sub-zero temperatures.

Nevertheless, they understood the necessity: Combat, McClure said, "was something you just had to do. It was the day's work as far as we were concerned."

There would be many days of such work ahead of them, as the Allies resumed their advance. McClure's battalion crossed into Germany and began taking towns. "Lots of little towns," McClure recalled. "After you took one, you could look and see the next one up ahead."

Herbert McClure
The Kansas native fought with the 90th Infantry Division in Europe in 1945. After the war, he served as a prison guard at Landsberg Prison holding Nazi war criminals, many who were connected with Mauthausen concentration camp in Austria.

Landsberg Prison
Capacity: 800
Population: 724 average
Opened: 1910
Former name: War Criminal Prison No. 1
Adolf Hitler served 264 days at Landsberg Prison in 1924, where he wrote his book "Mein Kampf" with assistance from Rudolf Hess.

SOURCE: Jewish Virtual Library; U.S. Holocaust Memorial Museum

Mauthausen-Gusen concentration camp
Mauthausen started as a single camp but expanded over time, growing to be one of the largest labor camp complexes in the German-controlled part of Europe.
Operational: August 1938 - May 1945
Number of inmates: On May 3, 1945, 64,800 men and 1,734 women were officially registered as inmates, in addition to some 15,000 non-registered prisoners.
Killed: Between 122,766 and 320,000 (estimated)

STEVEN RECKINGER/Tulsa World

Serving with a mortar crew, McClure's main job was carrying the shells, passing them to be fired from the 60 mm mortar guns. Being a mortar man offered at least one advantage, he said: In taking a town, "the machine gunners were out front, then the riflemen. We were next. That kept us out of some of the small arms fire. The ones in front took more casualties."

Some hazards were unavoidable. "We'd go to take a town and sometimes they'd bring in the tanks to soften it up first. The tanks would level those 105 mm howitzers and fire away. We'd be laying on the ground, the shells firing just a few feet above us. The snow and dust would just fly."

His hearing, he said, has never been the same, and now he relies on hearing aids.

March 16, 1945, was McClure's 21st birthday. But it would be important for more than that. In fact, McClure would come to think of the day they took Pfaffenheck, Germany, as his most memorable of the war.

"All we were told the day before," he recalled, "was that we were going to take this town and that it wouldn't be easy — it was filled with SS soldiers." Many members of the elite Nazi SS, they knew, were devoted Hitler fanatics who would never surrender.

As expected, American casualties were heavy and a number of tanks were destroyed. "Those SS-ers wouldn't give up," McClure said. But by the end of the second day the town was secured.

"We counted 100 dead SS troopers. No survivors on their side."

McClure missed out on the end of the war in Europe in May 1945. He, Estes and several other members of their unit had bad cases of jaundice and had to be flown to Paris.

When the news broke of Germany's surrender, McClure was still in a hospital ward. "Oh, those nurses and doctors like to have blown the roof off (celebrating)," McClure said. "But we were so sick we really didn't care. We just stayed in bed."

After they recovered, McClure and Estes drew assignments that would separate them for the first time. "Poor ol' Bob got sent to Nuremberg to stand guard at the (war crimes) trials," McClure said. "I got lucky. I was sent to beautiful Garmisch in the Bavarian mountains."

Date with the hangman

Following his months in Garmisch, McClure would spend the last part of his European service as a guard at Landsberg Prison.

Landsberg was where, two decades earlier, a young Adolf Hitler had been imprisoned and from which he had written "Mein Kampf." By the time McClure arrived after the war, it had been converted to hold Nazis convicted in the trials at Nuremberg and Dachau.

A number of them were facing death sentences, including several connected with Mauthausen concentration camp. As part of his duty, McClure stood guard in the courtyard during the hangings.

The hangman, a burly Army sergeant, was good at his work, he said. "He was as big as Hoss Cartwright," McClure added, describing him as he often has over the years when repeating the story.

Recently he was shocked to see the man's face again. This time it was staring grimly up at him from the cover of a WWII magazine. The article identified him as John C. Woods. The only American hangman in the European theater, he had deferred demobilization to stay on and hang top Nazis.

As a guard, McClure made regular rounds, stopping at each cell door to peer in through its small eye-level window. The principal concern, he said, was to make sure none of the inmates tried to commit suicide and escape justice.

It was in the process of making those rounds that McClure first came into contact with Dr. Erich Wasicky. Wasicky was a Nazi SS captain and pharmacist who had been convicted in the Dachau trials for his role in gassing prisoners at Mauthausen. Trial testimony indicated that Wasicky installed the gas chamber there, supplied the gas

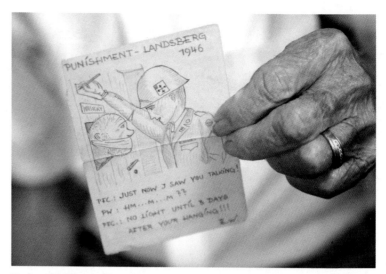

Herbert McClure holds a cartoon drawn by Nazi war criminal Dr. Erich Wasicky. McClure received the cartoon while serving as a prison guard in Landsberg Prison. MATT BARNARD/Tulsa World

and selected victims. The number of his victims is still not known.

Wasicky's killing days were over, though, by the time McClure arrived on the scene. Instead, the condemned man passed the time drawing.

McClure found this out by accident when one day during his guard rounds, through the small aperture in the cell door Wasicky suddenly presented him with a cartoon that he had drawn.

And he continued to do this periodically. He never said anything, McClure said, just handed him a slip of paper. McClure still has the dozen or so cartoons. Signed "E.W.," they depict scenes from daily life at the prison, with Wasicky's ironic commentary.

Conversing with the inmates was forbidden, so McClure never really talked to Wasicky. He remembers from brief exchanges, though, that he spoke perfect English.

When McClure's time was up, Wasicky was still imprisoned at Landsberg. But he would eventually keep his date with the hangman.

Flag still flying

McClure, meanwhile, had another date to keep.

Exactly 30 days, he said, after he got back to Neodesha, he and Bonnie were married. They celebrated their 70th anniversary on Aug. 4, 2016.

Moving to Tulsa in 1949, the couple raised two children, while McClure went to work for the furniture business he would eventually come to own. McClure Furniture Refinishing and Gentry Job Shop is still going, now with McClure's son in charge.

McClure said he's never suffered from nightmares like other veterans. "It's over and behind me," he said of the war. "I wouldn't volunteer to go through it again, though."

But he still carries the physical toll. With his hearing and vision problems, and varicose veins in his legs that he says are related to marching, McClure is a 100 percent disabled veteran. He said he has a generally good opinion of the Army, though, and feels like it has taken care of him.

McClure was discharged from service on July 4, 1946 — a date he still likes to point out to people, as though proof his patriotism had been divinely affirmed.

Also testifying to it is the flagpole that stands in front of his home, from which he proudly flies his American flag.

McClure received a number of decorations for his service, including two Bronze Stars, which he displays in a shadow box.

"(But) the honor I'm most proud of," he said, "is being able to fly my flag 24/7 in my yard."

Musician at war

Glen McGuire almost didn't survive Los Negros

After a battle, it wasn't always easy to tell the wounded from the dead.

But thankfully, in Glen McGuire's case, someone was paying close attention. Just as he was about to be stacked among the slain for burial, a fellow soldier saw a sign of life: one of his fingers twitched.

So instead, McGuire was moved in with the wounded.

However, while very much alive, he was far from all right. A regimental musician who doubled as a stretcher-bearer, McGuire had been caught up in the thick of the fighting on the Pacific island of Los Negros. While there, a line had been crossed somewhere deep inside him. Triggered possibly by the stress and the horrors he'd seen, McGuire lost his grip on his sanity.

Brought back among the wounded at Los Negros, he went into

a mental free-fall that would mean not only the end of the war for him, but a long, terrifying period of intensive treatment.

McGuire — who, as a poet, would later put these experiences into words — refused to give defeat the final word, though. Although he would continue to battle the effects of post-traumatic stress disorder, he would live fully and well, enjoying a rewarding career as an educator.

Late in life, McGuire even took up, of all things, running marathons. It was as though he had one final exclamation point to put on his triumph over trauma.

Pawnee proud

At 96, McGuire has long since retired from all that. He ran his last marathon in 2001 at age 84.

A resident of Saint Simeon's retirement community in Tulsa, McGuire sat for an interview with the Tulsa World in 2016.

A proud member of the Pawnee Nation, McGuire grew up in Pawnee, Oklahoma, where he and his younger sister were raised by their grandparents on their father's side. McGuire's ties to the

'WW II,' by Glen McGuire

Dug-in on Los Negros
a night of bunkers and foxholes
programmed for death
a cicada silence clicking clicking
suddenly exploding
dazzling light-shows that shadowed
waves of banzai breaking through
stuttering machine guns and BARS
M-1s and hand-grenades, echoing into silence.
somewhere a snapping twig
a sliding metal a moan a thud.
Come day our dead to be counted —
the enemy to be stacked and bulldozed
into a mass grave. . . .

Los Negros campaign phasing out
left time to think, but voices, whispering voices
drove me sleepless out of the camp.
AWOL and lost in a tangled rain forest,
voices swarmed my head
while at hand a machete hacked away
the snarling vines.
and diving green birds roundly complained
the cursed trespassing.

Moments of fragile sanity:
a straight-jacket half-awakening
bound on a plane to The Promised Land
while an angel in white soothed my sweating brow —
"There now, there now, war's over for you.
You're going home."

Re-routed to Buna — rows of white beds,
sedations, blackouts in a naked wire cage
where I was ordained a brown-skin Moses
among the nude disciples.
of a raving, chest-thumping Jesus Christ . . . .
Moses awoke stunned and stumbling
to an en masse attack against the guards
who finally gagged and bound him
to an electro-shock-treatment machine.

In Phoenix, full of truth serum,
I cried out to a prying face
a flood of childhood fears and
schizophrenic logic.

In a strain of voices (each day cloning the last)
nothing was hoped-for but ever-lasting silence —
eluding my guard, I jumped off a speeding train
and later near drowned head first
in a barrel of Oklahoma rain . . . .

Months went by.

At last a panel of jurors reviewed my case. and
I was detailed to a VA cafeteria,
where, in a store room alone one day,
I found myself clutching a butcher knife!
Suddenly, in one overwhelming moment,
I chose to live.

Oceans and time zones and pain to this day —
not entirely sane. . . .

Oklahoman Glen McGuire was assigned to the 1st Cavalry where he played in a regimental band. COURTESY

Pawnee tribe run deep. His grandfather on his mother's side was a Pawnee chief.

At 14, McGuire was sent to Haskell Indian School in Lawrence, Kansas, at the time a boarding school. It was there, McGuire said, that he took up the trumpet. Its main appeal at the time, he added, was that "it was loud." McGuire graduated from Haskell in 1939.

Although he knew the proud warrior tradition of the Pawnees, he admits that wasn't what he was thinking about when he volunteered for the Army. "I was adventurous," he said.

Assigned to the 1st Cavalry Division and sent to Fort Bliss, Texas, McGuire, like other cavalry troops, was trained on horseback. At the time, the Army wanted cavalry units prepared to fend off any potential invasions from the south through Mexico. But with the war in the Pacific heating up, that plan changed and the 1st Cavalry Division was sent there instead.

For McGuire, the plan would change even more dramatically. Among his papers, he still has the yellowed handwritten letter requesting he be reassigned to the 1st Cavalry's 5th Cavalry Regiment Band. "This young man will be of more value to the service as a musician," it reads in part, written by the regimental band leader.

McGuire couldn't have agreed more. He was glad when the transfer was approved.

"We had a band director who was also a composer," said McGuire, who played the trumpet, tuba and sousaphone. "We played marches — Sousa marches."

The band's primary role was to bolster troop morale, but the musicians took on other duties as needed. In combat zones, that included assisting medics in the field and serving as stretcher-bearers.

And it wasn't only the wounded who would need bearing. "Everybody that was killed," McGuire said, "had to be brought in from the front."

Musicians played their part

The musician's introduction to this grim task came in February 1944, when the 1st Cavalry Division was dispatched to help capture the Japanese-held Admiralty Islands north of New Guinea. The campaign was to start with the chain's third-largest

World War II veteran Glen McGuire (second row, fourth from left, with oboe) and other members of a military band. COURTESY

island, Los Negros, and go from there.

When the invasion began on Feb. 29, McGuire's 5th Cavalry Regiment was in the thick of the action. Three days in, it came to a head for the 5th when it had to face down, together with a unit of Navy Seabees, a furious nighttime assault.

The 5th withstood everything thrown at it. By dawn, when it was over, more than 750 Japanese troops were dead, compared to only 61 Americans. The 5th Cavalry received a Presidential Unit Citation, and one of McGuire's comrades, Sgt. Troy McGill, was awarded the Medal of Honor.

For their part on Los Negros, McGuire and other band members were singled out for praise by 5th Cavalry commanding officer, Col. Hugh Hoffman. When duty demanded they set their instruments aside, the musicians had stepped up, Hoffman said in a letter: "Transporting, often by hand, ammunition, water and rations to troops in battle ... evacuation of the wounded by litter over tortuous trails subjected to enemy sniper fire. ... A great deal of your work was performed under enemy fire. ... I am proud of you for the part you played in the distinguished victory won by your regiment."

Los Negros, mostly secured by March 11, would be used by Allied forces as an important air and sea base through the end of the Pacific war. The overall Admiralty Islands campaign itself would continue through May 18.

For McGuire, however, the war ended on Los Negros. It was there, with the fighting winding down, that he began to hear voices — the prelude to his mental breakdown.

Choosing to live

Initially mistaken for dead after one battle — before an alert medic saw his finger twitching — McGuire was brought back for medical examination. It was just the beginning of the horrors to come.

Ultimately, with his sanity unravelling, he had to be sedated and restrained by straitjacket. Returning first to New Guinea and then to the U.S., he would also undergo shock treatments. It was a harrowing time that he would remember only in fragments.

In a twist verging on the cinematic, McGuire actually escaped briefly, jumping from a train en route from San Diego to a veterans treatment facility in Little Rock, Arkansas. He was quickly apprehended.

But the real jumping-off point was yet to come: Sometime later, McGuire found himself, knife in hand, determined to take his own life. What stopped him he later recalled in one of his poems: "Suddenly, in one overwhelming moment, I chose to live," he wrote.

He's been choosing to live every day since.

After recovering sufficiently, McGuire began to put his life back together. He attended the University of Tulsa and then Phillips University in Enid. He earned a bachelor's in music, embarking on what would be a successful career in education, teaching both music and English. It included serving as band director at his alma mater, Haskell Indian School and eventually teaching for several years at Sherman Indian High School in Riverside, California.

Music has been a constant in his life. At one time, he was bandleader for his own group, traveling and performing.

He also found a creative outlet in poetry. A book of his poems, titled "Spider Spins Between Two Worlds," was published. McGuire won awards for it, and gave poetry readings around the country. In July 2016, he was recognized by the Pawnee Nation as its poet laureate emeritus.

Running to the finish

The marathons came later on, after McGuire had retired and moved back to Tulsa in the early 1990s.

Taking up running in his mid-70s seemed like a worthy challenge. "I just wanted to be an all-around athletic person," explained McGuire, who also became a tournament-winning senior tennis player.

His first marathon was the Los Angeles Marathon in 1996. He was 76 at the time, and placed first in his age group. In between marathons, he participated in other events, including several Tulsa Runs and the Oklahoma Senior Olympics, where he continued regularly to finish tops in his age group.

Because there wasn't much information for marathon runners his age, he developed his own training regimen. He became a regular on Tulsa's River Parks trail along Riverside Drive, his favorite spot to work out.

He ran his last marathon, the Chicago Marathon, in 2001. "I just got tired of it," he said of his decision to retire at age 84.

As good as McGuire was on his feet, he knows there's no running away from the war. He still has nightmares after all these years. But when he's awake he tries not to think about it, he said.

"It makes me unhappy."

Instead he chooses to think about the future. His big goal now? "I want to live to be 100," he said.

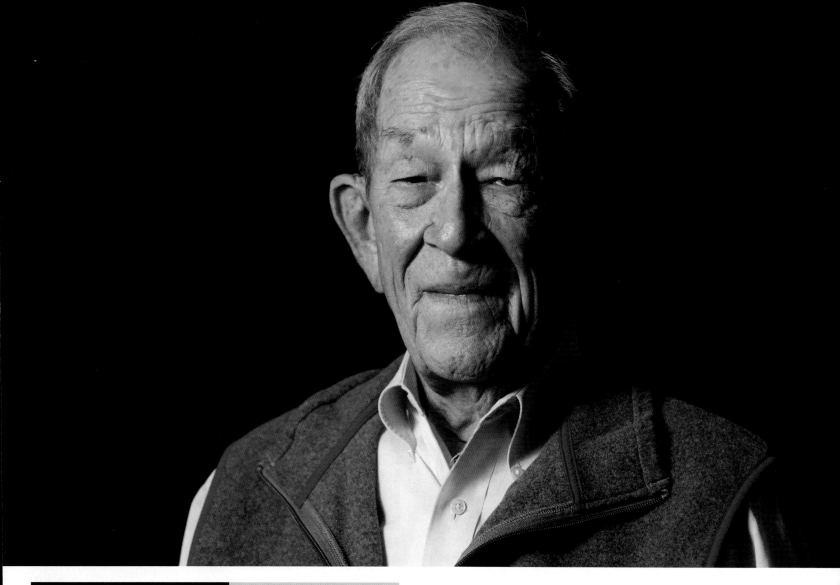

No glory in war

McKee was an Army paratrooper in Europe

Five jumps — four daytime and one at night. That was all you got.

"Then you were ready," said Calvin McKee. "As far as the Army was concerned anyway."

Taking place over a week, the five jumps from airplanes marked the culmination of paratrooper school at Camp Blanding, Florida. By the time you got around to the actual parachuting, McKee said, it could be intimidating. Occasionally a man would back out.

But that was rare, he said. Most completed all of their jumps successfully. McKee, who would go on to make multiple combat jumps in Europe, explained the psychology of it:

"You've been in a situation with a bunch of your friends and you're going to do something," he said, "but you're not sure you want to. But because you're with your friends, you go ahead. That's what it was like.

"You did it," he added, "because you didn't want to be the wimp."

'There's no romance about war'

When the Tulsa World met with him in 2016 at Montereau retirement community, McKee, 93, clearly wasn't jumping to be interviewed.

He consented. But on one condition: That nothing he said be presented in a way that could be interpreted as glorifying war. "There's no romance about war," said McKee, former president of Warren Petroleum in Tulsa. "It's a bloody,

Key dates in airborne warfare

World War II marked the first time paratroopers had been used in warfare. Some key dates:

July 1940: First U.S. airborne unit formed.

Nov. 8, 1942: First U.S. Army combat jump takes place in North Africa.

June 6, 1944: 13,100 American paratroopers participate in the D-Day invasion of Normandy.

Aug. 2, 1944: The 1st Allied Airborne Army is officially formed and will control all Allied airborne forces in Europe through the end of the war.

Sept. 17-25, 1944: Operation Market Garden, still the largest airborne operation in history, drops over 34,600 airborne troops into the Netherlands, including 20,000 paratroopers.

degrading thing. Horrible, nasty, degrading."

But back in October 1942, when he volunteered for the Army paratroopers, McKee didn't know any of that. One of seven children and a graduate of Tulsa's Marquette High School, McKee at the time was two years into the University of Tulsa's engineering program. His parents wanted him to stay in school, he said. But he made up his mind to put his education on hold.

Why he chose to jump out of airplanes as his way to serve in the war, McKee can't remember. "I can't put myself in the same frame of mind," he said. "It's been too long."

At the time, the use of paratroopers in warfare was new. The first U.S. airborne unit had been formed in July 1940, with the first combat jump following more than two years later.

For most of his action, McKee was assigned to the 18th Airborne Corps, part of the 1st Allied Airborne Army, which controlled all American and British airborne units in Europe, after it was formed in August 1944 by order of General Dwight Eisenhower. McKee served in airborne intelligence and reconnaissance units. His job, after dropping into an area, was to gather information on enemy weapons, troops and commanders, which would help the Allies plan their movements.

McKee was first stationed in North Africa, and began making jumps in Europe. By then a master sergeant, he saw action in Sicily, Italy, France, Belgium, Holland and Germany.

Drop zone

McKee's gear included main and reserve chutes and a drop bag, which contained his disassembled M-1 rifle. By the time you had all of it on, he said, you could do little more than "waddle" onto the airplane.

It didn't get any more comfortable. The harness on your main chute was kept so tight, McKee said, "you ached by the time you got ready to jump."

The jumps were made from C-47 transport aircraft that carried about 12 to 15 paratroopers. A typical combat jump, McKee said, was done from about 800 feet up flying at roughly 90 mph. But pilots often couldn't hold their position — antiaircraft fire was a constant threat once you crossed enemy lines — so it could be much lower than that.

But there were other things to worry about. Like "making absolutely sure your static line was still hooked," McKee said. Connecting the paratrooper to the plane, the static line had to remain hooked as the trooper jumped. Then it would break free and automatically deploy the chute. If the chute failed, you had to manually deploy the reserve one.

When they arrived at the drop zone, the jump commenced. The paratroopers jumped one after another in rapid succession, McKee said, "jammed up as close together as you could get, so you'd get minimal dispersal on the ground." Keeping dispersal to a minimum meant troopers were able to find each other quickly, then proceed to their designated assembly point. From there, "you went about your objective," McKee said.

He doesn't remember how many combat jumps he made. Except for his drop into Holland for Operation Market Garden, they were all at night.

But while the details of most are fuzzy now, one — a jump into southern France — McKee couldn't forget if he tried.

The silhouette

It was a cloudy night, McKee recalled.

Passing through low-hanging clouds on his descent, he landed in a vineyard, where he began preparing to move out. "Another man from our (group) landed not far from me. I knew where he hit because I could hear him putting his rifle together."

At that moment, McKee saw something loom up beside the other

Paratrooper Calvin McKee waves from a train as he leaves home for his service in World War II. COURTESY

man.

"This silhouette came up. The light was dim but I could see it. I can still see it vividly. It came up and then I heard the gun shot. I don't know if it was a German or not. But he shot and killed my man."

McKee raised his own weapon.

"I shot him," he said. But he doesn't think it was fatal. When his fallen comrade was recovered later, no one could find a second body. "I guess I just wounded him."

Whatever the case, McKee can still see that silhouette: "It was very impressionable on my mind."

At least one of McKee's parachuting memories is amusing. But to get him to tell the story he calls "The Time I Fell Out of the Plane," you have to catch him in the right mood, and still must almost twist his arm.

"It was horribly embarrassing," he said, smiling wryly and shaking his head. It was during an assignment to train French airborne units to jump out of American C-47s. McKee was serving as jumpmaster on one training flight.

"As jumpmaster," he said, "you count parachutes in the air. So if there is any malfunction you can radio back to medical people on the ground and they can be on the lookout."

Peering out the door after the troopers jumped, he had started counting chutes when with no warning the plane banked sharply left. McKee was unable to brace himself.

"It was sheer stupidity on my part," he said of tumbling out the door into mid-air. "I wasn't holding on to anything and it just caught me unawares."

McKee's luck held and he was able to deploy his chute and

land safely. His buddies, he said, weren't going to let him off easy, though. They gave him a hard time.

"It took a long time to live it down," McKee said.

Pulling the drawer shut

McKee said his job and duties kept him too busy to worry.

Which is one reason, he said, he's glad he wasn't in the infantry. Infantry troops often had a lot of down time. And down time meant thinking.

"I think the combat soldier reaches a point," McKee said, "where he puts his memories — of home, mom and dad, friends, the old bicycle, the first car — in the desk drawer and pulls it shut. ... For me, I had no free time to let my mind go there.

"The ideal soldier is totally mentally involved in whatever his assignment is. He can't think about those things."

When the war in Europe ended in May 1945, McKee pondered his next move. He could've stayed in Europe, he said. And "just for fun," he made several parachute jumps testing new equipment.

But in the end, he volunteered to go to the Pacific. Japan surrendered, though, before he could get there and McKee was discharged in October 1945.

Looking back, McKee is bluntly dismissive about the importance of his war service. Yes, he jumped out of planes, he said. "But everybody did that."

He does take pride, though, in one aspect of his service, he said: Making master sergeant. Just 20 at the time, the promotion came a year and nine months after he joined — an unusually short amount of time.

Coming home from the war, McKee resumed his studies at TU, going on to earn a degree in petroleum engineering.

Again, though, he would put his career on hold. Offered a direct commission as an intelligence officer, he accepted it and served with an intelligence battalion of the 18th Airborne. The Korean War was underway then, but he was never sent to Korea.

Finishing his second stint in the Army as a first lieutenant, McKee then got back to his career and his family. He and his late wife,

Patti, raised six children together, and he enjoyed a long career with Warren Petroleum. He retired in 1983 from his post as company president.

What patriotism means

McKee picked up a couple of pastimes as a soldier that, 70 years later, are still with him. One of them is smoking: "My Uncle Sam started me on that — our K-rations always came with four cigarettes," he said, as he fished one out from the pack of Marlboro 100s he keeps handy.

Then, there's the shooting. Trained on various kinds of weaponry during the war, McKee took up competitive shooting when he came home, and went on to win many championships. He was inducted into the Oklahoma State Skeet Association Hall of Fame in 1999 and named to the National Skeet Shooting Association All-American Team in 2006. He still tries to shoot as often as he can, he said.

When it comes to taking up arms as a nation, though, McKee, who's had a long time to think about it, is adamantly opposed to anything other than defensive war.

"It's the only conclusion I can draw. It's the only justifiable war. I am opposed to anything else. ... World War II was an absolutely defensive war to protect our country. It was a totally defensive war and it was done well."

"Patriotism," he added, "means the obligation of every citizen to rise to the defense of their country."

While that obligation is shared equally by all, McKee doesn't believe in equal distribution of honors. "I don't mean to denigrate (noncombat roles). They did what they were called to do," he said. "But it's the true combat veteran that should be honored. They are the ones who carried the brunt of it."

His own role, he said, kept him mostly out of combat. Still, there was plenty of danger, and McKee knows his story could have turned out quite differently.

"The Lord looked after me," he said. "There's no doubt about that. I was very fortunate."

Bombs away

Jerry McKinney flew 90-plus combat missions in two wars

Jerry McKinney's daily walk on the grounds at Heatheridge Assisted Living center wouldn't be complete without a cigar.

"Mostly it's just to chew on," the Tulsan, 91, said, adding that he rarely lights one up. Wherever he goes, he said, he tries to keep a cigar or two handy, usually tucked in his shirt pocket.

A habit that goes all the way back to World War II and the beginning of his aviation career — when he liked to chew one while in the air — nowadays McKinney's cigars only accompany flights of memory.

McKinney, a retired lieutenant colonel and former Strategic Air Command pilot who fought in WWII and Korea, flew more than 90 missions in B-26 aircraft between the two wars, starting as a bombardier.

He talked about his experiences in a 2016 interview with the Tulsa World. Growing up in Lone Wolf, a small community in southwest

Oklahoma, McKinney worked on the family farm, picking corn and cotton and milking cows, before joining the Army Air Corps.

A high school senior at the time, he was allowed to finish the school year and graduate before being called up. That was June 1943. McKinney finished flight training, he said, and as a newly commissioned second lieutenant was ready to ship out for Europe. But first he had other business to take care of.

A couple of years earlier, at a Sadie Hawkins dance, he had met Dorothy Jo Peck from nearby Hobart. What started, he said, with a "hello, Miss Brown Eyes" would last well beyond that night. The two soon got serious. And before McKinney left for the war, they got married.

'It always came back'

When he arrived in Europe in November 1944, McKinney would be assigned to the 344th Bomb Group, 494th Bomb Squadron, of the 9th Air Force, and stationed at a base several miles northeast of Paris. It would be several weeks before barracks were built, so the airmen slept on the ground in four-man tents.

The missions, however, began without delay. Flying a Martin B-26 Marauder known as "Boomerang" — a previous pilot had named it that because "it always came back" — McKinney was the bombardier-navigator of his six-member crew.

They typically flew in formations of six groups of six airplanes each, bombing ahead of ground forces to impair the Germans' ability to keep fighting. Flying at 8,000 to 10,000 feet, they primarily targeted airfields and factories in Germany. "We didn't know what they were making, but they were damn sure making something," McKinney said.

As bombardier, he sat in the nose of the plane.

For their first mission, "I remember doing a lot of praying. But we came out all right. We were shot at and shot up, but we didn't get hit too bad." But the threats kept coming with future missions — enemy fighter planes in the air, and powerful anti-aircraft guns from the ground below.

"If we counted three shots of flak in front of us and then three behind us, that meant they had us zeroed in. We had to take evasive action." There were close calls aplenty. The plane was equipped with cameras, and McKinney still has pictures that were snapped of a couple of the neighboring B-26s in flames.

"It could've been us. But it wasn't. … It made you feel lucky. I kept wondering when my luck would run out."

Thankfully, it wouldn't — not for McKinney or his crewmates. Over their 31 missions, not one was lost or even injured. McKinney received several decorations, including a Distinguished Flying

Cross. The cross, to the best of his memory, was for "bombing a German runway and taking out a lot of planes," he said.

By May 1945, when the Germans surrendered, bringing the war in Europe to an end, McKinney was stationed in Belgium. From there, he would move on to Germany. It gave him a chance to see from ground level what the bombs he had dropped could do. "One airfield we took over (near Munich) had been bombed and lost most of its hangars. The town, too, had been pretty well pulverized."

He has to admit — it made him kind of proud. "I felt good. I thought, 'Great!' "

Also while in the Munich area, McKinney took the opportunity to visit Dachau concentration camp. He didn't have to go, he said, but he wanted to. His commanders wanted the men to see it and never forget. The camp had already been liberated. But the smell from the place — where more than 30,000 prisoners had been killed over 12 years, and most of the bodies burned — hit you from several miles away, he said. Some former inmates, having no place to go, were still there, and showed them around the camp, McKinney said.

"It shook me up, the things the (Nazis) did to people," he said.

He can still visualize the rooms where the dead had once been stacked. There were "red stains on the walls — and not from paint brushes," he said.

'Thank you for your service'

By the time McKinney got home in January 1946, he had a 1-year-old daughter waiting for him. Dorothy had given birth to

World War II bombardier Jerry McKinney (third from left) stands with other members of his crew. COURTESY

An aerial photo taken by World War II bombardier Jerry McKinney shows another plane in flight. COURTESY

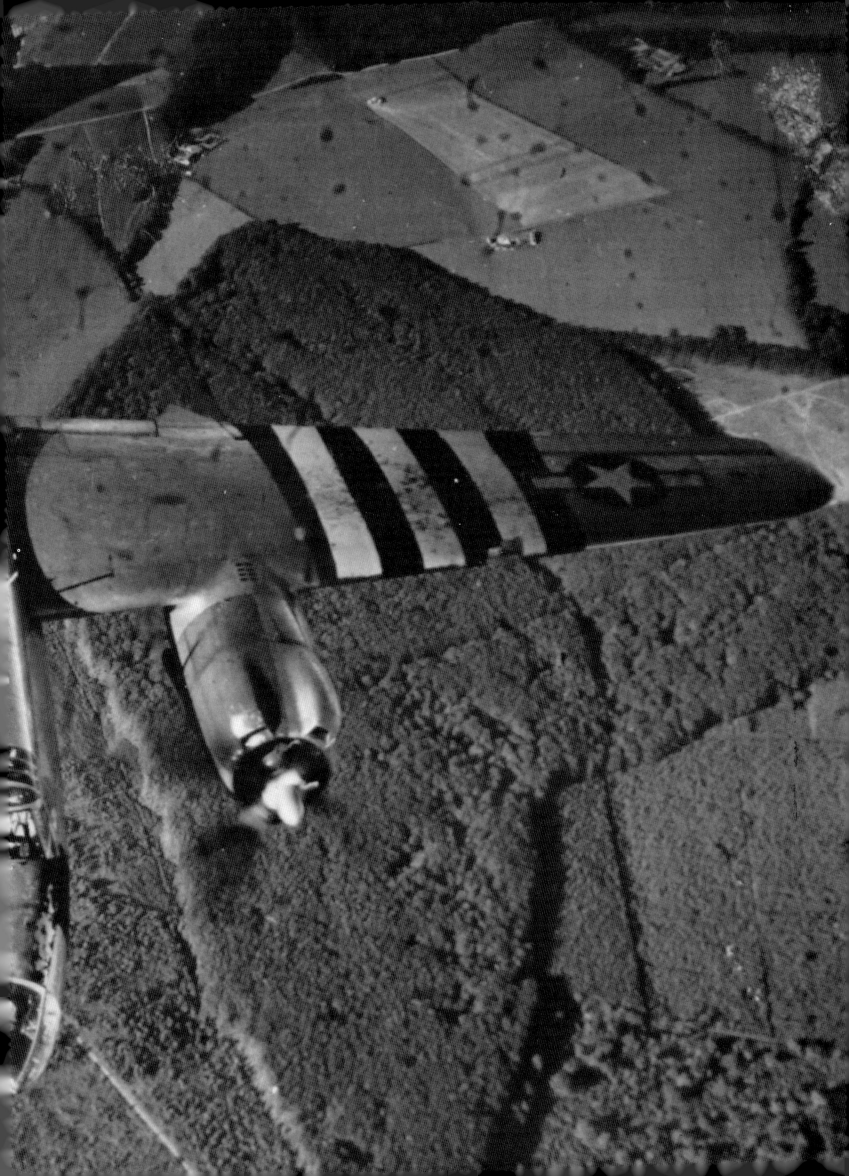

Boomerang was the plane Jerry McKinney flew in during World War II. COURTESY

their first child, Jo, while he was in Europe. When he first got the news, he "was on cloud nine," he said.

Now, finally getting to meet Jo, "we did a lot of catching up."

The couple would go on to raise three daughters. They were married for 58 years up until Dorothy's death in 2001.

McKinney was recalled to active duty with the Air Force in 1948, and would make a career as a military pilot. "I decided I hadn't had enough flying. I wanted to see other places." In Korea, he would fly 62 combat missions in a Douglas B-26 Invader.

"I didn't like them shooting at me," he said of combat flying in two wars. "Once or twice my airplane looked like it had been torn up and then put back together." But overall, he said, he enjoyed the experience.

The Cuban Missile Crisis, on the other hand — not so much. McKinney, who flew B-47s and B-52s for Strategic Air Command,

participated in the crisis as a pilot. He was on high alert for four days, he said, his plane loaded with hydrogen bombs. "The targets had been predetermined. We were only a phone call away from an atomic holocaust," he said. "Thank God it never happened."

After retiring from the military as a lieutenant colonel, McKinney flew private jets for Rockwell International. Later in life, he began to talk more about his war experiences. As a member of the group World War II Veterans of Tulsa, he spoke at schools, and enjoyed the cards and thank-you notes he got from students.

When people tell him, "Thank you for your service," McKinney is always quick to reply:

"You would've done the same for me, I'm sure."

His standard response, it pretty much sums up his feelings. "Somebody had to do it," he said.

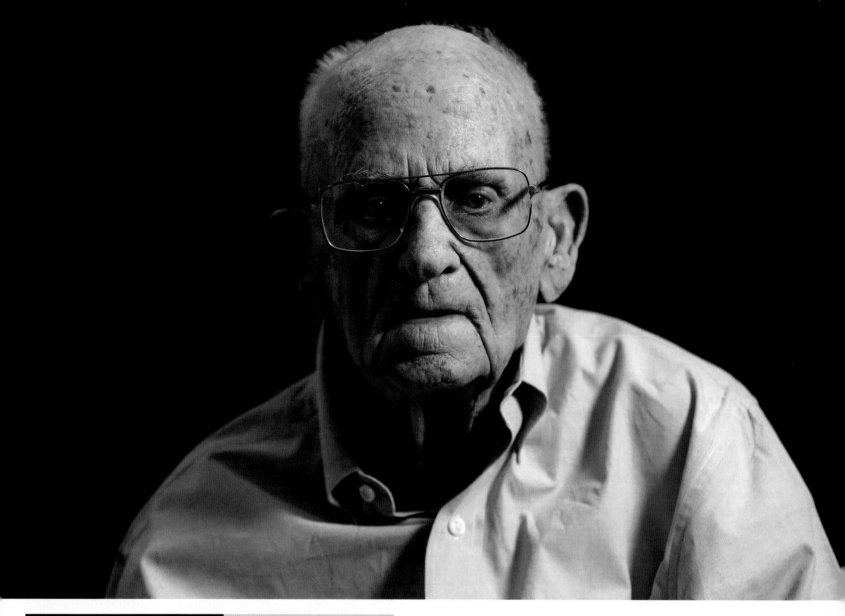

Leader of the team

Marvin McKissick led an Army survey team in Europe

Ask Marvin McKissick what the hardest thing about the war was, and he'll probably tell you being gone so long from home.

McKissick, who grew up near Haskell on his family's farm, was away for two years during World War II, his only connection the letters he exchanged with his parents and siblings. But in a twist that still, 70 years later, makes him chuckle, McKissick found one connection to home where he never would have expected.

In Germany after the war, McKissick was one of the officers tasked with discharging German prisoners of war back into civilian life. One of them, when asked about his plans, surprised McKissick.

In perfect English that "was better than mine," he said, the German proudly announced: "I'm going back to Haskell, Oklahoma, and buy me a farm."

The soldier, it turned out, had been one of the many POWs who had been transported to Camp Gruber in Oklahoma. During his

confinement, he had been part of a detachment housed at an armory in Haskell, and had worked on local farms.

"I said: Haskell — that's where I'm from," McKissick, now 97, recalled, adding that the man had his heart set on farming in the area's Choska Bottoms. "We visited about his time spent there," he said. It was the first time in a long time McKissick had felt so close to home.

Farm living

As a boy growing up, McKissick had shared that home with nine siblings, seven of them brothers. On the family farm, everyone worked together, he said. "We grew just about everything we ate."

After high school, McKissick joined the National Guard. He'd been itching to do so ever since three of his older brothers had joined.

"Money was hard to come by back in the 1930s," he said, adding that the pay was his main motivation. A younger brother also joined soon after, making five McKissick boys serving with the Oklahoma National Guard's 160th Field Artillery Regiment. Marvin was the first, though, to go full-time with the Army. He went on to officer candidate school, and from there, the new second lieutenant shipped overseas to the war.

Landing at Omaha Beach, Normandy, on Sept. 17, 1944, McKissick was put in charge of an Army survey team with the 691st Field Artillery Battalion. From France, they moved through Belgium, Holland and ultimately Germany. Their primary job was helping fighting units know the lay of the land to better engage the enemy, and helping them position their guns.

The work kept them back from the front lines, and generally out of harm's way, McKissick said. But there were constant reminders that harm was close at hand. Like when an enemy shell hit a building and killed six members of McKissick's unit, men who he knew.

Another time, when German 88-mm guns opened fire on them, he and his men had to dive under a tank. Luckily, he said, the only casualty was a cow a few yards away. But as the weeks went by, it was clear that Germany couldn't last much longer.

Once, on a scouting trip looking at sites for a command post, McKissick entered a small village where he was met almost immediately by the town's mayor and several German soldiers. They had come out to surrender.

"We were at a loss as to what to do," said McKissick, who was with his sergeant and the jeep driver. "So we advised them to bring their guns and stack them in the street and we would send someone."

Finally, the fighting ended for good. McKissick, who was using some R&R time to take a trip to Paris, happened to arrive on V-E Day. With news of the German surrender, "things were sure rocking," he said. "Dancing in the streets for three nights."

The war in Europe officially over, McKissick stayed in Germany. He helped provide security in Marburg and from there, Kassel, where he was assigned to discharge captured German soldiers. "My job," he said, "was to match the man with the discharge papers and sign the papers in three places."

'Willing to do anything for the country'

What became of that German soldier who had dreamed of Haskell, McKissick doesn't know. As far as he could tell, the man never followed through on his plan. "I asked around, but I never heard anything," he said.

McKissick, on the other hand, did follow through. Coming home from the war to his wife, Nadine, they raised two children, a son

Veteran Marvin McKissick has war mementos at his home in Tulsa.
MATT BARNARD/Tulsa World

and a daughter, while he pursued a career in banking. He became vice president of F&M Bank. He and Nadine had been married 56 years at the time of her death in 1999.

There was one interruption in McKissick's family-career plan when he was called back for active duty in Korea. He finished his military service with the rank of major.

McKissick remains proud of his generation's involvement:

"It was a generation that was willing to do anything for the country," he said. "We had very little griping ... We were patriotic — we thought a lot of our country and were willing to fight."

Marvin McKissick's graduating class at officer candidate school. COURTESY

Going for broke

Soldier fought in Europe with a Japanese-American unit

For Makoto Miyamoto — like a lot of other young Japanese-Americans in Hawaii at the time — Pearl Harbor was the spark that lit the fuse.

"My heart and soul was America; I was born and raised in Hawaii," he said, adding that he volunteered for the Army primarily because of the infamous attack. The fact that it was Japan, his ancestral homeland, behind it, only made him more determined to do his part.

Miyamoto, 91, who goes by "Mike," talked to the Tulsa World in 2015 about World War II and his service with the Army's renowned 442nd Regimental Combat Team. Known for its motto and battle cry "Go for Broke," the 442nd was a fighting unit made up almost entirely of second-generation Japanese-Americans.

Miyamoto said many of the older generation of Japanese in

America maintained sympathies for Imperial Japan's cause. But not so his young contemporaries: They "did not hesitate to disagree" with their elders. Still, for Miyamoto, it was "the hardest part (of the war) ... the fact that my family was from Japan and here I was fighting against them. It kind of confused me."

The fighting 442nd

Part of the Army's 92nd Infantry Division, the 442nd first joined in the fight to liberate Europe in 1944, landing at Anzio, Italy, in May. Italy, as a member of the Axis, had already surrendered to the Allies. But with the German Army still fiercely defending the peninsula, much brutal fighting lay ahead.

The 442nd's first battle followed in late June, as it distinguished itself in capturing the town of Belvedere. From there, it engaged in various fights, driving German forces north. Miyamoto, who was 18 when he joined the Army, would participate in nine campaigns during the war, most of them in Italy and France.

One of the most memorable was the "Lost Battalion" rescue, as it would later become known.

It happened in late October 1944, when, just after liberating the French city of Bruyeres, the 442nd was called to the aid of infantry units that had been cut off near Biffontaine. Although up against both the Germans and an unforgiving terrain — the area's tree roots made it difficult to dig in — the rescuers were ultimately successful.

It cost them, though. A lot of good men were killed, Miyamoto said. But that's a part of the war — the bloodshed — he prefers not to talk about.

'That's war'

Miyamoto was born in Hawaii, which at the time of the war was still an American territory. His parents were poor and had immigrated from Hiroshima, Japan, for work. Therein lies one of the twists in Miyamoto's tale — the fact that Hiroshima, where his family came from, would be the target of the first atomic bomb.

The bombing is a difficult subject; but he summed up his feelings in his usual soft-spoken and reflective manner: "A lot of innocent people died. But that's war. ... And it (the bomb) brought peace."

Miyamoto takes the philosophical approach with other potentially hot topics, as well. The internment of Japanese-American families on the West Coast, for example. Miyamoto's family was not affected, but he had comrades whose families were.

The internments, authorized by President Franklin D. Roosevelt, were unfortunate, he said. But, at the same time, he believes it was a "necessary thing to do to protect — to be on the safe side. One of the things war can cause is unhappiness."

'The other side of the fence'

When he talks about how he met his future wife, Mirella — a native of Italy — during the war, Miyamoto's solemn expression relaxes and a broad grin breaks out.

"She was on the other side of the fence," he jokes, meaning that Mirella was once, at least in principle, his sworn enemy. They met after Italy's surrender: He was an occupying soldier, she a nurse's assistant in the Italian Army's women's corps.

Technically an Allied prisoner, Mirella, as medical staff, was allowed to continue her work. He still remembers their first meeting — on a bridge over the Arno River at Pisa. The romance followed later, he said, but those are details he prefers to keep private.

After the war, since the Army was the only thing he knew, Miyamoto would decide to make a career of it. Retiring as a master sergeant after 20 years, he then worked in the hotel business in New York, where he also helped Japanese newcomers and businesses get established in America.

Mirella, meanwhile, earned a degree in finance and made it big selling stocks on Wall Street, a fact that her husband is still proud to recall. The couple, who were married for 65 years before Mirella's death, would raise one daughter. They moved to Oklahoma in 1983.

The making of a man

Miyamoto, who turned 92 in May 2015, lives in Owasso on the same property with his daughter and son-in-law. He was still driving up until a few months ago and though slowing down a little, remains vibrant, family members say.

Not long ago, with his grandson accompanying him, Miyamoto had the special joy of visiting the Go for Broke Monument, a memorial to the 442nd unit, in Los Angeles. Miyamoto's name, along with those of other 442nd veterans, is engraved on the monument.

Makoto "Mike" Miyamoto poses in Italy during World War II. Miyamoto was born in Hawaii to Japanese immigrant parents and fought in Europe with the U.S. Army's 442nd Regimental Combat Team, a fighting unit made up almost entirely of Japanese-American soldiers. He made a career of the Army, retiring as a master sergeant. COURTESY

WWII taught him many things, Miyamoto said, foremost among them how delicate life can be.

It also "made me a man. I was a young kid, but when I got out of the war, I was a man."

To any young kids today who might ask, Miyamoto, as an old warrior, has a little life wisdom to offer: "Be honest with yourself," he said. "Know what you are fighting for and defend it with your life."

About the 442nd Regimental Combat Team

The 442nd "Go for Broke" Regimental Combat Team, which consisted mainly of second-generation Japanese-Americans, remains the most decorated military unit in U.S. history for its size and length of service.

For its WWII service, the 442nd received eight Presidential Unit Citations, with 21 members — including future U.S. Senator Daniel Inouye — awarded the Medal of Honor. In 2010, the unit was presented a Congressional Gold Medal.

A formal military portrait of Makoto "Mike" Miyamoto was made shortly after the end of the war. COURTESY

'Liberty has a price'

Tulsan guided 30 successful missions with bomber group

The war in Europe, to tell the truth, was barely on Don Myers' radar. But the reality of it couldn't be avoided forever.

"We all knew that our life was going to change," said Myers, who before joining the war effort as a B-24 Liberator radar man was an undergraduate at Oklahoma A&M College.

The event that triggered that change came one Sunday just after lunch. In his dorm, Myers was listening to the radio when President Roosevelt interrupted to announce that Japan had attacked Pearl Harbor. Suddenly, the details of college life, like the time and place of Myers' next wrestling match, didn't seem so important.

"(Volunteering) was the thing to do. Everybody joined up," he said of his decision to leave. "There were a few slackers, but very few."

Mickey operator

"Some of it is just like it happened yesterday. Some of it is kind of hazy. Until something prompts my memory."

His voice soft and raspy — at least until he has a reason to raise it — Myers sat for an interview with the Tulsa World in 2015 and revisited his service in the war. Myers served with the 445th Bomb Group, 8th Air Force, as a "mickey operator," as the guys were dubbed who manned the planes' on-board radar. Radar was still a fairly new innovation then. Myers used the H2X system, which improved flight navigation on overcast days and at night.

"We could come within half of a mile of the target if we had a good checkpoint, like a railroad we could pick up. Then we'd turn it over to the navigator."

Only the planes that flew in the lead position of their formation were equipped with radar. That was Myers' plane. From September 1944 to March 1945, operating out of Tibenham and other bases in England, he flew lead on all 30 of his missions. On some of them,

Don Myers was a radar operator during WWII on a B-24 bomber. Only the bomber leading the mission formation flew with a radar man. COURTESY

given his proximity to the bombsights, Myers even dropped the bombs, he said.

The Kassel mission

As member of a lead crew in his group, Myers flew alternate missions, he said. Fortunately, Sept. 27, 1944, was not his day to fly.

On that mission — to bomb targets at Kassel, Germany — the 445th would fly straight into a nightmare. A swarm of German fighters attacked the bomber group; in the end, just four of 39 mission aircraft would return safely to their base. It was the highest loss percentage for one mission of any single group during WWII.

"I had been on several missions where we lost a lot of airplanes," Myers said. "It was just the luck of the draw" that he wasn't on this one.

Of 336 airmen involved in the Kassel mission, 117 were killed. Another 120 were taken prisoner. Myers knew one of the men shot down well, he said. "He had one mission to go to finish his tour."

The man survived the attack, but was held prisoner through the end of the war. Myers noted that one of the four aircraft that made it back to base was the plane his crew normally flew.

The Kassel mission didn't get "much publicity ... until after the war," he said. "A lot came out after that."

In 30 missions, Myers made it back every time. For that, he counts himself lucky. His principal plane did get pretty shot up, though, he said. A grumpy crew chief once "claimed I must have lead up my ass and that was attracting all the flak."

"I don't know whether he was kidding me or not — but he didn't want his airplane shot up."

Myers is proud not only of the role bombers played in waging the war, but in how they helped end it. Consequently, the subject of the atomic bomb is a prickly one with him. Blue eyes lighting up, he sits up a little straighter and fixes you with a hard gaze.

"There was a lot of resentment about" dropping the atomic bomb on Japan, he said. "But we would be damn fools to even think it was not the thing to do. ... It ended the war."

'Coolness and determination'

Over his 30 missions, Myers tallied 210 hours of combat flying. According to surviving records, he displayed "coolness and deter-mination while under attack by enemy aircraft." Despite the two Distinguished Flying Crosses and other honors Myers received, he gives all credit to his crewmates. Especially those at the controls.

"I didn't fly with any lead pilots who weren't extraordinary," he said.

Equally memorable were his commanders. One of them, commander over the 445th for part of Myers' time there, was Jimmy Stewart, the actor. The Hollywood star-turned-volunteer had distinguished himself with exemplary service and among his fellow airmen, his reputation was sterling, Myers said.

"He was a gentleman from way back," he said. Once, after a mission gone awry, Myers was debriefed by Stewart personally.

"We were 35 miles from the target and I lost it. ... They were able to jam the radar in some way," he explained to Stewart in his "country boy accent."

Stewart didn't hold the failure against him. He did seem amused by his accent, Myers said, and "just smiled. Then he moved on to question the next man."

'The best deterrent'

Myers enjoys watching TV news personality Bill O'Reilly and has read his books. O'Reilly, he said, "tells it like it is."

For his part, Myers has tried to do the same. War "is terrible. There should be a better way, but you can't avoid it," he said. "The best deterrent is to be prepared."

A native of Kay County, Myers graduated from Ponca City High School, where he was a star wrestler. But the decision to volunteer for the war was not one he had to grapple with. He knew what he had to do, and says the experience "made a man out of me."

"I had good training all the way through till I got my commission. That training is still with me."

After WWII, he continued to serve in the Air Force reserve. During the Vietnam War, he was called to active duty and served as a military auditor. Over the years, Myers has attended WWII reunions and conventions around the world.

It's an opportunity to remember, above all, that "liberty has a price. You have to make sacrifices and do what you think is right."

The enemy might change over time. But one thing is still true, the old airman says with certainty. "Good overcomes evil," he said.

Witness to history

Oscar Nipps watched Japanese surrender

Sometimes, even a walk in a park is no walk in the park. Oscar Nipps found that out once in Manila when, cutting through a park on their way to headquarters, he and his unit were set upon by Japanese artillery fire.

But what stood out the most — and why he remembers it so vividly to this day — is who kept walking in spite of it.

As "everybody hit the ground," Nipps said, he looked up to see Gen. Douglas MacArthur, who was just a few steps ahead of him, still on his feet. In fact, the general had not missed a stride.

"It made the impression on me that he was either awful brave or awful something else," Nipps recalled, laughing.

Nipps can actually take credit for helping the legendary leader stay upright. A short time later, as they approached the hotel where headquarters had been set up, MacArthur "hung his toe on some

barbed wire, almost hit the concrete." Fortunately, Nipps was right there.

"He reached out and put his hand right on my shoulder," he said. Regaining his balance, "he gave me this little ol' cocky grin," Nipps added. "He didn't say thank you. But I didn't expect him to."

'Not a dry run'

A Broken Arrow native and longtime resident, Nipps, known to friends and family as "Junior," welcomed the Tulsa World to his home in February 2016 to talk about his experiences in the war.

A rifleman and company cook with the 1st Cavalry Division, Nipps participated in the bloody, hard-fought campaign to liberate the Philippines from the Japanese, including the islands of Leyte and Luzon, and the Philippine capital city of Manila.

In Manila, Nipps was among the soldiers helping to liberate more than 3,000 internees — most of them American civilians — from Santo Tomas prison camp.

Nipps grew up in Broken Arrow, and attended school there through sixth grade. "I decided that was as far as I would go. My folks needed more help on the farm," said Nipps, one of five children.

Later, when his older brother entered the Army, the family pulled up stakes and moved to California to be closer to him. Nipps went to work in the shipyards there. In 1943, shortly after he turned 18, he was drafted into the Army.

Before he shipped out, during a 10-day furlough, Nipps and his girlfriend, Melza, talked about the future. She wanted to get married. But he thought the right thing to do was to wait.

"I didn't know if I was coming back," Nipps said, "and I'd rather leave a sweetheart behind than a widow." Reluctantly, Melza agreed and they settled for writing to each other.

Shipping out for the Pacific in July 1944, Nipps' first stop was New Guinea. At his next destination, the Admiralty Islands, he was assigned to the 5th Cavalry Regiment, 1st Cavalry Division. Shortly after he arrived, the division moved in to begin the liberation of the Philippines. The island chain had been overrun by the Japanese early in 1942.

The war for Nipps started for real on Oct. 20. He remembers the captain's voice breaking in over the PA as they sat anchored off Leyte. They had been practicing beach landings, but this time he "told us this was not a dry run, it was the real McCoy."

The exact time stuck in Nipps' mind: "10:20 a.m., the 10th month, 20th day."

The men had no idea what to expect of the landing, and feared it would be "hot," he said. Before they could get to the beach, though, the landing crafts had to stop. The water was too shallow to proceed.

So for the last 100 yards, they were forced to wade through waist-high water carrying 120-pound machine guns and ammo. Fortunately, the landing didn't attract the attention of the Japanese.

But the fight was not long in coming. Later that afternoon, Nipps said, "the bullets started flying. ... They fired at us, we fired back." It was the 19-year-old's first experience of combat.

"I don't know how to explain how it felt," said Nipps. "We fought them all over the island. Every day for a few weeks. Out in the fields hunting them down. They were still putting up pretty good resistance."

Santo Tomas

When they moved on to Luzon, the fighting would only get more intense. From the time he arrived in early 1945, Nipps would be on the front lines for 63 days "with no relief and very little food," he said. The hardest part was losing your friends.

"It was pretty rough to stand there and see those guys (die) who you had been with almost a year," Nipps said. "You was just like

Oscar Nipps Jr., and his future wife, Melza. COURTESY

brothers. That's how it felt — like you'd lost a brother."

Some of the fiercest fighting took place in the capital, Manila. "We were 88 miles from Manila when MacArthur sent the trucks to get us," Nipps recalled. "He wanted the 1st Cavalry Division to be the first ones in Manila. We made 88 miles in 66 hours, driving through a combat zone."

One of the first orders of business in Manila was to liberate Santo Tomas internment camp. Santo Tomas, set up on the campus of the University of Santo Tomas, was the largest of several prison camps in the Philippines where the Japanese held enemy civilians.

At the time, there were more than 3,000 prisoners confined there, many of whom had been there since the camp opened in January 1942. Conditions had deteriorated as the war went on, and many internees were near death from starvation.

Japanese soldiers in the camp fired on the liberators, Nipps said, "but we went in behind the tanks so they couldn't hit us. The tanks tore down the (fences). It didn't take much fighting to get them out of there."

The prisoners "were in very poor shape. Really, more or less skin and bones." Nevertheless, he added, there was much "hollering and screaming and yelling for joy that they were finally freed. ... It made you feel real good and feel real bad at the same time — that they had gone through so much misery."

High cost

The brutal fight to clear Manila took almost a month. Nipps recalls one particular night when the fighting was at its most furious. At one point, after relieving a machine gunner, he gave the gun back to the man, only to see him take a hit just seconds later.

"It blew his bottom jaw off," he said. Later a friend of Nipps' was

Oscar Nipps Jr. after he finished basic training. COURTESY

killed when the "back of his head was blown off."

It was that kind of night.

Another thing about combat zones, he said, was you couldn't get mail. So, his letters would often pile up, and he'd receive several at a time. Not all mail brought good news.

While he was in Manila a letter arrived from his mother informing him that his 5-year-old brother, Ervin, the family's youngest, had died. By the time Nipps received the letter, weeks had passed since the funeral. "That was tough to find out," he said.

Nipps was sitting in a foxhole, and had to read the words more than once. He remembers the day well. Later the same evening, he said, a rocket shell landed next to his foxhole but thankfully, it didn't go off.

Another shell hit next to a nearby foxhole and exploded, killing both of the soldiers in the foxhole. Once again, Nipps said, "the good Lord was looking after me."

The cost of liberating Luzon was high: 10,640 American troops were killed. But it wasn't anywhere near the number of soldiers the Japanese lost: 205,535 troops. Luzon was the largest American campaign of the Pacific war, involving more troops than had been used in North Africa, Italy or southern France.

At the time, though, Nipps and his fellow soldiers thought the worst was yet to come. Shipping out in August for Japan "loaded with ammo, weapons and everything," they fully expected to have to invade the island. Then, en route, they heard about the atomic bombs. There was a lot of celebrating on the ship, Nipps said.

Witness to history

On Sept. 2, 1945, Nipps was on board a ship in Tokyo Bay. It was anchored alongside the USS Missouri where Japan would officially surrender, ending the war. Nipps watched from the deck as the Japanese officials arrived. He was able to see the entire ceremony, he said.

"I was close enough I could almost see the pen they were using."

Not lost on Nipps was the significance of the moment to him personally. "I knew if they didn't (surrender) I was going to be one of the first ones to go in."

Historians have estimated that more than 1 million American lives would've been lost had an invasion of Japan been undertaken.

After finishing his overseas service, Nipps, who reached the rank of sergeant, shipped back to the states, arriving on Jan. 31, 1946. "Did it ever feel good," he said of coming home to Broken Arrow.

He and Melza married and raised three children together while he worked at various jobs, including many years in construction, hanging drywall and wiring houses. At the time of Melza's death in

A medal received by WWII veteran Oscar Nipps Jr. is seen at his home in Broken Arrow. MATT BARNARD/Tulsa World

2003, the couple had been married 57 years.

After the surrender, Nipps stayed several months in Japan as part of the occupying forces. He said while there he could have visited Hiroshima and Nagasaki, where the atomic bombs had been dropped.

"A lot of guys did. But I chose not to," he said, adding that his reason kind of sums up his feelings in general about the war. "I'm kind of a soft-hearted guy. And I'd already seen all I wanted to."

Taking the shot

Edmund Orwat was part of an anti-aircraft gun crew

Edmund Orwat doesn't remember how his parents first got the news that their family homeland had been invaded. Probably, it came over the small radio that sat on the kitchen table of their Buffalo, New York, home.

But Orwat does remember his mother's response. In the months to come after the Germans invaded Poland — the act that officially began World War II in September 1939 — she would periodically round up clothing and other items and package them up.

"She would get a letter every so often, saying that they needed this or that," Orwat said. "We were very poor. But as little as we had, she still wanted to help." Orwat remembers helping carry the packages for her to send to relatives back in Poland.

"I was a youngster and didn't know much about what was going on," he said. As for what the future might hold, Orwat knew even less. For one thing, he would've been surprised to learn that, as a member of the Army, he would be fighting the Germans himself.

The breadwinner

Orwat, who moved from New York a few years ago with his wife, Irene, to be close to family, welcomed the Tulsa World to his home in 2016 to talk about his service in World War II.

Orwat, 91, was born and raised in Buffalo, and lived there much of his life. The family originally came from Poland. Orwat's father was born near Kraków and immigrated as an adult. He never attended school, and was never able to read or write English. He was a hard worker, though, and found work at a company that manufactured elevators.

Orwat's mother, who was born in Buffalo after her family immigrated from Poland, had only a fourth-grade education.

Tragedy struck early and often during Orwat's childhood. He was one of eight children, but both of his older brothers died young:

one from polio, the other from a fall while playing at a quarry. Later, Orwat's father lost an arm in an accident at home, and it affected his ability to work.

Although only 5 at the time, as the oldest surviving son, "I became the breadwinner," Orwat said. He looked for ways to make money. He shined shoes in the neighborhood taverns. He delivered an evening newspaper. And every penny he earned, he said, he gave to his parents to help pay the mortgage.

Orwat's father saw potential in his industrious son. "I remember him pointing his finger at me," Orwat recalled, "and saying 'I want you to be an engineer.'"

It might well have been the hand of destiny. Orwat attended Buffalo Technical High School, taking classes in chemistry and other subjects with an eye toward an engineering career. After graduating, he began college part-time, continuing to work to help support the family.

He decided he wanted to volunteer for the Army Air Corps. But his mother talked him out of it. "She depended on me," he said.

When he was finally drafted a short time later, in May 1943, "she could have appealed to the draft board, saying as breadwinner she needed me. But I don't think she knew that was an option."

Aiming high

Orwat remembers the first ship he boarded in New York Harbor, leaving for England to join the war. He had no more climbed on board, he said, when suddenly everyone was told to get off again.

"I don't know why, maybe a mechanical problem or something," he said, adding that they would be delayed and then leave later on another vessel. The ship he had first boarded, he said, was later torpedoed and sunk. Orwat's crossing was uneventful. His troop ship traveled in a convoy, escorted by battleships for protection.

"Our ship had no guns. We were just targets."

But there was no protecting them from the effects of sea travel. The "up and down" motion made Orwat and other first-time seafarers sick. "I heaved my guts over the side," he said, laughing.

Orwat was assigned to the Army's 838th Anti-Aircaft Artillery Battalion. There, he became part of a crew that manned a ground-based 40mm anti-aircraft gun. The gun crews' role was to support the infantry troops, trying to protect them from attacking enemy aircraft, he said.

The 40mm gun, joined by quad mount 50-caliber machine guns, was pulled on a cart behind a truck, and could be moved and positioned quickly. Orwat's main job on the crew was to help target enemy planes as they flew over. He remembers planes exploding in the air when they scored a direct hit.

From England, they moved on to France, where they joined the 7th Army under Gen. Alexander Patch.

Crossing the Rhine

Orwat's war service would never take him to Poland. But he would get to help strike at the heart of the German Reich, joining up with the Allied forces advancing into Germany itself.

Entering France at Omaha Beach, Normandy — "they flopped open the gate (of the landing craft) and into the water you went" — Orwat's first combat experience would come in late March 1945 at the Rhine River, as 7th Army units prepared to cross over into Germany.

Bridges had been destroyed, Orwat said, so they looked for spots to construct temporary bridges. The units were under German fire much of the time, from the ground and the air. Orwat's unit lost an officer and several men. It was a new experience for Orwat and many of the others.

"The chaplain was going back and forth, making his rounds. He yelled 'Get your asses on the ground!'" Orwat recalled with a chuckle.

The gun crews immediately got to work, setting up and providing protection so the engineers could build the bridges. The entire

Edmund Orwat shared this photo of a 40mm anti-aircraft gun. COURTESY

crossing operation took several days. The aerial attacks came from German fighters.

"You try not to be frightened," Orwat said. "You have an obligation. ... We either got them or they got us."

According to accounts, during one night raid, guns from the 838th and other units took out 10 of 12 enemy aircraft.

"Who shot how many I couldn't say," Orwat said. "And I'd hate to venture a guess. ... It was a team effort."

The crossing was a success, with three infantry divisions and one armored division reaching the other side and establishing a beachhead. After crossing the Rhine, the units moved from town to town. There were still occasional attacks from the air. The gunners' job remained to protect the infantry troops.

From Germany, Orwat's unit moved into Austria, stopping at Brenner Pass just above Italy. That's where he was when the war in Europe ended in May 1945. At news of Germany's surrender, Orwat said, "I felt relief — 'I'm alive and I'm going home.'"

At one point, Orwat's unit had a chance to visit Dachau concentration camp. "It was a sight you will never forget," he said.

Liberated only days earlier, many of the former inmates were still there. Orwat remembers all the outstretched arms: "'Help me, help me, help me,' they said."

Life after the war

Finishing his service in June 1946, Orwat resumed the career path his father had envisioned for him. After graduating from the University of Buffalo, he became a civil engineer for the state of New York, raising three children with his wife, Irene.

Liberation for Poland would be a long time in coming. Under Nazi occupation for more than six years, longer than any other country during WWII, it eventually fell under the control of communist forces. All told, it would be almost 50 years before Poland was free.

Orwat never had the opportunity to visit the family homeland. But he's happy that his granddaughter got to make the trip as a participant in Catholic World Youth Day 2016 in Kraków.

Orwat has gone to many military reunions over the years. The survivors' numbers dwindled, though, and they eventually stopped having them, he said. Not dwindling as much are his memories from the war. "Sometimes you look back and wonder 'Did all of that really happen?'"

A sympathetic ear

Iris Painter was a radio operator in England and France

Iris Painter had no way of knowing who was on the other end of her radio. They were hundreds of miles away in many cases, and communicated only in dashes and dots.

But there were some interactions that were done face to face. Those are the ones she remembers most. Soldiers and airmen coming back from the Battle of the Bulge and other combat zones "had stories," said Painter, an Army radio operator stationed in France during World War II.

"They did a lot of things they were not proud of. And they liked to have somebody to talk to about those things."

Painter was always ready with an encouraging smile and sympathetic ear. Being a radio operator, relaying messages to and from units on the front lines, was a valuable service. But sometimes she "felt that the best thing we did was talk to the soldiers. Just be

their companions, dance once in a while, have a little fun. So that it wasn't just war, war, war."

'A great shock'

Painter and her family — she was the second of 13 children — moved to Tulsa in 1918, she said, just in time to march in the World War I victory parade downtown. She was too young really to remember anything about it.

Remembering WWII, though, has never been a problem. The Dec. 7, 1941, Pearl Harbor attack "was a great shock to us all," said Painter, 97, in a November 2015 interview at her home in Tulsa.

"Everybody wanted to do something — be part of the most important thing happening in the world at the time."

By that time, Painter was a 23-year-old psychology major at the University of Missouri. But with two of her brothers going off to serve, one in the Army and one in the Merchant Marine, she decided to do her part as well. As soon as its formation was announced in May 1942, Painter applied to the new Women's Army Auxiliary Corps, or Women's Army Corps as it was soon to become.

Iris Painter was stationed in Chantilly, France, during her service as a radio operator in the WACs during World War II. COURTESY

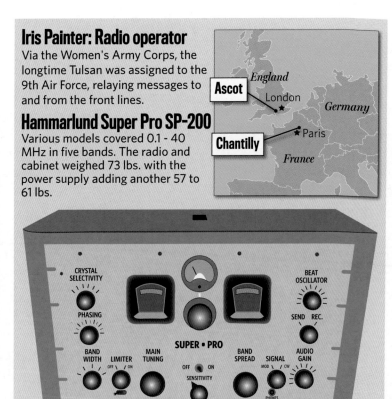

Iris Painter: Radio operator
Via the Women's Army Corps, the longtime Tulsan was assigned to the 9th Air Force, relaying messages to and from the front lines.

Hammarlund Super Pro SP-200
Various models covered 0.1 - 40 MHz in five bands. The radio and cabinet weighed 73 lbs. with the power supply adding another 57 to 61 lbs.

STEVEN RECKINGER/Tulsa World

"I didn't know what it was exactly," she said. And she almost didn't find out. Painter was rejected on her first attempt for being 10 pounds underweight.

It was nothing a few malts couldn't fix, she said. Quickly gaining the weight she needed, she went on to become a member of the first WAAC group in St. Louis. The women's unit was still so new, they weren't properly equipped, Painter said, recalling the man's overcoat she was issued, which came down almost to her toes.

From basic training in Des Moines, Iowa, Painter went on to become a radio operator. She was sent to radio school, where she learned to send and receive messages in Morse code.

Getting used to danger

After several transfers in the states, Painter, assigned to the 9th Air Force, shipped out for England. "It was all a brand-new experience to me. I'd never been anyplace in particular." For the next six months, Painter worked as a radio operator in Ascot, England.

Britain was still being bombed by the Germans, who had just introduced the V-1, an early type of cruise missile. Dubbed "buzz bombs" by the British, "you could hear them overhead," Painter recalled. "When the motor stopped, you knew a bomb was going to (hit)."

Maybe it was their youth, but Painter and her friends adapted quickly, she said. "You just got used to things," she said. London was the most frequent target of German bombs, as Painter found out during off-duty outings to the nearby city.

"The sirens would go off. If you were at the movies, they would interrupt. You were supposed to go to the metro tunnels."

Painter admits she and her cohorts were a little too nonchalant about it all. They would try to hide, she said, so they wouldn't have to go to the shelters. And they positively hated the helmets and gas masks they had to wear.

The reality of what the bombs could do, though, was ever-present. She remembers seeing one building in London that had been reduced to rubble overnight.

New worlds

The war opened up a whole new world to Painter. Once, during a

trip to see the horses run at Ascot Racecourse, she had a brush with royalty. Britain's Queen Elizabeth and her daughters, Princesses Elizabeth and Margaret, came out for the races from nearby Windsor Castle. The queen was friendly. She talked to Painter's group, asking them about their unit and their duties.

"They were like real folks," she said of the royal family.

Painter came to like the British people in general, although they were a little different, she said, from what she was used to.

"I dated one English soldier. I remember him saying, 'Would you mind awfully much if I hold your hand?'" she said, mimicking the accent. The British were "more formal like that." And, of course, there was tea time. She learned to expect no radio communications from the British at that time of day. Painter's stay in England was destined to be cut short.

"We knew from the rumors," she said, "that D-Day was coming."

But when it finally happened — on June 6, 1944 — it still came as a "horrible shock to all of us," Painter said. With the Allied invasion of Europe underway, the pace picked up in the radio room.

"We got lots and lots of messages," Painter said. "We were working full speed."

A few weeks after D-Day, Painter's unit moved to France, where Allied forces were advancing. Crossing the channel on a landing craft, she first set foot in France at Omaha Beach, which had been one of the invasion points for U.S. ground forces and the site of intense German resistance.

"The wreckage (from D-Day) was still all there," she said. "The fighting was over, but destruction was left behind." Outside of the bombings in London, it was her first experience with the devastation of war.

Chantilly

From Omaha Beach, Army trucks took Painter and her comrades to Chantilly, France, where they spent the next several months based at a chateau. The previous occupants, the German military, had apparently left in a hurry, Painter said. "Food was still on the table," she said.

Painter worked out of a trailer next to the chateau. Her fellow

Iris Painter (second from right) is seen in an Army promotional photo shot in Paris, showing off duty uniforms for enlisted personnel, during her service as a radio operator in the WACs during World War II. COURTESY

radio operators included both men and women. When the Battle of the Bulge began in December 1944, however, all the men were sent to the front lines. Painter and the women were left behind to continue handling radio messages.

As their male colleagues departed, "they gave us a Tommy Gun (Thompson submachine gun) for 'just in case.' But we didn't know how to use it," she said, laughing.

News about the war was always hard to come by. The women knew conditions were bad, though. At one point, each of them donated a blanket for troops at the front.

Painter's thoughts were not always on work. Chantilly was not far from Paris, and she saw much of the City of Lights on side trips. She bought small gifts to send to her brothers and sisters back home. She missed them terribly, she said, and made friends with some of the local French children.

With the end of the war in Europe in May 1945, Painter's job duties didn't change. And from France, they soon moved on to Germany. During this time, she turned down an opportunity to visit one of the liberated concentration camps. Others went, but "I wouldn't go," she said. She felt she had seen enough already.

In August, Painter was given a choice of being transferred to the French Riviera or going home. She didn't have to think about it. "I hadn't seen home in two years," she said.

A big adventure

The war is not a topic Painter revisits often. In fact, she can't imagine why anyone would still be interested, she said — "it was

such a long time ago."

Painter's two brothers who served rarely brought up the subject. She remembers someone once asking her brother Bill if he'd ever killed anyone. "He just got up and left the room."

Painter is quick to emphasize, though, that her experience was different from those who fought. The war "was a big adventure for me. It was no sacrifice on my part. It was an opportunity I never would've had under any other circumstances."

It even allowed her, through the G.I. Bill, to achieve one of her dreams: learning to fly. That, in turn, paved the way to a career, starting as a commercial pilot and flight instructor, and then going into air traffic control.

Painter eventually finished her psychology degree, and went on to become part of the original staff of what was then Tulsa Junior College, in 1970. She retired in 1984.

Painter has enjoyed a rich family life. Although she never married, she's been like a mother and grandmother to her younger siblings and their children. Perhaps it's them she's thinking of when she offers her final verdict on war.

"I don't want there to be any more wars now," Painter said. "An enlightened nation needs to find another way to settle problems."

As for her war, she still doggedly insists that her contribution was minimal.

"Everybody had a service and I think sometimes that the folks who stayed at home did as much," Painter said. "They had to make sacrifices and do without. ... The Army provided everything I needed."

Storming the beach

Bill Parker helped lead first invasion wave on D-Day

Whether Bill Parker was indeed the first D-Day invader to set foot on Normandy's Omaha Beach is impossible to know for sure. But there's one fact that he believes makes a good case for it.

"I didn't see any bodies in front of me yet," Parker said.

With German resistance at peak intensity, the stretch of French coastline would be littered with the dead and dying within minutes of the invasion's launch. Many of the bodies would belong to Parker's 116th Infantry Regiment.

The leaders of the first wave on June 6, 1944, the unit sustained 96 percent casualties. Parker, somehow, made it through unscathed. And he learned something, he said, that would serve him in the dangerous months to come.

"I made up my mind if you were first and the quicker you got

across there, the better chance you had," he said. "So, all through the war, when we attacked, I tried to be first."

Born a cowboy

One of Tulsa's dwindling number of D-Day veterans, Parker, 91, represents an even rarer subset of that group: the soldiers of the first wave. Although the distinction means a lot to him, he said, there's another title that he wears even more proudly.

"I was born a cowboy, and I'll die a cowboy," Parker said.

Hailing from McCurtain in rural Haskell County, Parker — who is part Choctaw — grew up around horses. All of his life, while employed in different jobs including home construction, he continued to work with them, he said, training roping horses as a sideline. He still rides when he can.

Probably the best roping job Parker ever did, though, was of his wife, Colleen. The couple, who have lived in the same house in north Tulsa since 1954, have been married 71 years. Just four months apart in age, the two were both students at McCurtain High when they met. Things got serious, Parker said, after he attended a pie supper fundraiser that Colleen had entered.

"Dad give me a quarter," he said, "and when her pie came up, I bought it."

Afterward, as she was walking home, Parker rode after her on horseback.

"When I caught up," he said, "I got down off the horse and I took her hand. And she didn't pull away. And I've had her hand ever since."

The two waited to marry, however. First, Parker had to go to fight the war. Drafted in 1943, he was called to report the summer after his senior year in high school. He was short a few credits, and the school withheld his diploma, but it was too late then to do anything about it.

Parker remembers saying goodbye to Colleen as he boarded the troop train in McAlester.

"That was the loneliest day of my life," he said.

The longest day

"They kept telling us the war would be over before we had to invade France," Parker recalled. "But of course it wasn't."

Arriving in England in January 1944, Parker was assigned as a replacement troop to the 116th Infantry's 2nd Battalion — part of the larger 29th Infantry Division. The only real question about the invasion, he said, was when.

The inevitable finally arrived on June 6, 1944. Helping to kick off D-Day, Parker's 116th was tasked with leading the first assault wave at 6:30 a.m., landing on Omaha Beach — the code name for a 5-mile stretch of shoreline, and one of five Allied invasion points.

In the choppy waters of the English Channel, he said, it was trouble enough just climbing from his ship onto the landing craft that would take him to shore. As leader of a six-man wire team, Parker had to be the first out, so he sat in the front of the vessel. In all of his training experiences on water, he had become ill. But for some reason, this time, he didn't get sick, he said.

Once on the beach, his team's first job was to blow up a barbed-wire obstacle the Germans had erected, clearing the way for the rest of the 30-something soldiers from their craft. Fire from German guns was already heavy as Parker and his team waded in from the drop-off point. Due to extensive training, they were able to detonate the obstacle successfully. From there, armed with rifles and grenades, they made their way to a ridge of sand, where they took cover and returned fire.

Focused on what was going on ahead, Parker didn't realize until later what had happened behind them — that no one else had made it off their landing craft. Apparently, he said, it had been hit by a shell just seconds after his team's departure.

'Dead people everywhere'

On their own, Parker and his companions stuck to the plan — to reach the top of a hill overlooking the beach. He remembers the machine gun fire coming from a German pillbox and the "sand kicking up about three feet in front of me" from the bullets.

Eventually, they were joined by a group of about 20 other soldiers who had landed farther down the beach. Together, shooting as they went, they were able to get up the hill, where they spent the night.

In the chaos of the day, all of the men had been separated from their larger units, Parker said. "We decided to stay put till daylight. It was dark that night. We could hear shooting on both sides of us but nothing out front."

Parker didn't grasp the full scope of what had happened at Omaha Beach until the next morning. Running out of ammunition and knowing there would be plenty to retrieve off dead soldiers he decided to go back to the beach.

"You can't imagine what that was like," he said of the nightmar-

Soldiers from World War II veteran Bill Parker's group cross the snowy landscape of Europe. COURTESY

ish scene that awaited him. "Dead people everywhere. In the water. Washed up on the sand. The water was plumb bloody.

"Down the beach they had gathered the wounded. They were being doctored. ... One boy that was in my company, he had a big bandage on his head. I tried to talk to him, but he wasn't able to talk."

All told, the 116th took 1,000 casualties on D-Day.

Reluctant leader

It's funny, Parker said, the things you remember from a war. Like a simple piece of gum.

Chewing one as he stormed Omaha Beach, he still recalls how "the gum got so dry I couldn't open my mouth."

Then there are the things you can't remember, which can be frustrating. For example, Parker can still see the faces of the five other men in his wire crew. But he can't for the life of him recall their names. Although Parker was a private like the rest of them, he added, "everywhere we went, it seemed like I was expected to lead."

The other 20 or so who had joined them followed him, too, he said. "We were on our own for a while," he said.

Eventually, they were able to join the rest of the 116th Infantry at Saint-Lô.

From D-Day on, they were in and out of combat. Parker didn't get to shower or shave, he said, for 43 days. By the time he got the chance, he had a thick red beard.

The 116th participated in three more campaigns: Northern France, Rhineland and Central Europe, with Parker taking part in daytime operations and many night patrols.

"My whole thought was to live," he said. "'Don't do nothing fool-ish. Do what you got to do.'"

'I shot Hitler'

Parker was awarded a Bronze Star and two Purple Hearts among other decorations. He hasn't seen them in a while, though, and is not sure now where he put them. But one memento from the war he's never lost track of: his Colt .45 six-shooter.

Formerly a tank commander's, Parker traded him for it and then personalized it: On each side of the handle are small photos of Colleen, held fast by glass he repurposed from a German aircraft windshield.

These days the gun mostly stays in its holster in a drawer. During the war, though, it sat on Parker's hip, ready for action.

"I shot Hitler with this," Parker announced suddenly, as he showed the gun during his interview.

It happened one night in Germany, he began, eyes twinkling. He and some soldiers had entered a house where, in the partial darkness, Parker thought he saw a man. He drew his .45. And when the figure refused to respond to orders, he fired. To Parker's surprise — and his companions' amusement — it turned out to be "a chalk bust of Hitler," he said. "I had shot the head right in two."

"My boys kidded me about that for months," he added.

As for himself, despite dozens of near misses and brushes with the enemy, Parker was never shot. But he didn't escape harm entirely. Once in Normandy, he was hit in the foot by shrapnel from an exploding shell. He walked on it for several days but eventually had to seek treatment. By then, it had become gangrenous.

Lying in the hospital, he was alarmed, he said, to overhear two medics say of his foot: "There's nothing to do but take it off."

Luckily, a wiser captain intervened, Parker said. He told them not to amputate, rather "soak the foot in hot water with Epsom salt." The method worked.

"They would've had trouble from me," Parker said, "if they'd tried to take my foot off."

Eddie

It was in March 1945, while stationed at Lippstadt, Germany, that Parker and his unit first met Eddie. An 8-year-old Lithuanian orphan, the boy had been living in a refugee camp.

"We fed him. He began to learn English," said Parker, adding that Eddie would wait behind for them when they went out on their missions. The soldiers grew attached to Eddie, whose parents had been killed by the Germans.

"Some of the officers had an officer's uniform made for him," he said. The boy took a particular shine to Parker, and Parker to him.

"I kind of felt like he was my own," he said.

Parker even decided he wanted to adopt Eddie. "But I wasn't married at the time, and I was told that it wasn't going to happen."

Later another man in his unit, who was married, was able to adopt the boy. Parker, who has old photos of him, was happy for Eddie, who eventually settled in Virginia with his new family.

"It was for the best," he said.

Unfinished business

For decades afterward, Parker didn't bring up the subject of the war if he could help it.

He was aware that his older brother, Jim, had been a tail gunner on a bomber over Europe. But it was only last year, at Jim's funeral, Parker said, that he learned he'd flown more than 50 missions.

"We just didn't talk about it," he said. "I wanted to forget it."

Even so, Parker had some unfinished business related to the war: that high school diploma he had missed out on.

At the time, he said, "the superintendent told me if I came back to

World War II veteran Bill Parker holds a revolver that he carried in the European theater. Parker put a photo of the woman he later married, Colleen Parker, under grips that he made from the windshield of a German aircraft.
MATT BARNARD/Tulsa World

school that summer he'd see that I got my diploma. But I told him I couldn't. I had already been called up to the Army."

But a few years ago — almost 67 years exactly since he'd gone off to war — Parker found himself back at McCurtain High for graduation ceremonies. Taking advantage of an initiative allowing WWII vets to obtain their honorary diplomas, Parker walked across the stage at last and was handed his.

"The best thing that happened to me that day: This little girl came out of the audience, maybe 7 or 8. And she said, 'I want to hug you,'" Parker recalled, his voice cracking. It was a meaningful gesture, even to a man who prefers to downplay his part in the war.

"I was just an old foot soldier, trained to fight. We weren't anything special. Just soldiers."

Thinking back on the war — especially on blood-soaked Omaha Beach — Parker can't help feeling that he's been living on borrowed time ever since.

"You get to feeling you weren't supposed to get through it," he said.

But it had to be done, regardless of the cost.

"If we hadn't," Parker added, "we'd be speaking German now. We had a maniac we was fighting."

Bill Parker (right) and another soldier in Europe after the invasion of France. COURTESY

Proud to serve

Gordon Patten enlisted in the Marines in 1944

At 5-foot-10, Gordon Patten wasn't the tallest Marine recruit in boot camp at Parris Island, South Carolina. But as it turned out, he was just the right height when it counted most.

Patten remembers it well: the moment when a mere inch became the deciding factor not only in where he was going but quite possibly in his fate.

"I was marching with my platoon one day," he said, "when this major stopped us. He ordered our sergeant to 'divide these men up' — all of us 5-foot-10 and over to one side, everyone else on the other."

Told to get their things together, he and the Marines in the taller group were jubilant when they learned their destination: They were being assigned to sea duty.

"If I'd been 5-foot-9," Patten added, "I would have been in the infantry. I would have been hitting those beaches."

On beaches like those at Iwo Jima, Okinawa and other Pacific islands, young Marines would die by the thousands in 1944 and 1945.

"I was very fortunate," Patten said.

Welcoming the Tulsa World to his home early in 2016, Patten, now 89, talked about his World War II service, which would see him serve aboard the battleship USS Iowa. A native Tulsan, Patten joined the military right after graduating from Central High School in May 1944. He and three buddies went down to join together, he said, and chose the Marines.

"Seagoing Marines," as they were called, could be assigned to Navy destroyers, cruisers or battleships. Patten landed on a battleship — the Iowa. One of a contingent of 100 Marines assigned to it, he remembers his first glimpse of the ship in San Francisco.

"It was in drydock there, back for repairs," Patten

said. "I didn't know they made a ship that big. It was magnificent."

Launched in 1942, one of the Iowa's first missions had been to carry President Franklin D. Roosevelt across the Atlantic to a war conference. In fact, the ship had some custom features just for Roosevelt. Patten remembers seeing a special bathtub designed to accommodate the president, who had polio and used a wheelchair.

After its debut in the Atlantic, in 1944 the Iowa had been transferred to the Pacific fleet. Patten came on board after that. He remembers waving goodbye from the deck, as the Iowa passed underneath the Golden Gate Bridge on its way out to sea.

Drop out of the sky

One of the battleships' duties, Patten said, was to protect the aircraft carriers, which sailed at the center of the convoys.

The Iowa's biggest guns were its 16-inch cannons. When they fired, the ship would rock back and forth, Patten said. The 40mm antiaircraft guns manned by Patten and other Marines were not as big. But they were just as vital, defending the ship and adjacent carriers against the dreaded Japanese suicide planes known as kamikazes.

"(Kamikaze pilots) could just drop out of the sky," he said. "You'd better be ready. Sometimes we were sitting on those guns all night."

Kamikaze pilots "were smart," he said, adding that they often would follow American planes back to the carriers. "Our radar couldn't distinguish ours from theirs, so they would come up with ours and then separate and attack."

"They didn't give a hoot if they lived or died," he said of the Japanese pilots, who attempted to crash their explosive-laden planes directly into ships. "You just had to do your best to kill him. It was you or him."

Before the Iowa left Hawaii to join the fight, Patten saw the results of a kamikaze attack. The USS Franklin aircraft carrier was there, undergoing repairs, and from one end to the other "the deck was twisted metal."

"That was the first time I knew what they could do," Patten said.

Too busy to be scared

Patten was trained as a loader on the antiaircraft guns.

"I'd rather have been the one shooting the damn thing," he said, but still he's proud of his role. The handler would pass him a clip, and he'd quickly but carefully drop it into the hole of the gun.

"You had to be perfect at it," he said, "or it would jam the gun. I could still do it now," he added, demonstrating the repetitive loading motion.

Each clip had five shells, and just as he let go, the gun would fire them, "boom-boom-boom-boom-boom" in quick succession, he said. The focus required for the task helped keep any nerves at bay.

"We were never scared," Patten said. "You had so much to do. You didn't worry about it."

The Iowa left Hawaii to join the Navy's 3rd Fleet. In the weeks to come, the battleship and its guns would support Allied air and ground operations, including in the Philippines and the Marshall Islands. The ship endured a number of attacks. But no kamikazes ever scored direct hits on the Iowa. One came close, though. Patten can still see it. It flew over the bow of the ship, he said, but missed and "went down into the drink."

World War II veteran Gordon Patten (top row, sixth from left) and others pose for a photo aboard the USS Iowa battleship. COURTESY

For Patten's part, he felt more threatened by nature. The ship was so massive, ordinarily you couldn't even tell you were at sea — "it was like riding in your backyard," he said. But during storms, when you were swaying back and forth, you definitely knew it, he added.

"The only thing you ever had to worry about was hurricanes. We were in one or two."

Japanese surrender

In the days leading up to the dropping of atomic bombs in August 1945, the fleet pulled back, its guns going silent, Patten said.

"We were just floating," waiting to be part of the expected invasion of mainland Japan.

When the bombs were dropped, "we only heard that the war was over — we didn't know how or why," Patten said. "We were like, 'What happened?' The next thing we knew we were headed into Tokyo Bay for the surrender."

There, on Sept. 2, 1945, the Iowa was anchored right alongside when Japanese officials boarded the USS Missouri to officially sign the terms of surrender.

Patten wasn't present for the historic moment. He and his Marine unit had been dispatched to Yokosuka to occupy a naval base there. But like any Iowa veteran, he's still a little sore at how the surrender went down.

"The peace was supposed to be signed on the Iowa," which was the flagship of the 3rd Fleet and carried Adm. William F. Halsey. "But President Truman was from Missouri, and he wanted it done on the Missouri," Patten said. You don't get to argue with the president, he added.

Patten and his friends had their first real chance to celebrate victory a few weeks later. They arrived in Seattle in time for Navy Day, Oct. 27, 1945, a day declared to honor the Navy's role in the war.

"We went ashore and had a great time," he said, adding that the best moment was seeing big-band icon Count Basie.

Why we fight

Patten has never been troubled by questions of why we fought the war. But if he ever was, he would only have to think about one experience that still haunts him.

Among its duties after the war, the Iowa helped carry liberated American prisoners of war back to the U.S. There were about 200 on board, Patten said.

"They sat on the deck of our ship," he recalled. "They were so emaciated, their minds gone so bad ... they would hardly eat. You had to spoon-feed them. It was terrible. They couldn't hardly walk. Most of them you had to pick them up, take them where they wanted to go."

When the ship docked in San Pedro, California, the POWs had to be carried off the ship. Patten remembers watching them, asking himself "How could anyone treat another human being like that?"

Even now, he often finds himself wondering about the ones from the Iowa.

"How did they live? ... Did they make a life? Did they get married? Did they have offspring? Were they able to make a living?"

Patten is not shy about admitting it: He still harbors a lot of resentment toward the Japanese for their treatment of POWs.

After his discharge, Patten was ready to go home to Tulsa, which he hadn't seen in two years. He hitchhiked all the way. It was a common way to get around back then, he said, and if you had on a uniform, you never had to worry about getting a ride.

Seeing Tulsa at last felt "out of this world," he said.

Marrying and going on to raise four children, Patten attended law school at the University of Tulsa and built a successful career as an attorney. He retired from practice three years ago, at age 87.

These days he finds himself thinking often of his service.

"I'm so thankful I was able to give to my country," Patten said. "All my Marine buddies felt the same way."

World War II veteran Gordon Patten is shown aboard the USS Iowa.
COURTESY

An "expert rifleman" badge is among war decorations earned by World War II veteran Gordon Patten. MATT BARNARD/Tulsa World

Total destruction

Clarence Pleake fought at Iwo Jima, helped occupy Japan

Clarence Pleake's most recent bus was a Greyhound double-decker. But unlike those he spent his career in, this one is a little too small for him to climb behind the wheel.

A former Greyhound bus driver, Pleake has to content himself these days with making miniature versions in his home wood shop.

"I gave it (the double-decker) to my daughter," he says, describing his latest creation with pride.

For all mass transit has meant to him, though, there remains one example Pleake would just as soon forget: The train that — with him on board — pulled out of Kansas City's Union Station one long-ago day in 1944. Bound for the West Coast — and after that the war — Pleake had no way of knowing then what horrors lay ahead of him and his fellow Marine enlistees. All he knew for sure, as he pulled away, was what he was leaving behind.

"I couldn't hardly stand it, and neither could she," Pleake said of his wife, Virginia, whom he can still see clearly, standing with their twins to see him off.

The station was the site of many a tearful farewell that day. In fact, the crowds were so heavy, Pleake's family "had to stand in the back," he said. "They couldn't get close."

On to Iwo Jima

Pleake, now 94, welcomed the Tulsa World to his home in 2015 to talk about his WWII service.

The oldest of four siblings from Hollister, Missouri, Pleake was 21 and married by the time the U.S. entered the war. And he soon had two more mouths to feed — twins, a boy and a girl. But neither his family situation nor the good job he had in Kansas City would ultimately hold him back.

"All my friends were joining," he said, adding that military service was something he felt duty-bound to do.

Joining the Marines to fulfill that duty, Pleake would soon find himself headed to war in the Pacific, assigned to the 5th Marine

Division, 27th Regiment. A member of an 81-mm mortar squad, he would see no real combat at his first few stops: Wake Island, Eniwetok and Guam.

"Guam had just been secured, but there were still a lot of snipers," he said. "But I was more afraid of the snakes there. The snipers were not very good shots."

Pleake's next stop, Iwo Jima, would be a whole different story. There, on Feb. 19, 1945, the Fighting 5th would take part in the brutal Allied invasion of the Japanese-held island.

Going in with the second wave at Iwo Jima's Red Beach, Pleake remembers having to crawl forward over the sand because of all the shells exploding around them. Eventually, he and his mortar squad found a spot to set up, and from there, began returning fire, trying to take out enemy pillboxes and machine gun nests. It was a routine they'd repeat countless times over the next few weeks, as the unit helped fight for and ultimately secure the island.

"You were always under fire in some way," Pleake said. "Even if you were off the lines for a few hours, there were still snipers. It just wasn't safe."

One sniper was picking them off from the side of Mount Suribachi, and Pleake volunteered with two others to take him out. Finding a cave in the mountain side where they believed he was hiding, they set off an explosive charge inside. It wasn't the smoothest operation. The force of the blast sent them tumbling backward down the mountain.

"We were pretty bruised and cut up," Pleake said. But apparently it worked.

"We must have got the sniper. We never had any trouble from him again."

Mass burials

One night, Pleake was sharing a foxhole with a Marine from another squad when a shell hit the hole. Pleake was somehow uninjured. But his companion "was blown almost in half," he said. The memory of it is still too much for Pleake. As he recounts it, he leans over, choking up.

"I dragged him back in the hole," he said, "and stayed with him all night. But he died."

Of all Marine divisions at Iwo Jima, the 5th would sustain the most casualties: 1,098 killed and 2,974 wounded. Many of the dead were buried in mass graves. Pleake, whose platoon lost nine of its roughly 40 members, witnessed the grim rite more than once.

"The (Navy) Seabees would bulldoze a trench out — about 5, 6 feet deep," he said. "The bodies were sewed up into blankets, and then they'd be laid side by side with their dog tags in the trench."

The bulldozer would then cover them with sand, and a single cross would be erected at one end, he said.

Keeping Pleake going amid such horrors was the encouragement he received from home. He and his wife wrote each other every day. It wasn't perfect: His wife's letters to him sometimes would arrive several at once. And those Pleake sent home were always censored. But regardless, they were an important lifeline.

After his wife's death several years ago, his letters to her, which she'd kept, were found.

"I read every one of them," Pleake said. "It got a little boring," he added, laughing.

Raising the flag

While on Iwo, Pleake witnessed a scene that would go on to provide one of the war's most iconic images: the American flag being raised on Mount Suribachi. There were two flags, actually: A small one to start, and then a larger one later to replace it — the one captured in the famous photograph.

"The dumb thing was," Pleake recalled, "I stood up when I saw it — bullets still going everywhere. I thought (the fight) was over."

After 20 seconds, I decided I better get back down."

Pleake would be on Iwo Jima for 36 days. During that time, with the almost constant fighting, he wasn't able to brush his teeth or shave, he said, and often went a couple of days at a time without rations. He went as many as four days without eating at one point, he said. But finally their job was done. Pleake and the battered, depleted 5th went back to Hawaii to rebuild.

A full-scale invasion of Japan still loomed, though, and they expected to be called back to take part. But it never came to that. One day in Hilo, Pleake stopped at a newspaper rack where he saw the headline on the latest edition of Stars and Stripes. It read: "Atomic bomb dropped on Hiroshima."

"I thought 'Oh boy, the war is over!' " Pleake said. Actually it would take one more atomic bomb drop — on Nagasaki — to bring Japan's surrender. But for all practical purposes, Pleake was right.

A new mission

Pleake would still be going to Japan, as it turned out. But now, as part of occupying forces, it was with a different mission. Assigned to an intelligence unit, Pleake joined in breaking down Japan's war infrastructure.

Starting in Sasebo in southern Japan, moving from there to what is now Saikai, they burned ammunition and other Japanese war matériel as they went. Pleake remembers his interaction with the Japanese people clearly. In Sasebo, "After about three days, they realized we were not there to hurt them," he said. From their K rations, the Americans shared hard candy with the children.

Pleake noticed that at first girls walked two or three timid steps behind the boys.

"But it wasn't long before they were walking down the streets together, holding hands. Things changed so much in just the short time we were there."

'Nothing was standing'

Situated a few miles from Saikai was the city of Nagasaki, which just weeks earlier had been leveled in the second atomic bomb blast. One day, Pleake and two buddies decided they wanted to see it. Catching a ride on a jeep headed that way, he said, there was no way they could've prepared themselves.

"Looking at it I couldn't believe it," he said. "Ordinarily with destruction you see a few structures still rising up, maybe eight or 10 feet. But the part we saw, nothing was standing. I never saw destruction like it. It was complete."

Pleake and his companions wandered through Nagasaki's abandoned streets until military police made them leave.

"We weren't supposed to be there. It was still radioactive. It never dawned on us about the radioactivity. We hadn't been warned."

Pleake never suffered any ill effects, though. Not long after that, he would finish his service and come home to his family in Missouri. He eventually became a Greyhound bus driver in Tulsa. He retired after 32 years.

Marine Corps blues

When Pleake first decided on military service he intended to become a Navy submariner. But that all changed when he went to enlist. The sight of a Marine master gunnery sergeant in his blue dress uniform — "the prettiest suit I ever saw" — impressed Pleake beyond measure. So he joined the Marines instead.

As it turned out, though, the Corps had stopped issuing dress blues through the end of the war; so Pleake had to be content with the basic green.

A few years ago, as a birthday surprise, his family had a special blue uniform made for him.

"I joked that I'd had to wait 50 years," said Pleake, who proudly

Clarence Pleake (left) and Conway J. Perry served with the Marines' occupying force during the rebuilding of Japan after the end of World War II. COURTESY

posed for pictures in it.

These days, Pleake finds that he's still waiting for some things. Like for the day when he will finally come to terms with all he saw.

"Wars are so horrible," said Pleake, whose two brothers served in Europe while he was in the Pacific. "It's impossible to explain exactly what the horrors are like. You've got to see it.

"I just think of all the guys we left over there."

For years, Pleake had trouble sleeping and lived with an unset-tled feeling he says is hard to describe. But despite the bad things he saw, he remains an irrepressible optimist.

"I've had such a wonderful life," Pleake said, "that I'd be ashamed to complain about anything. And it's all because of the freedoms we have defended."

"Our flag means so much to me. I'd urge every young person to remember that flag and do whatever you have to do to defend it. Our freedoms are so wonderful here."

Mortars not biased

Powell fought with segregated Army unit in the Philippines

One thing about mortars: They don't discriminate. Roland Powell learned that early on in his combat experience, observing how the shells cut down everyone, race or skin color notwithstanding.

The sound of them being fired in the distance "was an eerie feeling," recalled Powell, who served in a segregated Army unit for black soldiers. "Then, you got real nervous," counting off the seconds to see where they'd hit.

Powell, 94, a World War II veteran, welcomed the Tulsa World to his home in 2015 to talk about his experience in the war, including his part in the Philippines campaign of 1944-45.

As a motor sergeant charged with keeping a fleet of trucks running, he was often in the thick of the action.

"We worked and we fought," he said.

Besides hauling ammunition, food and supplies to the front lines, sometimes Powell's trucks were called on to carry the wounded.

"We'd have guys with half an arm or a leg tore off, hollering for help," he said. "I did all I could to help."

Liberating the Philippines

Powell was drafted into the Army in April 1942. He was 21 at the time.

Several stops stateside and then at Pearl Harbor would follow, though, before he got his first taste of battle. That would come in the Philippines, as the 6th Army led the effort to liberate the island chain from Japan.

"I think they knew we were coming," Powell said of his first stop, Leyte island. "By golly, they put the fire to us."

Hoping the mortar shells wouldn't find them, he and his fellow soldiers hunkered down in foxholes. It was more of the same, he added, at Mindoro: "I think they knew we were coming, too. They had us a welcoming party."

But, he said, "the (U.S.) Navy was awesome — they lit that place up before we got there."

By the time Powell arrived on Mindanao, the fighting wasn't as bad, he said, "but we still lost guys there."

Even 70 years later, he's able to rattle off the names of fallen comrades.

"We lost a lot of guys (in the Philippines). A lot of trouble."

Powell grew close to a number of his fellow soldiers during his time in the Army. Many of them couldn't read, or in some cases, even spell their own names, he said.

"I read for them and helped write letters home for a lot of guys," he said.

'You didn't want to do it, but you had to'

The sight of children running up to you, their arms outstretched, would've been welcome in most settings. But not so in the Philippines, Powell said: There, it was something soldiers learned to fear, representing a side of warfare so horrific it haunts him to this day.

The enemy "had put grenades under the children's arms," he said. "They killed a bunch of us that way."

To protect themselves, soldiers took desperate measures, he said, shooting anyone who came running at them.

"You didn't want to do it, but you had to do it. That's tough right there. I still don't like it. They (the children) weren't responsible."

With the surrender of Japan, Powell's unit would move on from the Philippines to Japan to assist in the occupation.

In December 1945, Powell received his discharge. A technical sergeant, he could've stayed three more months and been promoted to master sergeant. But he missed home badly and decided it was time.

As a member of a unit that was all black except for the white officers, Powell's military experience was a reflection of the segregated culture at large. And while he was gone, not much had changed back home.

"Many places were still off limits to us. You had black toilets and white toilets. ... But we made it — we made it. In spite of it all, we survived."

Proposing on Pearl Harbor day

Longtime Beggs residents who moved to Tulsa last year, Powell and his wife, Hattie, have been married for 72 years. They raised three children and have many grandchildren, great-grandchildren and even great-great-grandchildren. In fact, Powell represents the first of five living generations of Powells.

It all started in Beggs, he said: He and Hattie had walked to school together as children and began dating in high school. Powell proposed the same day as the attack on Pearl Harbor, and they married nine months later, Aug. 15, 1942, while he was on leave.

After returning from the war, Powell went to work for Dyer Construction in Tulsa and would enjoy a 30-year career there.

"If I had to, I'd do it all over again," he said, reflecting on his war experience, his wife and the family they raised. "I'm blessed, son. There's a man upstairs," he said, shaking a gnarled forefinger at the ceiling. "The Lord took care of me. That's what brought me through. Lord, yes. That's who keeps me going now."

'The greatest country'

For years, Powell wouldn't say much about the war, family members say. He did have one special confidant: A nephew who had been a prisoner of war in Korea. But it wasn't until his grandchildren were getting older that Powell began to open up.

Recent years have also seen Powell begin to experience side effects from the war that he didn't when he was younger. Diagnosed with PTSD, he has nightmares and moments of paranoia, family members say; at times he even shouts, lost in some bad memory.

Age is also catching up. Powell doesn't hear as well and uses a walker to get around. But his memory is as good as ever. Of the many things he hasn't forgotten, he said, one is what a great honor

Roland Powell, who served in the Army from 1942 to 1945 in the Pacific Theater, is shown near the end of World War II. COURTESY

About the Philippines campaign

More than two years after the Japanese captured the Philippines, the U.S.-led liberation of the Pacific island chain would begin Oct. 20, 1944.

The islands would be secured by the end of June 1945, although fighting would continue up until mid-August 1945, almost through the end of the war.

Among the casualties, U.S. forces saw 13,973 killed. Japan suffered 336,000 deaths.

With control of the Philippines, the Allies expanded their blockade of Japan, almost completely cutting off its supply of oil.

it was to serve his country.

"I'll tell you one thing: This is still the greatest country in the world. I haven't been everywhere, but everywhere I have been, people say, 'I want to go to America. I want to go home with you.'

" 'My country 'tis of thee — of thee we sing,' " Powell suddenly recites. "I'm not saying we don't have our faults. But it's still a great country, my boy."

Driving force

Price saw action at the Battle of the Bulge

"I want to challenge Gregory Hines."

That was all, Al Price swears, he had to say. From there, his feet took over. Invited up on stage during a performance by Hines in Tahlequah, Price impressed everyone, including the late actor and dancing legend, with a lively demonstration of his tap-dancing skills. It remains one of his favorite memories.

In his 80s at the time, the Tulsan had only been tap dancing about 10 years, not exactly an age at which people look around for new hobbies.

"(But) I had always wanted to do it," he said, "ever since I was a kid and saw Fred Astaire."

As light as Price is on his toes, though, he's never been the kind to tap dance around difficult subjects. For example, the things he saw and experienced in World War II.

A co-founder of a veterans group in Tulsa whose members often speak publicly, Price has talked about the subject to countless school groups through the years.

"You'd be surprised," he said. "(The children) ask good, solid questions. They want to know the truth."

'Down and dirty'

Whenever he talks about WWII, Price, 91, has a couple of central themes he likes to drive home. For starters, "there's no such thing as a good war," as he noted during a recent interview.

"The Germans were a pretty tough enemy. They were dirty, and you had to get down and dirty with them. Or we would not have won. "The war brought out dirty things. ... We just did it a little better than they did."

The experience, for Price, began with the D-Day invasion of Normandy. Drafted into the Army at 18, he arrived at Omaha Beach just a few months later — on June 7, 1944, the day after the inva-

Al Price (kneeling, far right) pauses with his unit on a roadway by a destroyed vehicle during his service in the Army's 2nd Infantry Division in Europe during World War II. COURTESY

sion began. It was late in the evening, but he still "saw a lot of bodies ... lot of dead people all around. It was a horrible thing." It was his first experience with the realities of war, and it set the tone for the rest of his service.

Assigned to the 2nd Infantry Division, Price was a driver for a captain from his unit. From the time he hit Omaha Beach through the end of the war, he and his jeep would cover thousands of miles in and around combat zones. Often, the captain was checking on front-line troops and making sure they had the supplies they needed.

"How to explain being in combat ... It was not an easy thing," Price said. "It helped being so young. That helped us get through it. Our boys were very well-trained. The combat soldier was a tough cookie."

Battle of the Bulge

He was there for the whole shebang, so the Battle of the Bulge is a topic Price can address with some authority, and he has spoken and written about it.

On Dec. 16, 1944, when the Germans' "Bulge" offensive began, Price said he and his division had been fighting to capture dams along the Ruhr Valley, Germany's industrial heartland. As they were heading back to their base near Elsenborn, Belgium, they ran into the first convoys of American troops and military vehicles. They were retreating, he said; the German offensive had caught everyone off guard.

"The Germans did a real good job. They weren't sissies," Price said. "We had to stop them. And we did."

But not before the campaign became the bloodiest of the war for the Americans. Of the 500,000 American troops involved in the Bulge through Jan. 25, 1945, there were upwards of 81,000 casualties, including 19,000 killed.

Price saw his share of the fallen from the driver's seat of his jeep, as he crossed battle lines with his captain. The image of snowy fields strewn with dead Americans and Germans, bodies frozen solid, is fixed forever in his mind.

It wasn't just the soldiers killed in the fighting that made an impression. Another death he saw later, he said, is one of his worst memories. It was in Germany, he said, after the war was pretty much over.

"It was a little boy. About 3. He had a coat on. It was winter." Price believes the child had been hit by shrapnel. "He was just laying there like he was sleeping."

"There were some pretty sad things you were exposed to," he said.

Price came home from the war with a bad back. "Riding in a rough, tough vehicle with the jarring and so forth" will do that, he said. But it was a small price to pay, he added. For many others, the war demanded much more.

"I didn't get hurt," Price said. "But what kept me from getting hurt I'll never know. I was lucky to get through it."

For his role at the Bulge, Price received a Bronze Star. He doesn't remember what for, he said, and it doesn't really matter.

Al Price is shown with his M1 carbine. He served with the Army's 2nd Infantry Division in WWII. COURTESY

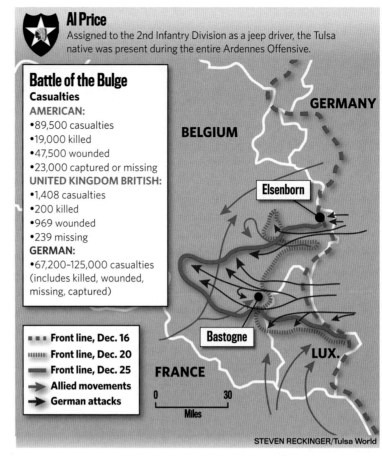

Al Price
Assigned to the 2nd Infantry Division as a jeep driver, the Tulsa native was present during the entire Ardennes Offensive.

Battle of the Bulge
Casualties
AMERICAN:
•89,500 casualties
•19,000 killed
•47,500 wounded
•23,000 captured or missing
UNITED KINGDOM BRITISH:
•1,408 casualties
•200 killed
•969 wounded
•239 missing
GERMAN:
•67,200–125,000 casualties
(includes killed, wounded, missing, captured)

GERMANY
BELGIUM
Elsenborn
Bastogne
LUX.
FRANCE

▪▪▪ Front line, Dec. 16
▥▥▥ Front line, Dec. 20
▬ Front line, Dec. 25
→ Allied movements
→ German attacks

0   30
Miles

STEVEN RECKINGER/Tulsa World

"You were there and you did your job."

Life after war

Price came from a troubled background. Because of an unstable situation at home as a child, he moved to Tulsa Boys Home, where he would live for five years. That, and a good experience at Central High School — legendary track coach Bill Lantz was like a father to him — made the difference, Price said. He graduated from Central in 1942, and was drafted shortly afterward.

The toughness that his early life experiences bred into him, he said, might have helped him deal better with war than some of the others.

"It was pretty tough coming home and adjusting to everyday life," Price said. "You didn't have anything to hang onto. You ran around pretty heavy. A lot of boys didn't get through it at all."

"Time makes it easier," he added. "But you still have the memories."

Price found different ways to deal with them. Military reunions — "being around those guys and being able to compare notes" — have played an important part, he said. He's been a regular at the 2nd Infantry Division's annual reunion, and even brought it to Tulsa in 2005.

There have been other opportunities, too, to talk about the war. Price co-founded World War II Vets of Tulsa more than two decades ago, and many of its members have spoken at schools and other events.

When he started speaking at schools, Price said, he noticed "a lot of these kids weren't getting any World War II in their courses. They were eager to know."

Price got married after the war. He and his wife, Margie, are still together. They share an apartment at Town Village senior living center in Tulsa. The couple's life together has been touched by tragedy. They had two children, but lost one.

For all he has seen and lived through, though, Price has found plenty of reasons to kick up his heels. A photo on the wall of his apartment shows one of them — a shot of him dancing with Gregory Hines. The memory of it still makes him smile.

"All in all, life has been pretty good to me," Price said.

Al Price (standing in back, center) stands with other soldiers and a casualty on a stretcher during his service in the U.S. Army in the European Theater during World War II. COURTESY

'This is reality'

Charlie Prigmore was an Army medic in Europe

It started as a simple shot of morphine for a wounded soldier. But for medic Charlie Prigmore, it came with a big dose of reality.

"I was upset and I think I said something like how sorry I was," Prigmore said, recalling the young man who lay before him, right leg missing below the knee from stepping on a land mine.

"He said, 'Doc, just give me some damn morphine. If you want to feel sorry for someone, feel sorry for these poor bastards that are staying.'"

About to be loaded onto a hospital ship at Cherbourg, France, "he was just happy to be going home," Prigmore added, recalling the soldier's "grateful look."

"He was my first wounded soldier," he said. "I

thought then, 'This is reality. This is what this war is all about.'"

Just months earlier, fresh out of Tulsa Central High School, Prigmore had been looking forward to the war as a "big adventure." Suddenly, he didn't feel so gung-ho anymore.

Going to war together

"Like I tell people, I was not physically at Omaha Beach or Utah Beach (sites of the D-Day invasion). I was not at the Battle of the Bulge. But mentally I was at all of them — because I worked with these boys who were there. I helped with the aftermath."

Prigmore, an award-winning high school coach in football and wrestling who retired as vice president of academic affairs at Northeastern State University in Tahlequah, talked to the Tulsa World in 2016 about his experiences as an Army medic, treating wounded soldiers on hospital ships.

Drafted halfway through his senior year at Central, 1943-44, Prigmore, now 90, was granted a deferment so he could finish and graduate. He said he couldn't help being excited at the time.

"We had 900 kids graduate, and almost all the guys had been drafted. We had played football together, wrestled together." Now they were going to war together.

The truth is, though, "an 18-year-old guy does not know anything about war," Prigmore said.

Because he had worked at a dentist's office during high school, the military apparently thought he would make a good medic, Prigmore said. He was trained to specialize in physical therapy, and then assigned to hospital ships, where his job was to work with wounded troops, helping them exercise and regain movement as they recovered.

Over the next year, as a member of the Army's 231st Hospital Ship Complement, he served on two ships — the Larkspur and the Wisteria — making five round trips to Europe to pick up the wounded.

Big ears, small mouth

No sooner had his work begun than Prigmore reconsidered his enthusiasm about war.

"I thought, 'Hey, this must be real.'"

Prigmore's ships carried between 500 and 600 patients. He was one of two physical therapists — or "physical reconditioning specialists" as they were called — on board. Over each two-week-plus voyage back to the states, he worked with 75 to 100 patients, he estimates.

"The physicians and nurses in charge were my bosses, basically — they told me who to work with."

Working one-on-one with the soldiers was no easy task.

"GIs are kind of funny about doing exercises anyway," he said. "And some of the things we had them do weren't very pleasant."

As part of his work, he often talked to the patients. Or listened, rather — "big ears, small mouth" is a principle he learned to put into practice then, he said, and would apply later as a coach and teacher.

Conversing with his patients "was not part of my written responsibility," Prigmore said. "But if I could help some of their psychological scars by listening to them, I thought 'why not?'"

'Sometimes, they cried'

The patients' moods, Prigmore said, ranged "from pretty jovial to pretty damn mad."

From the angry ones, "I heard a lot of obscene words. About their sergeant, the Army, President Roosevelt. They blamed everybody for what happened to them. Everybody but themselves."

Some, he said, were "pretty open and explicit about how they got hurt." Others, "you couldn't pry it out of them with a crowbar."

Sometimes, they cried.

"It's hard to be working on a grown guy who's lost an arm, that's crying," Prigmore said, the memory making him pause. "I don't like to think about it. Sometimes I almost felt like I was their wife, daddy, brother. They were trying to find something to hang on to."

The ships weren't carrying just the physically wounded. In fact, on the Wisteria, he said, there were four padded cells. Once he was assigned briefly to help give out the daily medication to the men held there — soldiers suffering from mental breakdowns.

"We opened one of the cells," Prigmore said, "and this big muscular guy inside pushed it open, and grabbed the nurse with me — Lt. Fox was her name. He grabbed her and ripped her blouse open."

Prigmore, the tough former high school football player, reacted instantly, hitting the man and subduing him.

"And I got chewed out for it," he said. "They told me 'You are not to hit our patients.' ... But I had no psychiatric training. I did what I thought I had to do."

Charlie Prigmo

The Tulsa native served as a medic on two Army hospital ships, the Larkspur and Wisteria. He personally provided physical therapy to hundreds of wounded soldiers.

	Knots	Patient capacity	Date first voyage	Destination first voyage
Wisteria (William Osler)	11	588	July 16, 1944	United Kingdom
Larkspur (Breslau Bridgeport)	10	592	Aug. 31, 1944	United Kingdom

Patients evacuated from overseas; debarked at Army ports

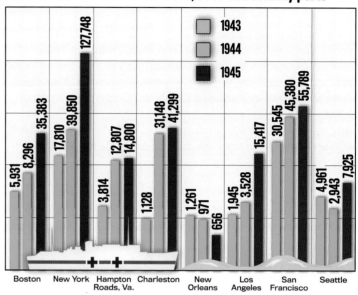

SOURCE: www.usmm.org   STEVEN RECKINGER/Tulsa World

On the lighter side, Prigmore occasionally had the duty of showing movies. Taking a 16mm projector from ward to ward, he treated the patients to "To Have and Have Not" starring Humphrey Bogart and other films of the era.

"They liked me a little more when I was showing movies," he chuckled.

One of Prigmore's most vivid memories of a fellow passenger happened after the war in Europe ended.

Carrying some German prisoners of war back to Germany, the ship had just pulled out of New York Harbor, Prigmore said, when one of the POWs jumped over a handrail trying to escape. Within seconds, as he thrashed about in the water, the ship's fan tail hit him. "Boom! He went under," said Prigmore, who was close by and saw everything. Per Geneva Convention rules, they had to search for him for two hours. But it "was pointless," he said. "I had seen the body parts in the water."

Prigmore said everyone wondered why the German had done it.

"My theory was: He could not face going back to his home country having lost."

Prigmore, who found he was good at knowing what people were thinking, later earned a degree in psychology. His experience with the soldiers in the war laid the groundwork, he said. He never saw any of them again after they arrived in the States.

"But sometimes I've wondered — still do — what happened to various ones."

Looking over his shoulder

Along with the soldiers he treated, Prigmore also thinks often of the players he coached.

One of them still frequently on his mind is Bob Kalsu, who

played for him at Del City. Kalsu went on to become an All-American offensive lineman at the University of Oklahoma, then got off to a promising start with the Buffalo Bills before he was killed while serving in Vietnam.

Prigmore remembers what he was thinking, attending the memorial service: "What a loss, what an unnecessary loss. He had a great future in front of him.

"It makes you think about your own life," he added. "I could've been like Robert (Kalsu). I could've been one of those guys hauled back on those ships."

But Prigmore's story turned out differently. After his discharge in May 1946, he made up for lost time, attending Northeastern State, where he played baseball and was co-captain of the 1950 football team.

Over the coaching career that followed, he directed football, baseball and wrestling at various schools, including in Tulsa, where he was named to the East Central Hall of Fame as a football coach and Edison's Hall of Fame as a wrestling coach. Four times he was recognized as Northeast Oklahoma Conference Coach of the Year.

After earning his doctorate from OU in 1968, he served as executive vice chancellor of the University of Arkansas for Medical Sciences in Little Rock before returning to Oklahoma and NSU.

At his side for all of those stops was his wife, Billie. The couple, who celebrated their 66th anniversary in 2016, met after the war. It was at a "hobo dance" at NSU — she was dancing with a buddy when Prigmore cut in. Two months and a day later they were married.

Whirlwind courtships, more common back then, aren't the only things that have changed since the World War II era, Prigmore said. For one, "everybody in the country was in that war — one way or another. People now, they are not part of Iraq or Syria or whatever. Unless they've got someone in it. But during World War II, everybody was in it. This country was 'all in.'"

Prigmore believes some things will never change, though.

"There will always be people who are willing to give their lives for this country. Regardless of who the president is. This country is bigger than that office."

Reflecting further on his life, Prigmore added: "I think everybody looks over their shoulder, wonders 'what would I have done different?' My answer: I wouldn't do anything different."

That includes his war service.

"If I was 18 years old again today, I'd do it all again in a New York second. ... I am proud of the little part I played."

World War II veteran Charlie Prigmore was a medic aboard the medical ship Larkspur. COURTESY

Fierce combat

Marine Bill Pummill survived three intense island campaigns

About two feet, give or take an inch. That's how far Bill Pummill's head was from the mortar shell that hit and blew up his field pack.

Seventy years later, he still can't quite figure how it missed him. Sometimes, it seemed, he was just lucky that way. On this occasion, Pummill had been taking cover from a mortar attack in his foxhole when his pack — which he'd left lying outside, a couple of feet from where he was huddled — suddenly exploded from a shell.

"I looked, but there wasn't a thread of it left," he said. Going forward, Pummill would continue to need that kind of luck. It was just his first night on Iwo Jima.

Without a scratch

Pummill, now 93, talked to the Tulsa World in 2015

about his World War II service and how, somehow, he made it through three fierce campaigns without a scratch.

A member of the 9th Regiment of the 3rd Marine Division in the Pacific, Cpl. Pummill was assigned to communications. Trying to set up radios and telephones in war zones often meant having to duck bullets while you worked. It was that way at both Bougainville Island and Guam, two of Pummill's stops before Iwo Jima.

Involved in the fight to secure both islands, he again needed his good fortune to get through. One time, while on Guam, Pummill and a group of men were trying to take refuge from a mortar attack when they dove for a nearby bomb crater. The last of the group, Pummill couldn't make it and jumped into an adjacent crater. Just as he did, a shell hit the other one and exploded.

"All seven of those guys were killed. ... I still wonder how I could be so lucky," he said.

From Guam, it was on to Iwo Jima. Pummill's unit went in two days after the invasion began on Feb. 19, 1945. The first thing he saw after his boots hit the island's black-sand beach gave him an idea of what horrors lay ahead: An American tank rolled up and stopped, and three guys jumped out. To his shock, he said, "they looked like charcoal. They had taken a direct hit from a Japanese anti-tank gun and were burned bad. I'm sure they died."

Although Pummill's primary job was still laying communication wire, on Iwo Jima, he said, he spent more time with a rifle in his hands. And in addition to fighting, he would also join in helping clear Japanese soldiers from the island's network of caves.

Pummill didn't see the famous flag-raising on Iwo Jima's Mount Suribachi. But he did go to an Easter service there afterward that his company chaplain organized. Church was important to him, and he attended services whenever they were held.

Pummill was discharged in October 1945, having served more than three years. Pummill, who hailed from Crocker, Missouri, met and married a Tulsa girl after the war, and the two settled here. He went on to a 21-year career with American Airlines.

Trying to forget

Looking back, Pummill remembers how surprised he was to have survived Iwo Jima.

"I'd been through Bougainville and Guam: I was thinking, 'Man, I'll never make it through this.' But I did — three campaigns, and never suffered an injury. I was very fortunate."

For many of those around him, that wasn't the case. Between Guam and Iwo Jima especially, Pummill saw many buddies and other Marines he knew die in action.

"When you were on Iwo, seeing all the guys killed going up to the front — it was an eerie feeling." After experiences like that, "you try your best to forget," Pummill said. For years afterward, he didn't talk about the war — not even with his younger brother, an Army veteran who had fought in Europe.

"We just said very little about any of it," he noted, adding that they seemed to have a silent understanding between them. More recently, though, Pummill has opened up. He has grandchildren and great-grandchildren now, and they want to know the story. If good can come from veterans telling their stories, Pummill hopes it's what this and future generations might learn from his.

"Stand behind your country and do what we did in World War II," he said. "Everyone pitched in. Everyone did their share."

The Yanks mop up on Bougainville. At night the Japanese would infiltrate American lines. At Dawn, the doughboys went out and killed them. This photo shows tank going forward, infantrymen following in its cover. NATIONAL ARCHIVES

KEN RENBERG   ARMY 1939-52

Talking the talk

Renberg, a German-American Jew, interrogated German POWs

Of all the places a German accent might have blended in, the American side of the line was not one of them.

So, 2nd Lt. Ken Renberg played it smart: He let his driver do the talking.

"I didn't open my mouth," said Renberg, a German-born U.S. Army officer whose duties during World War II once included checking his unit's roadblocks near the front lines.

Deferring to his driver to speak to guards, he added, was a good move. "One of the questions we were asked was 'Who was Babe Ruth?' And I didn't know much about baseball."

Seventy years since the war — and almost 80 since he immigrated to Oklahoma from Germany — Renberg, a longtime member of Tulsa's Jewish community, knows a lot more about baseball now.

And he still has his German accent.

During the war, his ability to speak German coupled with his family's long history were more assets than liabilities, he said. Because of that, Renberg, who served with the 1st Infantry Division, would come to specialize in interrogation, gleaning information that was important to his unit's combat plans.

Useful intel

Renberg, 94, a resident of Montereau retirement community, talked to the Tulsa World in 2015 about his war service. His work as an interrogator began in England in early 1944. A member of Army intelligence, Renberg interviewed German prisoners there, gathering information in preparation for the coming D-Day invasion.

Not long after D-Day, Renberg was assigned to lead an interrogation team, moving with the infantry through western Europe. Questioning German troops as they were captured, they aimed to get any information that might prove useful to the Allies.

Renberg says he always observed Geneva Convention rules. But regardless, coercive tactics rarely would've been necessary, he said. Most POWs talked easily. "A lot of them didn't like the war or Hit-

Ken Renberg (right) poses with two of his childhood friends in Germany during World War II. Renberg, who is Jewish, left Germany and settled in Enid. His family escaped Nazi persecution and followed a few years later. He enlisted in the Army after high school and became an intelligence officer. COURTESY

ler," Renberg said. "I never had any dyed-in-the-wool Nazis. These were just guys trying to save their own lives.

"Most were soldiers in forward positions. You didn't ask strategic questions, just tactical: 'Where are your minefields, guns? Who's your company commander? etc.' "

Leaving Germany

The war was personal for Renberg in a way that it could never be for most American soldiers.

Originally Gunter Renberg — he changed his name to Kenneth later — he was born in 1920 in Delmenhorst, Germany. With Nazi persecution of Jews on the rise, in 1937 his parents sent him to America, where an aunt and uncle lived in Enid. Renberg lived with them and attended high school there.

Two years later, his parents and younger brother also fled Germany for America, settling in Tulsa.

Graduating in 1939, Renberg didn't wait long before deciding what his next move would be. On Sept. 1, the Germans invaded Poland, officially beginning WWII in Europe. In response, Renberg signed up with the National Guard.

"I joined," he said, "to get even with Hitler. I am Jewish and Hitler claimed we were not Germans. I came from a family that had lived in Germany for many centuries."

The U.S. would not enter the war for two more years, so Renberg had to bide his time. As a member of the Guard's 45th Infantry Division, he served with an artillery battalion stationed in Enid that included many of his former classmates. But Renberg's military responsibility took a much different course than most of his friends.

Ken Renberg carried this notebook during his service during World War II.
MICHAEL WYKE/Tulsa World

Inside information

He was shipped overseas in December 1943, landing in Scotland on Christmas Eve. From there, he was assigned to the 18th Infantry Regiment of the Army's 1st Infantry Division. By that time, the 1st Infantry — known as the "Big Red One" — was preparing to spearhead the upcoming D-Day invasion of Normandy.

Renberg, who was by then an officer, trained in interrogation and went to work questioning German prisoners of war, seeking information that would help the Allies. "Units, positions, weapons, plans — what units were opposite us? Who was commanding them? We were trying to build up this information as much as possible," he said.

Renberg's work gave him access to a special intelligence room in London. It was always under heavy guard, he said, and required a pass to get in.

Reviewing maps and documents there as part of his job, Renberg was privy to inside information. He recalls how he and a colleague learned in advance that June 5, 1944, was the target date for the D-Day invasion. "Officially, nothing had been said," Renberg said, "but we surmised."

And they were almost right — ultimately, it would be pushed back one day, to June 6, because of bad weather.

Wounded in action

Among the forces storming Omaha Beach on D-Day, Renberg's division suffered the heaviest casualties. Luckily, he came through unscathed.

But a few weeks later, on July 26, his good luck changed.

His unit was caught in a bombardment outside St. Lo, France. With shells falling all around them, "everyone tried to find a hole. They were jumping into trenches. Some right on top of dead Germans," said Renberg.

He remembers vividly when a shell exploded close to him. He was standing beside one of his men when they both were hit by shrapnel. His comrade "just fell over," he said. "I tried to tear his shirt open — but he was gone."

Renberg was bleeding badly. Shrapnel had left about a 6-inch-wide hole in his shoulder. He would spend four weeks recovering in a hospital and received a Purple Heart.

But Renberg's personal mission was not done.

Why he joined

This time, again leading a team of interrogators, Renberg was assigned to the 102nd Infantry Division. By the time he arrived, the 102nd was at the German border. When the Battle of the Bulge began in December 1944, his division stayed where it was. A neighboring division was moved, though, and Renberg's was left to cover a two-division zone.

The German counteroffensive failed, and the 102nd crossed the Roer River and headed straight east through northern Germany.

Renberg says he never saw any of the death camps where so many of his fellow Jews were murdered. But he feels he did his part to bring them justice.

The regime's antisemitism was "why I got in the service ... joined

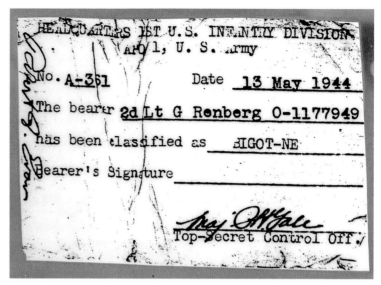

Ken Renberg's intelligence headquarters ID card bears his code name, BIGOT, an abbreviation for the phrase "to Gibralter" in reverse in the U.S. Army. COURTESY

the night Hitler marched into Poland."

"I figured doing something about it" was the best response.

While in Germany, Renberg took temporary charge of a prisoner-of-war camp that earned him a write-up in the Tulsa World. It was a former farm that had been "repurposed," and held 2,500 German prisoners at a time. Over Renberg's three days at the camp, he said, some 35,000 POWs went through — with only him and 15 military police officers in charge.

It was exhausting, he said. "We kept going on booze," he added, with a smile. "That's what gave us the energy."

Keeping the faith

By this time, Renberg had accumulated far more than enough points for his discharge. So after the German surrender, he decided to come home to Oklahoma. Once back, he didn't take any time off. Two weeks after returning he started classes at the University of Tulsa.

Renberg stayed with the Army as well. He remained a reservist through 1952.

Although he says the war made him a "realist" — "You don't dream. You just make decisions" — his story, and that of the Renberg family in general, embodies the American Dream.

One of Renberg's relatives, who also had immigrated, started the Renberg's clothing store chain. Renberg did well, too. Graduating from TU with a degree in engineering, he became successful in the oil business.

Renberg has returned to Normandy and Omaha Beach three times over the years. One of those was an Army-paid trip with current 1st Division members: "They wanted someone who'd actually been there," he said. "And, hell, I was only 80 at the time."

Renberg hopes American sacrifices in places like Normandy and elsewhere won't be forgotten. If he could speak to future generations, he says, he would tell them: "Believe in this country. Help it. Be prepared to defend it and maintain its institutions. ... Keep the faith."

Topflight service

Pilot led missions in his B-29 Superfortress

Bill Renfro wasn't going to let his flat feet trip him up again.

They had cost him already with the Navy, which had rejected him three times.

But this time, with the Army Air Corps, he was ready when the subject came up. "I said, 'Well, I didn't think this was the walking army, and I don't intend to jump out of this airplane very often.' "

The resident flight medic bought Renfro's reasoning. He was cleared for service.

And just like he thought, his feet would never get the chance to fail him. As the pilot of a B-29 Superfortress during World War II, not only would Renfro never have to bail out, both he and his plane — he flew the same one throughout — would come out of it unscathed.

The experience would take such a hold on Renfro, in fact, he would make a career of the Air Force, retiring eventually from Strategic Air Command.

'The Best'

Renfro, 99, who was still recovering from the effects of a stroke, sat down in 2015 for an interview with the Tulsa World at Oklahoma Methodist Manor.

The subject of the war is not one the veteran — who retired as a lieutenant colonel — talked about much over the years, except with a cousin who had been a prisoner of war. But he opened up more later, and even talked about it at length for a biography his family had written about his life.

Renfro doesn't mince words when it comes to his aircraft. Comparing B-29s to B-24s, which he also flew, he said: "It's like two different airplanes. One's a drag by comparison. The 29 flew like an airplane. The 24 flew like a boxcar."

And one B-29, in Renfro's mind, could beat all comers.

The "Ding How" was its name. As the plane's pilot, Renfro had the honor of christening it. He said the phrase is Chinese and means "the Best."

He had it painted on the plane in English and Chinese, and re-members how Chinese civilians would give him a thumbs-up when they saw it.

'See the cities burning'

Early on, Renfro's bomber didn't get to do much bombing.

Assigned to the 40th Bomb Group, 20th Air Force, his first experience of war came in the China-Burma-India theater. There, his B-29 initially doubled as a transport plane, carrying gasoline to China over the Himalayas.

Renfro made about 20 of these flights over the "Hump," as the mountainous route was called. There was a little bombing to do, including an 18-hour round trip once — the longest mission flight he ever made — to bomb targets in Singapore.

But the bulk of his bombing experience came after India, when his squadron was transferred to the Pacific Theater in 1945. There, based on Tinian island, Renfro and his crew carried out runs on the enemy's homeland.

This was a different kind of bombing — general areas rather than specific sites, he said. Using incendiary bombs, the idea was to start fires and turn large sections of cities into infernos. "(We) just laid down a line of those bombs ... burned the hell out of them," Renfro said. "You could see the cities burning for 200 miles."

A couple of days before each mission, leaflets were dropped on the cities warning citizens of what was coming. Still, there were many civilian casualties, Renfro said.

The raids would continue until one day in August 1945.

Renfro had no idea, he said, what an atomic bomb was. "When I first heard of it, it had been dropped."

'Then it got serious'

A native of Savannah, Oklahoma, and one of five siblings, Renfro moved with his family to the Tulsa area later. He graduated from Central High School in 1933. Soon after that, he said, he and a bud-dy hopped a freight train for a trip to Chicago and the World's Fair.

But the real rite of passage — the war — was still a few years away.

After trying and failing to get into the Navy, Renfro enrolled at what is now Southwestern Oklahoma State University in Weath-erford. There, majoring in math, he became a national champion wrestler and, in 1940, president of his senior class.

After graduating, Renfro again tried the military, and this time he was able to convince the Air Corps his flat feet wouldn't be a prob-lem. He went on to graduate from cadet school a second lieutenant, then trained as a bomber pilot.

To that point in his life, Renfro "hadn't been up in anything but an elevator."

"(But) I was fascinated by flying," he said. "So when I started out, I was flying for fun — and then it got serious."

Doing what he was supposed to

Before he left for the war, Renfro got married. His wife, Johnnie, welcomed their first child, Mike, while he was away.

"It bothered me," Renfro said of being away from his family, "but I tried to keep thinking about what I was supposed to do. You don't forget them, that's for sure." Letters from home "kept me going."

His B-29 crewmates were like a second family, he said. They were "a good crew, loyal crew ... They never bitched or growled. Which gives you more confidence (as the pilot). Never detected any of them not wanting to go. Never had any dissension in the ranks, so to speak."

His crew was loyal to him and he was loyal right back, he said.

Renfro said his biggest fear during the war was "crashing on one of those islands and becoming lost." But somehow "we made it back every time. We stretched those airplanes."

After the war, Renfro went to work for American Airlines briefly

Pilot Bill Renfro (sitting, front row, fourth from left) poses with other pilots in the Instructors Training Squadron at Barksdale Air Force Base in Shreveport, Louisiana, in 1941, during his service in the Army Air Corps in World War II. COURTESY

Pilot Bill Renfro (standing, back row, far left) poses with the crew of his B-29 bomber "Ding How" in Chakulia, India, in 1944. COURTESY

before returning to the Air Force. As a bomb commander with Strategic Air Command, much of his work was classified. He was stationed with NATO in Paris for a while, and later at the Pentagon in Washington, D.C.

No half measures

The title of the biography Renfro's family had written about him is "No Half Measures." It's a reference to the all-or-nothing way he's faced all challenges in life, including his most recent.

Renfro suffered a stroke a few years ago. He's worked hard to battle back, swimming and working out. But for a man who was still traveling and enjoying life, it has definitely slowed him down.

There are some things, though, that age and infirmity can't touch. Like who he is underneath. Still young when the war came along, the experience, Renfro says, laid a foundation. "I hadn't formed a real firm character by then. I developed that during the war."

It was there that he learned about duty: "Carry out your obligation, whatever that is." At the time, for him and his men, that meant, "Take the bomb and make the target."

And it has applied to the rest of life as well. The best advice he can offer, Renfro said, is to "know what you are supposed to do and do it."

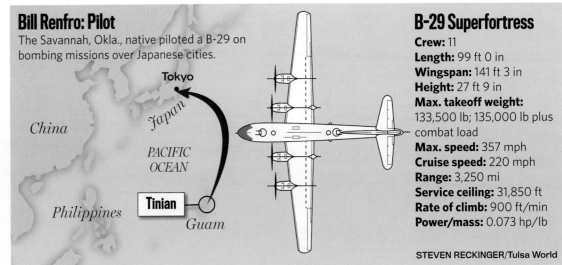

Bill Renfro: Pilot
The Savannah, Okla., native piloted a B-29 on bombing missions over Japanese cities.

Tokyo
China
Japan
PACIFIC OCEAN
Philippines
Tinian
Guam

B-29 Superfortress
Crew: 11
Length: 99 ft 0 in
Wingspan: 141 ft 3 in
Height: 27 ft 9 in
Max. takeoff weight: 133,500 lb; 135,000 lb plus combat load
Max. speed: 357 mph
Cruise speed: 220 mph
Range: 3,250 mi
Service ceiling: 31,850 ft
Rate of climb: 900 ft/min
Power/mass: 0.073 hp/lb

STEVEN RECKINGER/Tulsa World

Kamikaze up close

Bill Ryan was deck gunner on an aircraft carrier in the Pacific

The news that the USS Franklin had lost 807 men at sea in a Japanese attack hit Bill Ryan like a punch in the gut.

But he couldn't help, at the same time, feeling a little thankful. After all, it could easily have been 808.

Just a few days earlier, before switching voluntarily to the USS Essex to help fill a need for deck gunners, Ryan had briefly been a sailor on the Franklin.

Among its longer-tenured men, there had been a premonition, he recalled, that something bad was going to happen. "It was their third time out, and there was a rumor they were not coming back," Ryan said, recalling the experience in a 2015 interview. "I consider myself very fortunate to be here at all," he added.

It wouldn't be the last time, though, fate would intervene on his behalf. For Ryan, only a few months into his World War II service at

the time, the close calls and near misses were just beginning.

The view from the middle

From its spot at the center of its flotilla — surrounded on all sides by battleships, destroyers, cruisers and other war vessels — the USS Essex aircraft carrier offered an impressive view.

And over his 79 consecutive days at sea, Ryan had ample opportunity to take it all in. "There is a certain beauty in the majesty of all these men manning all these ships," said the longtime Tulsan, 91.

Still possessing the eye for beauty that helped him become one of Tulsa's most noted architects, Ryan can't help talking about his experiences, including war, in aesthetic terms. For instance, his carrier, too, was "beautiful," he said, "with its twin turrets at the end of the island."

But being in the presence of beauty only made all the ugliness that much worse. Like the death and havoc unleashed with each new wave of Kamikaze suicide planes and bombers.

"When you were below decks and heard the 20s start firing, you knew you were in trouble — that you were under attack," Ryan said.

As a deck gunner, manning a 20 mm anti-aircraft gun, it was Ryan's job to help protect the carrier, allowing it to keep up the air strikes that would prove vital to winning the Pacific war.

The most intense fighting would come during the carrier's support of the U.S. invasion and conquest of Okinawa in April and May 1945.

Ryan volunteered as a gunner, he said, because he had qualified as a marksman during training. But the 20 mm guns would require more of him than just aiming and pulling a trigger. Because there weren't enough volunteers, he had to perform each of the roles done ordinarily by a three-man crew. "I was loader, trunnion operator and gunner," he said.

Once the ammo was loaded and he strapped himself in, he could begin firing away.

Kamikaze close call

Still haunting to Ryan is a close encounter he had with one kamikaze.

He was at his gun station when the plane zoomed right by him, he said, close enough almost to touch. "For one instant, I looked at (the pilot) and he looked at me. I could see his expression, the white scarf around his neck."

What happened next he still can't fully explain. Zeroing in on the Essex, "at the last second (the kamikaze) banked left. If he'd banked right he could've had the whole ship. But he missed us. Crashed into the ocean. I'll never know why he did that."

Ryan says he still, 70 years later, sees that pilot's face in his dreams. "I'll never forget it. It was the closest I ever got to a kamikaze."

Ryan's battle station allowed him to see all the other ships in the Essex's vicinity. When under attack, their crews, too, had their hands full. "I saw five close up — ships being bombed." The Japanese "came in all numbers at all times, usually pairing off."

As if a steady diet of bombs, torpedoes and careening kamikazes weren't enough, there were also mines.

"Mine-laying aircraft ... would come in at dusk and lay mines all ahead of us (in the water)," Ryan said. Navy picket ships would do their best to shoot the mines, detonating them before anyone struck one.

'Landing on a postage stamp'

The Essex carried up to 100 aircraft at a time, including different kinds of fighters and bombers flown by Navy and Marine pilots. They were coming and going, day and night, on missions, Ryan said.

"I have the most respect for the pilots. ... They were the heroes — flying these planes and landing on a postage stamp." To land in so small a space as a carrier's flight deck, the planes needed a little help and relied on their tailhooks to catch cables and bring them to a stop.

It didn't always go as planned, Ryan said. Rescue attempts were going on constantly — for pilots who crash-landed in the sea or on the deck, where often they had to be pulled from a burning wreckage.

Inevitably, some could not be saved. Burial ceremonies at sea were solemn spectacles, Ryan said. Taps was played, and the wrapped body "just slid off the plank."

Bombs and typhoons

Although the Essex managed to avoid serious damage, one bomb did put it briefly out of commission. Ryan remembers it well. Readying to fire his gun, he had just adjusted his goggles, he said, in time to look up and see it: A Japanese bomber diving directly at the ship.

"I watched the bomb come loose. ... the explosion was devastating."

The force, he said, lifted the ship partly out of the water, "hitting me in the fanny."

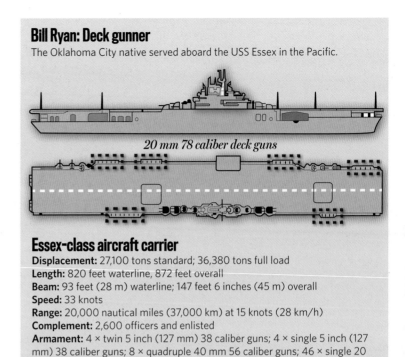

Bill Ryan: Deck gunner
The Oklahoma City native served aboard the USS Essex in the Pacific.

20 mm 78 caliber deck guns

Essex-class aircraft carrier
Displacement: 27,100 tons standard; 36,380 tons full load
Length: 820 feet waterline, 872 feet overall
Beam: 93 feet (28 m) waterline; 147 feet 6 inches (45 m) overall
Speed: 33 knots
Range: 20,000 nautical miles (37,000 km) at 15 knots (28 km/h)
Complement: 2,600 officers and enlisted
Armament: 4 × twin 5 inch (127 mm) 38 caliber guns; 4 × single 5 inch (127 mm) 38 caliber guns; 8 × quadruple 40 mm 56 caliber guns; 46 × single 20 mm 78 caliber guns
Aircraft carried: 90-100 aircraft

STEVEN RECKINGER/Tulsa World

Bill Ryan served as a deck gunner aboard the aircraft carrier USS Essex.
COURTESY

Bill Ryan (back row, second from left) gathers with shipmates on the flight deck of the aircraft carrier USS Essex during his service in the U.S. Navy. COURTESY

Fortunately, the bomb — a 500-pound armor piercer — had not hit the ship directly. "It was considered a near miss. But it still blew a 30-by-30-foot hole in the side of the ship. "It was bad enough," he added, that the Essex had to sail to the Philippines for repairs. It was the worst hit the Essex took while Ryan was on board.

Besides the Japanese, the ship also had to contend with nature. After surviving Okinawa, the Essex sailed through a major typhoon. Bracing as wave after wave crashed over the bow, Ryan couldn't help wondering "if we were going to hold together," he said.

To bring down an aircraft carrier, though, would have taken a truly mighty storm. Once while on watch, Ryan got a real sense of how massive the Essex was, walking between several different areas of the ship in the dark. "It was like being in a city," he said, "and you are going to places you've never been before."

That same watch was the occasion of another of Ryan's flirtations with disaster. With no light to guide him as he was walking along the carrier's catwalk, he stepped down, and before he knew what was happening, was dangling in mid-air.

A hatch door had been left open.

Thankfully, some of his gear snagged to keep him from falling. Otherwise "I would've gone into the sea," he said. "And they don't stop for you."

Among the good memories from Ryan's time on the Essex was getting to meet a childhood hero. World-renowned polar explorer Richard Byrd, who was also a top Naval officer, was on Ryan's carrier briefly. "It was a great thrill for me," Ryan said.

The first to call

An Oklahoma City native, Ryan was attending Capitol Hill High School when, at 17, he decided to quit and join the military.

At the time, though, there was a hold on volunteers. "The war had been going on about a year, and there had been so many volunteers up front," he said.

But Ryan was undeterred. He "signed up for every branch there was" and waited. The Navy was the first to call.

Ryan's best friend, Harold, would join him in enlisting. At the time, the two were dating the girls whom they would eventually marry. The girls, Ryan said, were also best friends, and accompanied each other to see him and Harold off at the station.

After the war, Ryan was able to complete his high school diploma. Although he had thought seriously about becoming a Naval officer — and would put in eight more years with the Navy Reserves — it was in architecture he would find his passion. Graduating from the University of Oklahoma, he went on to design projects in Tulsa such as East Central High School and the iconic Rose Bowl bowling alley, as well as school, church and commercial projects across the region.

Possibly his favorite, Chapel on the Hill in Broken Arrow, was the site of his 90th birthday party, thrown for him by friends.

Reflecting on his war service with the Navy triggers strong emotions in Ryan.

"I was part of something much bigger than anything I could ever experience," he said. "The sacrifices weren't viewed by most veterans as sacrifices. They were viewed as patriotic duty."

Waxing poetic at the memory, he adds: "It was so powerful, so beautiful to look across the water and see ... this formidable flotilla of ships, every size you could think of. You could see the might. You could see the pride. It was something you knew would never be defeated."

'A picture of hell'

Jack Sanders flew 31 successful missions, including 2 on D-Day

Jack Sanders' two missions on D-Day — taking out a big gun in a French coastal town, then destroying a main bridge over the Seine — were plenty exciting.

But compared to some of his other experiences as a B-24 pilot, he said, June 6, 1944, was, on the whole, uneventful.

Sadly, it was far from that for the boys on the ground.

Coming back from his first D-Day mission, Sanders would always remember how the clouds seemed suddenly to roll back, revealing Omaha Beach below and the Allied invasion that was underway. "It was an absolutely sickening sight," said Sanders, who, powerless to intervene, could only watch as waves of young Americans were being mowed down.

"Guys down there wallowing in that rough sea. ... It was chaos. The big guns were firing. If you wanted to get a picture of hell,

that was it."

It was because of that scene — the Germans were so preoccupied with the ground forces — that he and his crew faced minimal trouble, Sanders added.

But that kind of experience would be the exception. For many of his 31 missions, leading up to D-Day and in the weeks to follow, trouble would be the rule.

The fear factor

Talking to the Tulsa World in 2015, 93-year-old Sanders — a former Oklahoma state fire marshal — opened up about his World War II experiences.

"Fear," he said, "is a big factor in war of any kind. ... But you've got to get that out of your system because there are too many things to think about and to do to worry about getting killed." As a pilot, especially trying to fly in formation, "you've got to keep your mind on that aircraft" — and it's not easy to do with "flak busting outside the window."

But if you stay focused and trust in your training, he added, "there's a good chance you'll be there for supper tonight."

Sanders joined the Army Air Corps right after Pearl Harbor. He considered all his options, he said, but decided quickly he wanted to be a "flier." Assigned to the 453rd Bomb Group, 8th Air Force, Sanders would be stationed in Old Buckenham, England.

The group's targets — oil refineries, depots, aircraft factories, etc. — could be relatively close, such as on the French coast. Others, in Germany, required several hours of flight. But wherever the targets lay, they were well protected, Sanders said. German fighters were an ever-present threat, and the "ground-fire was deadly."

The 88 mm antiaircraft gun "was the best in the world," he said, "and they knew how to use it."

'A mortal shot'

Bomber crews tapped for the next day's missions were listed on what was known as the "hot sheet." It was posted in public places, and if your name was on it, Sanders said, you could expect to wake at 3:30 a.m. to a flashlight beam in your face. Breakfast would follow in 30 minutes or so, then a briefing on the mission.

Of the many missions Sanders and his crew flew together, one — to Hamm, Germany — came closest to being their last.

They completed it, destroying a principal supply depot. But bad weather had delayed them, and the return journey would be in the dark. That was never a good idea, he said.

Sure enough, as the plane was approaching the home side of the English Channel, "all of a sudden all hell broke loose," Sanders said. Appearing right on their tail, a German Junkers Ju 88 night fighter "just pumped us full of lead — blew my tail gunner out of his turret, injured my waist gunner, blew out the No. 2 engine."

"I knew instantly it was a mortal shot," Sanders said, adding that the plane began dropping steadily.

But luck would be with them. Just as a crash-landing seemed inevitable, a lighted runway appeared below. It was their neighboring field, Sanders realized. He knew then they could make it home.

WWII pilot Jack Sanders (back row, third from left) stands with his crew next to a B-24 Liberator bomber. COURTESY

A few tense moments later they were there.

"It was a hard landing," Sanders said, adding that ground crews moved in quickly to put out the fires. Three crew members had been wounded. But they all survived. "We got our wounded off and walked away," Sanders said.

31 and zero

Sanders is one of two members from his bomber crew still living, he said.

In all 31 missions, he didn't lose a soul, a remarkable record. He chalks it up to a little luck and a lot of discipline and professionalism.

"There was nothing in war," said Sanders, "as dangerous probably as taking a big bomber, loading it to capacity, with high octane gasoline, a load of bombs, taking it off the ground — and do that 31 times and get by with it. You can't imagine how vulnerable you are."

In taking on those risks time and again, Sanders' decorations would pile up, among them a Distinguished Flying Cross with Oak Leaf Cluster and an Air Medal with three clusters.

But don't call him a hero.

That word "in my opinion, should be reserved for those who lost their life, received serious injury or were left in a state of, let's say, disrepair," Sanders said. "Some of my best friends who are still buried in military cemeteries around the world — they are my heroes."

Sanders has many fond memories of the men he served with. One of them was Hollywood star Jimmy Stewart, a fellow bomber pilot and operations officer for the 453rd. Sanders knew him and would see him occasionally in the bar.

Stewart was highly respected among the men. "He was as much a soldier as anybody was," Sanders said.

Survivor's questions

Sanders was a graduate of Central High School, where he starred at football. He attended the University of Tulsa and was working for a local oil company when Pearl Harbor was attacked in December 1941.

After the war, Sanders went into fire service. At the time of his retirement as state fire marshal in 1984, he had held the position longer — 20 years — than any other state fire marshal in the U.S.

Sanders married his wife, Helen, before the war. At the time of her death in 2014, the two had celebrated 75 years together.

During the war, Sanders said, they wrote letters to each other every day. And after he came home, Helen helped him figure things out. Like many other returning service members, Sanders found himself asking questions:

Why did he survive when others didn't? What made him special?

"My wife told me ... and she was absolutely right: 'You have been blessed. I don't know why, and you don't know why. But ... maybe (God) has something else for you to do.'"

Sanders had attended church as a boy — his mother, a staunch believer, made sure of it — but it didn't mean much to him, he said. After the war, though, that changed. His faith helped him find meaning in his experiences and to "just be a better person."

Jack Sanders, B-24 Liberator bomber pilot, has his wings, Distinguished Flying Cross and 8th Air Force patch in a shadow box at his home in Tulsa.
MICHAEL WYKE/Tulsa World

"Lord, I hope I stood for something in these 93 years," Sanders said.

"I love America. I'm very proud of my country, patriotic. ... We're going through some tough times, but we'll get over them."

'Gung ho' to fly

Arnol Sellars flew a P-47 fighter on raids over Europe

The first time Arnol Sellars flew one in the skies over Europe, he was sold on the P-47 Thunderbolt.

"It was a good ol' airplane," he said. "You could shoot all kinds of bits off of it and it would still bring you home."

But it wasn't invulnerable. And on his 56th and final mission of World War II, Sellars learned that the hard way. Forced to bail out of his plane after taking two direct hits, he spent the last few weeks of the war in a German hospital with a broken leg.

Sellars knows he was lucky. Many other airmen who were shot down over Europe died, either there or later as a result of their injuries.

It was partly those airmen Sellars was thinking of a few years ago when he took on a project that remains close to his heart. The Tulsa

resident, who flew missions over Italy and later Germany, became the stateside liaison for a team of Italians looking for World War II aircraft crash sites.

"We left hundreds and hundreds of wrecked airplanes all around the (Italian) countryside, and there are a lot of efforts now to find these planes," said Sellars, 91. He has played sleuth for several of the sites that have been discovered, tracking down information about the pilot and family members. "(The Italians) were so glad to find a survivor. And I'm glad to do it."

"I'm glad somebody's interested enough to find out as much as they can."

Gung ho

Born and raised in Tulsa, Sellars graduated from Central High School in 1942. Joining the Army Air Corps on deferment, he started classes at the University of Tulsa but was called up for service soon after.

Sellars had dreamed of flying since playing with model airplanes

Arnol Sellars stands in one of the P-47 fighters he flew. COURTESY

At left, Arnol Sellars (third from left) stands with other fighter pilots in his squadron by a handmade sign that reads "The Lily Whiters Club" during his service in the Army Air Corps. Sellars flew P-47 fighters in Italy, France and Germany. COURTESY

Below, Arnol Sellars stands in a P-47 fighter he crash-landed at his home airfield after it was hit in the nose section by Nazi anti-aircraft fire. Sellars could not see out because of the oil on the windshield and was led back to the airfield by another plane. COURTESY

as a child, and was "gung ho" to make that a reality with the Air Corps, he said. By April 1944, he had his wings. Six months later, he arrived in Italy for assignment with the 522nd Fighter Squadron, 27th Fighter Group. "They put me right to work," he said.

To prevent supplies and arms from reaching German forces, the squadron carried out mission after mission, attacking and trying to destroy bridges, railroads and enemy supply trains and convoys. Sellars remembers his first mission well. The goal was to dive-bomb a bridge, and "I wasn't quite prepared. I missed the thing completely," he said. "But I got better."

Boasting eight 50-caliber machine guns with two 500-pound bombs under each wing, Sellars' P-47 was well armed. And it was elusive. It would "dive like a falling piano," he said. "So if you got in trouble you could get away."

By that stage in the war in Italy — Sellars flew most of his missions out of Pontadera in Tuscany — there were almost no enemy aircraft left, he said. But the antiaircraft fire coming from the ground still posed a serious threat. Wherever they flew over enemy-held territory, "huge, big puffs of black smoke" from German 88 mm guns greeted them, filling the skies.

It was the same way in France and Germany, where Sellars' squadron moved in January 1945. There, they continued assisting ground forces, "blowing up bridges, strafing ground troops, shooting up trains, cutting rail lines."

The bail out

April 2, 1945, started out like business as usual for Sellars. But it didn't end that way.

His assignment was to fly to Heilbronn, Germany, and look for "targets of opportunity." "It was a stupid mission," Sellars said. "But publicity was a very important thing to our leaders. They liked to be able to tell the newspapers how many sorties we flew each day. So somebody at headquarters said 'Gee, let's go get some more sorties' " so they could boast a bigger total than other squadrons.

Encountering heavy ground fire en route to Heilbronn, however, Sellars' plane and two others in his group of four aircraft were shot down. One pilot was killed. Sellars and the other were taken prisoner. The one who got away made it back to base, he said, but "his plane was shot to ribbons."

Sellars' plane had been hit twice. After the first hit, to the nose section, he still hoped he could fly it back. "But I tried and I couldn't. It was like I was sitting there flying a 7-ton glider. Then they shot me again."

The second hit took off part of his left wing, and Sellars was forced to bail out. As he did, the tail of the plane clipped his left leg, breaking it below the knee. He didn't realize it until he landed.

On the ground "I was thinking I'd better get up and get out of there. Then I looked down." His leg was pointing at a 90-degree angle, foot sticking out awkwardly.

So there would be no getting away. Picked up shortly after by German soldiers, Sellars was taken to a field hospital. "There were a lot of German soldiers there missing limbs, etc. I was in good shape compared to most of them." He was there only briefly before being taken to another hospital.

It looked like Sellars might not make it there, though. During a stop in one town, residents wanted to take him out of the jeep and hang him, he said. "But the soldiers, bless their hearts, said, 'No. He's a POW.'"

Deeply grateful

The last part of Sellars' brief time as a prisoner of war was spent at a hospital in Ludwigsburg, Germany. Staff there were friendly and took good care of him, he said.

The fact that Germany's defeat was imminent probably had something to do with how he was treated, Sellars admits. In fact, he added, "all of the Germans kept coming by to practice their English with me." But whatever their motives, Sellars remains deeply grateful. He still has a letter that the hospital director wrote him congratulating him on his freedom.

With the arrival of Allied forces, Sellars was evacuated from Ludwigsburg to a U.S. Army hospital in Paris. That's where he was, confined to his bed with a cast on his leg, when the war in Europe officially ended a few days later.

"What a celebration that was!" Sellars said. "Any patients who were ambulatory went out and came back talking about the free drinks and how many kisses they got." In his condition, though, there would be no party for Sellars. All he could do, he said, was "lay there, seeing it out the window and wishing I could get out there."

A 'big, common experience'

Several years ago, Sellars tracked down the hospital in Ludwigsburg where he had been cared for and wrote officials there a letter. "I thanked them for being so nice to a frightened little guy," he said. He also donated money to a program at the hospital that cares for children with special needs.

Even in the madness of war, it seems, Sellars had found things to be grateful for.

He's particularly grateful for the man it made out of him. His basic character didn't change, he said, but he definitely grew up. "I had been to foreign countries I had only dreamed of, had been in a lot of peril and had the fool scared out of me."

After the war, Sellars went to college on the G.I. Bill. He married his wife, Betty, and they raised three children together. At the time of her death, the couple had been married 64 years.

After the war, Sellars continued his service with the Air National Guard, attaining the rank of captain. He flew P-51 Mustangs, which were like "sports cars" with wings — "a joy to fly." But he still can't say he prefers them to his old P-47s. "Both were excellent airplanes," he said.

Sellars didn't talk much about the war for years. As he's grown older, though, he's become an amateur historian on the subject, making friends and contacts all over the world, especially through the crash-site project.

"Each generation has got their war to fight," Sellars said. "They just have to stand up and do what seems to be best. I hope that all of them, whatever their crisis, have theirs solved with everybody in the country behind them. That was so gratifying." With WWII, he added, "everybody in the country was involved in it. You either had somebody in it, or you had a defense job. Everybody contributed to it. We had this big, common experience."

Arnol Sellars' P-47D fighter is getting re-armed and re-fueled for another mission. It was one of several P-47s he flew in the Army Air Corps during his World War II service in Italy, France and Germany. COURTESY

Kissing the sky

Frank Slane helped invade Germany in a CG-4A glider

When Frank Slane volunteered for the Army Air Corps at 18, he had a picture in mind of what his service would look like. The CG-4A was not it.

"It was a big box kite with wings," said Slane, recalling his first time to pilot one of the military gliders. Used during World War II, the gliders had to be towed to their destinations by C-47s because they lacked a power source of their own. For a would-be fighter pilot like Slane, it was "about as far away as you could possibly get when they take your engine away."

Still, Slane, who co-piloted a CG-4A in the Allied invasion of Germany in 1945, is proud of the role the aircraft played in the war, carrying troops and equipment. And it didn't keep him from enjoying plenty of air time later in their fuel-powered cousins.

Now a retired lieutenant colonel with the Oklahoma Air National Guard, Slane over his career would tally more than 13,000 hours flying airplanes and in the process become the first guardsman to fly one around the world.

'Antsy' to join the fight

Welcoming the Tulsa World to his home in 2015, Slane, 91, revealed how it was that he came to fly gliders. After registering for the draft on his 18th birthday, about one month after the Pearl Harbor attack, he got "antsy," he said, waiting to be called.

"I thought 'Gosh, I ought to be doing something to support this effort.'"

So Slane, a freshman at Kansas State Teachers College in Pittsburg, Kansas, volunteered for the Air Corps. He graduated from training as a second lieutenant and single-engine pilot, and was assigned to be a flight instructor. But Slane wasn't satisfied with that role.

Keen to "volunteer for anything that would get me out of that and into combat," he found the opportunity in an unlikely place: the Army's glider program. Three flight hours and 10 landings later — all it took to qualify — he was bound for Europe.

'In the hands of God'

Slane's first experience of the war would not be with gliders. Assigned to the 437th Troop Carrier Group, 9th Air Force, he was a copilot on C-47 transports, dropping supplies to the troops during the Battle of the Bulge.

In March 1945, with the airborne invasion of Germany's Rhineland, Slane would finally "find out why I had glider wings."

As copilot of a glider carrying troops, Slane took off from Coulommiers, France. His formation ran into heavy flak after crossing the Rhine. From there, it only got worse. When one of the tow planes ahead of him was shot down, suddenly "my enthusiasm for war was gone," Slane said.

But, "I put my life in the hands of God and said 'If it's my day to die, well then ... that's how the cookie crumbles.' "

The hardest thing about gliders, Slane said, isn't landing so much as finding a place to land. Once the tow rope is cut, "there's no way to go but down." And then you have only minutes to get it right. Slane and his pilot managed to get it right, though, even as they dodged enemy fire. However, once safely on the ground, the danger did not subside.

"The machine guns opened up on us," he said.

The glider was riddled with holes from wing tip to wing tip, and one of the troops on board was killed. Slane turned in his seat and reached for his carbine, just as a round pierced the windshield. He wouldn't know until later how close he'd come to dying.

"The path of the bullet was right where my head had been," Slane said. "Reaching for my carbine when I did, saved me."

But right then, he was too focused on surviving to notice. Finally seizing their chance, he and the others got safely away from the plane and walked about a half-mile to the command post.

From his foxhole that night, Slane could see the artillery lighting up the sky "like the Fourth of July." It would take the light of day to see the results.

"The impact of what war really looks like really hit us" the next morning, Slane said. "It was sickening. Bodies everywhere. ... dead paratroopers hanging from trees and power lines. One guy had been hit by a mortar. He looked like a pile of hamburger."

That was Slane's only glider mission and his lone experience in ground combat. From then until the war ended, he flew C-47s.

Aviation in his blood

Slane finished his service in 1946 and returned to college. But the war had changed him. The "enthusiastic kid" — the one who four years earlier had been so gung-ho to fight — was gone, he said, replaced by a "responsible adult."

Slane completed a degree in education and taught high school in Galena, Kansas, for the next three years. But aviation, he said, was in his blood. In 1951, he moved to Tulsa to attend Spartan School of Aeronautics. He went on to teach there.

He also flew as a test pilot in P-51s, as well as other planes. But the P-51, he said, was his favorite. It was also in Tulsa that Slane began his long association with the Oklahoma Air National Guard. He joined in 1952, and in 1957 became a full time flight training supervisor.

By the time he retired as a lieutenant colonel in the Oklahoma Air National Guard in 1975, he had racked up 13,500 total flight hours. During that time, Slane was frequently on active duty as a transport pilot, including missions during the Cuban Missile Crisis, and later, off and on for seven years during the Vietnam War.

When cows fly

In 1962, flying for what was then the National Guard's 125th Air Transport Squadron, Slane became the first guardsman to fly around the world. It was an unusual mission: transporting some purebred cattle, a gift from the Kennedy Administration to the King of Afghanistan to help build his private herd.

"For some reason they picked our unit," Slane said. "They built a barn inside a C-97, pens, hay, all that kind of stuff."

Pilot and commander on the mission, Slane successfully delivered the cattle to Kabul, Afghanistan. Since they were already halfway around the world, he said, they took an eastern route home, completing the circuit.

'All comes back to service'

With his community volunteering, Slane is, in a sense, completing another circuit, one that began all those years ago when he volunteered for the war.

"It all comes back to service," he said. "We are privileged to live in this country and we owe the country some service. ... Not just the country, but our communities and churches."

Slane is an RSVP Tulsa board member, and through the nonprofit organization has taught basic computer skills to senior adults. He still delivers for Tulsa's Meals on Wheels, one of his favorite organizations, filling in as needed.

"Volunteering is so important," Slane said. "There are a lot of organizations that need some extra help."

Another organization that gets a lot of his time is Oklahoma Toastmasters. He's been part of it for more than 50 years and remains a member of three Toastmasters clubs in Tulsa. Honing the public speaking skills that the club emphasizes, Slane is good at articulating the things he feels most strongly about. Like how we ought to serve those who serve us.

"War is the worst possible way for nations to resolve their differences. ... (But) military service is a noble calling. Those who have served and those who are serving deserve all the respect we can give them."

Full speed ahead

J.D. Smith was torpedoman on a naval PT boat in the Pacific

At the time, J.D. Smith just assumed he would get his helmet back. But sadly, the friend he loaned it to never got the chance to return it.

"I was looking at him — and suddenly his head just disappeared," Smith said, recalling the moment the "daisy-cutter" bomb hit near their PT boat, sending metal fragments in every direction. Severed at the neck, the sailor's "head rolled right off into the water. Still with my helmet on it."

It was another case of wrong place, wrong time. On a PT boat — with a crew of only a dozen or so, and sharing such a small space — any loss is a big loss, Smith added. "Everybody's a close friend."

Unfortunately, during his time in the Pacific in World War II, Smith and his mates experienced that loss more than once.

'Devil boats'

The first time Smith laid eyes on a Navy PT boat, he liked what he saw.

"I thought, 'that's pretty neat.' They really are a high-class looking boat," recalled Smith, 89, in a December 2015 interview at his home. Originally trained to fire torpedoes on a destroyer, he was surprised to learn he would be serving instead on a PT boat.

The PT boat was a dramatically different naval experience. Small at roughly 80 feet long, the vessels were highly maneuverable. And they were fast, Smith said. Running on 100-octane gasoline and powered by three 1,600-horsepower Packard engines, they "could go up to 50 to 60 miles per hour if they have to. Not advisable, but they could."

PT boats stuck to coastal waters, on the lookout for enemy vessels to attack. They patrolled in pairs, and almost always at night. During the day, the crafts were highly vulnerable to enemy aircraft, Smith said.

Patrolling in the darkness "was kind of spooky," he said. "Usually you'd run across (the enemy) like they came out of nowhere. And they might start firing at you first. But a lot of times you initiated it."

Almost every night they had an engagement of some kind, he said. Hailed by the Americans for their daring, PT boats would come to be hated by the Japanese, who had another name for them: "Devil boats."

Ahead of the draft

Smith's journey to the Navy began, he said, in Stillwater, where he grew up. One of five children and the only boy, Smith enlisted in December 1943 when he turned 18.

"Everybody was getting drafted," he said, and the Army didn't appeal to him. "I didn't want to wear those big ol' field boots."

His decision to go with the Navy, he said, "worked out pretty good." From San Diego, Smith sailed out for Australia. There he was assigned to a PT squadron as a torpedoman.

He would serve most of his time on PT 126. His crews had 12 men typically, though at times up to 14. Starting from Australia, Smith's squadron moved up the coast of New Guinea, then operated for a while out of the Indonesian islands of Biak and Mios Woendi. From there, they moved on to the Philippines. That's where Smith's

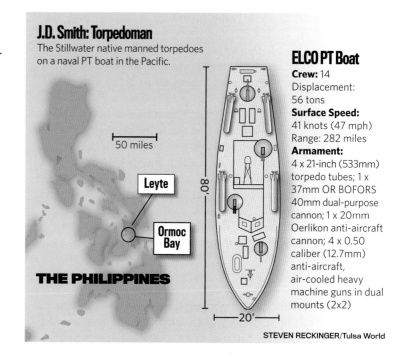

J.D. Smith: Torpedoman
The Stillwater native manned torpedoes on a naval PT boat in the Pacific.

50 miles

Leyte

Ormoc Bay

THE PHILIPPINES

ELCO PT Boat
Crew: 14
Displacement: 56 tons
Surface Speed: 41 knots (47 mph)
Range: 282 miles
Armament: 4 x 21-inch (533mm) torpedo tubes; 1 x 37mm OR BOFORS 40mm dual-purpose cannon; 1 x 20mm Oerlikon anti-aircraft cannon; 4 x 0.50 caliber (12.7mm) anti-aircraft, air-cooled heavy machine guns in dual mounts (2x2)

80'

20'

STEVEN RECKINGER/Tulsa World

A PT boat patrols off New Guinea in 1943. U.S. NAVY

biggest engagements would come, including, in October 1944, the invasion of Leyte.

Arriving three days before the invasion, Smith's and other PT boats were the first vessels to enter Leyte Gulf, followed by the minesweepers, which came behind them, clearing the waters of mines ahead of the bigger ships.

One of his most vivid recollections is from later at Leyte's Ormoc Bay. With American ground forces on the island on their tails, Japanese troops tried to escape on barges.

"We'd watch them and then come along and sink them," he said. On one occasion, Smith and his boat sank about five of the barges close together, each containing about 40 of the enemy. "Water was full of (Japanese troops)," Smith said.

Since shooting them would've violated international law, he added, his commander had another idea. "We ran over them with our propellers."

Food and drink

Smith knew his designated weapon intimately. The torpedo was a "delicate, precision instrument," he said. Every PT boat carried four of them, at a cost of $10,000 to $12,000 each. It was Smith's job to take care of them, he said, and when the time came, to fire them.

About 20 feet long and packing 600 pounds of TNT in its warhead, a torpedo had its own engine. When it hit the water, the engine would kick in, and could propel it as far as 15 miles.

Not that you ever needed it to go that far, Smith said. His targets were at most 600 to 800 yards away. He said he fired about 12 total during his time at sea, with only three missing their targets. One of the interesting facts about torpedoes is what they were fueled on, Smith said.

"Each one held 22 pints of 100-proof alcohol." Eventually, somebody wised up and the formula was changed, he added. But until then, sailors frequently indulged.

"I was pretty popular at Christmas time," Smith said, chuckling, adding that as torpedoman, only he knew how to get the alcohol out. By the time the 1944 holidays had passed, he recalled, "two of our torpedoes would not fire at all. All the alcohol was gone."

The alcohol was commonly mixed with orange juice, he said, and canteens of it were stowed around the boat. The food on board wasn't bad, either. Particularly prized, Smith said, were the gallon cans of beef and the chocolate pudding. Each boat also had a cook.

Smith remembers how he and his crew once toiled all day repairing the boat only — to their chagrin — to be served peanut butter sandwiches for dinner.

"All the cook had to do, while we did all the work, was make us something good," Smith said. "We took turns throwing him over the side."

Going home

From the Philippines, they eventually went on to Okinawa. By that time, after weeks of fierce fighting, the island was mostly secure, Smith said. Their next stop was a small island about 25 miles north of Okinawa. There, they began preparing for the expected invasion of mainland Japan.

"Fortunately, they dropped the bomb," Smith said of the Americans' atomic bomb attacks on Hiroshima and Nagasaki, making invasion unnecessary.

When he and his crewmates got the word, they knew finally "we were gonna go home." There was no feeling like it, he said. By that point in the war, "you felt like you could be there forever."

It hadn't helped that, over his three years of service, Smith never had one day of leave. "I was never in a situation where I could take any," he said.

He had gone from basic training to torpedo school, and then on to the South Pacific, where he had an assignment virtually every day.

Nothing to hide

One of the first things you notice about Smith are his tattoos. Drawn in blue ink on each tanned forearm, one is a profile of an Indian chief, the other an Indian woman. Letters above the former, faded but still just legible, spell out "Oklahoma." He got them, he said, in San Diego when he was in torpedo school, just before he shipped out for the Pacific.

After the war, when he rose to become a chief engineer with Borden, he kept the tattoos concealed under shirtsleeves, he said. These days, however — long since retired — the longtime west Tulsa resident has nothing to hide.

That includes talking about the war, although he admits the effects of dementia are beginning to rob him of some of the details.

It also includes the public life he actively maintains. Smith, a longtime volunteer, was Oklahoma Legionnaire of the Year in 2008, and when it comes to serving his fellow military veterans, he is still present and accounted for.

He was commander for seven years of American Legion Post 17 in Sand Springs, and remains active in both the Legion, Tulsa's Veterans of Foreign Wars Post 577, and at the VA Medical Center in Muskogee, where he's donated his time for many years.

A few years ago, he helped lead the statewide fundraising effort for "Operation Homecoming," which brought area troops home for the holidays from Texas where they were training for Iraq.

"Somebody has to do it," he said when asked what motivates him. "The guys who did it before me — I was real proud of them and respected them tremendously." If his health holds out, Smith has no plans to stop volunteering. He knows what can happen when you have nothing left to do.

After their job was done in the war, most of the surviving PT boats were completely dismantled, he said. "They took out the engine, the radar and other vital parts. They boxed those up and shipped them off. Then they burned the hull."

He didn't feel too bad about his boat's fate, though. By then, "it was getting pretty old," he said.

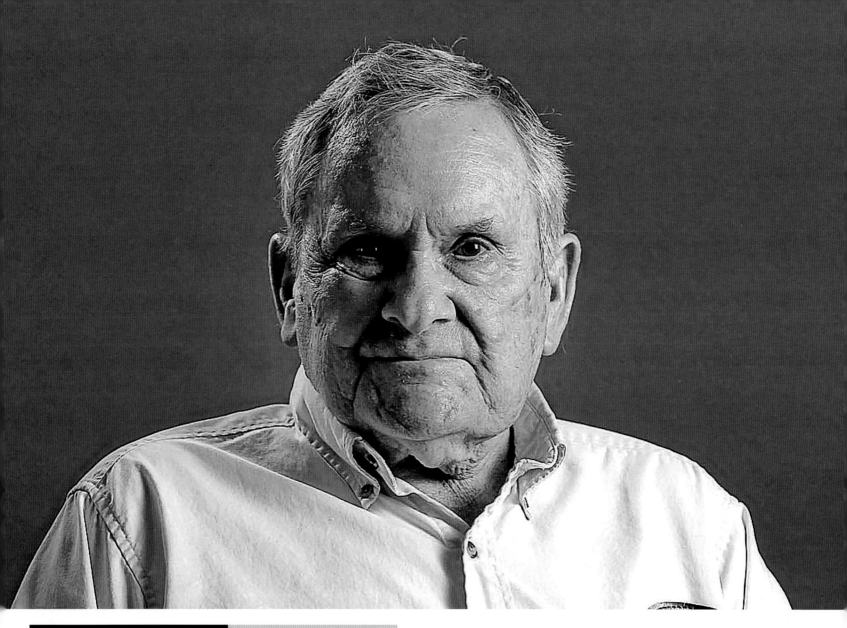

Battle-hardened

Recon soldier served in five European campaigns

"There's no shame in a man knowing how to sew." Nelson Smith's mother had always told him that. But if he hadn't believed her before, he certainly would after the Battle of the Bulge.

With nightly temperatures dropping well below zero — and he and his Army unit ill-equipped to endure it — the small sewing kit his mother had mailed him might well have been the difference between life and death.

"We tore up blankets; I think I put three more blankets in it ... making it thicker," he said of the extra lining he sewed into his sleeping bag. Smith's skill with a needle and thread certainly came in handy.

But overall, he admitted, his survival would continue to depend on other tools of his trade. Like his Thompson submachine gun and .45-caliber handgun.

A Sand Springs resident who retired from a long career as a building and remodeling contractor, Smith talked to the Tulsa World in 2015 about his experience as a reconnaissance soldier during World War II.

Reconnaissance was a tough and often dangerous job, said Smith, who spent 308 days on or behind enemy lines. On paper it was about moving ahead of the main force, locating the enemy and reporting back. But as often as not, Smith said, once you found the enemy, you ended up in a fight.

"If they thought you could handle it (the situation), they'd tell you to go ahead and take it," he said. Reconnaissance, Smith added, was often more than advertised. He and fellow "recon" men were used pretty much wherever and however needed.

Hard cases

Before D-Day, in England, one of Smith's jobs was tracking down and capturing downed German airmen. Because it spared them from the wrath of British civilians, the Germans were usually happy to be taken prisoner, he said. After D-Day, Smith's unit worked for a few weeks with French resistance fighters.

"They were a bunch of hard cases," he said, recalling his first rendezvous with a resistance group. The leader, known as "Patch," wore a black patch to cover a missing eye. His girlfriend and fellow fighter was also missing pieces — the first joint of her forefinger, which the Nazis, who had held her prisoner once, had cut off during interrogation.

"She was just as tough as those men," Smith recalled. He and his unit provided the French ammunition and supplies, and even assisted with operations behind enemy lines. For the first of these — preventing a German troop train from reaching the front lines — they planted explosive charges on the tracks ahead.

"We stopped the train," Smith said matter-of-factly.

Hard times

In some ways, Smith's life had prepared him for the fight to come. Growing up in a bad part of town, he said, he had to learn to take care of himself.

"I fought all the way to school and all the way home," Smith said. "They were hard times, I'll tell you."

At 17, he tried to join the Navy with a buddy. But he was underage and his parents wouldn't give the required permission. So, Smith stuck around and graduated from Webster High School. When he was finally drafted in April 1943, he had been married three months to his wife, Gloria.

There were certain things, though, Smith's hardscrabble youth could not prepare him for. His first encounter with death in warfare, for example. Smith can't forget it — the row of dead Americans lined up against an embankment, the first thing he saw upon arriving on Omaha Beach on D-Day.

"It was one of the most disheartening things," said Smith, who went in six hours after the first wave of troops.

Smith's unit, the 21st Cavalry Reconnaissance Troop, would continue working with the French Resistance until Gen. George Patton arrived and they were assigned to provide recon for his 2nd Armored Tank Division, known as "Hell on Wheels."

From the hedgerows of Normandy, Smith's unit moved through northern France toward Belgium, fighting pretty much all the way, he said. When patrolling ahead, there was always danger. If you weren't dodging artillery or ducking mortar barrages, Smith said, you were getting strafed and bombed from the air.

Once he eluded an attack only to find later that a round had pierced his canteen and field jacket. Close calls like that were common, he said. Also, recon troops behind enemy lines could easily be cut off from their unit if they weren't careful.

Moving backward

Mail helped keep Smith going. The letters that arrived from Gloria and his parents were read and reread, he said, and kept handy in his knapsack, to read yet again.

Also arriving by mail from Tulsa was the small sewing kit. After all these years, Smith still has it. It was just the basics: a small pair of scissors, needle and thread, a few extra buttons.

Tucked inside is a handwritten note, edges now cracked and brown, from his mother: She thought the kit might be useful, she wrote, to darn a sock or sew a button. Just how useful it would prove — helping reinforce a sleeping bag in dire conditions — she could have no clue.

The winter of 1944-45, when the Germans launched the last-gasp counteroffensive known as the Battle of the Bulge, was

Nelson Smith sits in a jeep during his service in the Army in the European Theater during World War II. COURTESY

historically brutal.

"Water froze. Guns froze up on us. Everything froze," Smith said. "We were on foot all the time."

He would remember the Bulge as his most demanding experience. Assigned by then to the 32nd Cavalry Reconnaissance Squadron, he and his mates were driven back 26 miles, he said. But the counteroffensive couldn't last. The tide turned against the Germans. The Allied advance resumed.

As Smith's unit moved deeper into Germany, they took five or six towns a day.

"If they had up a white flag, we wouldn't fire at them," he said. "But if they didn't, we'd flatten that town." For years afterward, the smell — bodies slain from the artillery and bombs burning in the rubble — would stay with Smith. "Every time I smelled a trash fire, I was reminded of human flesh burning," he said.

Smith also took part in the liberation of prison camps. At one small one — a farm and a big barn surrounded by a fence — he and a team arrived just in time to prevent another Nazi atrocity.

Knowing the Allies were nearing, six or so SS guards had herded all the prisoners into the barn, shut them in and "had thrown gasoline on the front of the barn, fixing to burn it," he said. Smith and his companions intervened, though, and saved them.

A Tulsa World newspaper from April 30, 1945, is among Nelson Smith's war memorabilia.   MICHAEL WYKE/Tulsa World

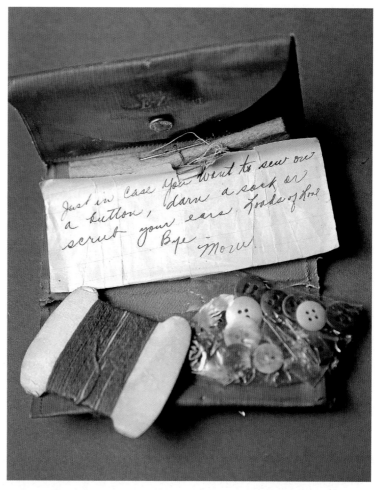

Nelson Smith still has the sewing kit sent by his mother that he carried with him across Europe during his Army service.   MICHAEL WYKE/Tulsa World

"The people were just skin and bones," he said of the prisoners. "They had worked them to death."

Always a soldier

After the war, Smith returned to Tulsa and his wife. The couple were married for 70 years and raised a family together. Gloria died in 2013.

After thinking about it for some time, Smith finally, at the encouragement of his son, Ward, wrote his war experiences down. It turned into a small book. Titled "I Was a Soldier! I Am a Soldier! I Will Always Be a Soldier!," a family friend had it published as a surprise. Intending the account for family, Smith left out much of the profan-

ity, blood and gore, he said. But what's left is a pretty good chronicle of his experience.

"Most of the time I did my very best at a particular job and to look out for my friends," Smith writes, "but there were times when I was so tired and disgusted I didn't give a damn. When you exist on cigarettes and adrenaline, it doesn't take long to change your attitude."

Over the five major campaigns of the European war he participated in, Smith saw death everywhere he turned. But "seeing an American dead or mortally wounded," he said, was the worst. "I can still see the faces of some of them I was close to."

Sometimes, war is necessary, Smith said. "But there's no glory in it."

VIRGINIA STEELE   ARMY 1943-45

A battle star

Okinawa was eye opener for Army nurse Virginia Steele

It started with one set of dog tags. From that, Virginia Steele had an address to go with the name. Twice more in her hospital ward, when servicemen died from their wounds, the Army nurse would check their tags, and write down their personal information.

"I have no idea why I did it," said Steele, who was stationed on Okinawa during World War II.

Many months later, though, after the war was over and her service completed, she found a use for the information. Deciding she wanted to visit the young men's survivors, she was able to track them down and contact them. They were open to her visiting.

"I went just to give closure to the families. I wish I had a lot more names. I just had those three," Steele, now 93, told the Tulsa World in February 2016. To the best of her memory, the servicemen had all been about 18 years old — "young, really young. ... One was an only child."

The families had "little things they wanted to ask," she said. The men had been buried on Okinawa, and "mostly they wanted to know about the burial place, which they had never seen. So I told them about it, the beautiful cemetery there."

Thinking about it often in the years since, Steele is glad she took the opportunity to reach out to the families. "I think if it had been my child," she said, "I would've liked it — to have someone who knew him to visit."

A nurse goes to war

Deaths actually were not that common at the 381st Station Hospital where Steele worked while on Okinawa. When the serious cases arrived from the field hospitals, they would be stabilized and then transported to better facilities on hospital ships. Typically, the ones who stayed at the 381st were those who could be treated and soon sent back to their units.

"I never heard one of them say they didn't want to go back," said Steele, a longtime Tulsan who resides at Inverness Village. "They had left their buddies back there, you see."

Arriving in the spring of 1945, when the battle for the island was raging, Steele was introduced to medical practice on Okinawa and life there in general would come in crash-course fashion. After disembarking, the nurses' first stop was their camp, she said. But they didn't stay long, other than to discover its location — the middle of a bean patch — and that their tents had not yet been set up. From there, they were taken straight to the hospital and put to work, she said. There had been some fierce fighting in the past few hours, and the casualties were pouring in.

"It was a real eye-opener," Steele said of that first shift.

The facilities themselves took some getting used to. Just a collection of large connecting tents held up by poles, the 381st had "not one permanent building," she said.

The newly arrived nurses tended the wounded for several hours until they were relieved. Thankfully, she said, when they got back to camp, their tents were up and ready for them. But they had no more than climbed into bed than they had to get out again. A siren was going off.

"It was an air raid," Steele said, adding that the nurses were sent to a designated ditch near the camp to wait it out. "After an hour or two, 'all clear' sounded." Back to bed. Steele had barely closed her eyes, though, when the siren sounded again. "We had two that first night," she said. "I may have gotten three or four hours of sleep."

Four in the Pacific

Steele, formerly Virginia Timm, grew up in Superior, Wisconsin. She was one of five siblings, of whom four would serve in the war. Her two older brothers, Warren and Franklin, were Marines. Her older sister, Madonna, was a Navy nurse on Guam. All served in the

A military insignia was part of Virginia Steele's uniform. COURTESY

Pacific Theater, she said. All came home safely.

As for Steele's route to the war, it first took her to Chicago. A nursing school student at Michael Reese Hospital, she remembers someone from the Army coming by after the Pearl Harbor attack to recruit medical personnel. Steele signed an agreement that if the war was still going on when she graduated in a few months, she would serve.

It was. So she did. She was 22 at the time. Completing basic training at Fort McCoy, Wisconsin, Steele wondered where she might be sent.

Virginia Steele and her fellow nurses pose at a military hospital in Okinawa, Japan. COURTESY

"They issued us winter clothing," she said. "So we thought we might be going to Europe."

Ultimately, though, they traded it in for tropical clothing, and shipped out for the Pacific. Even then, Steele wouldn't learn her destination until they left Hawaii.

"My first thought was 'Where was that?'" she said of hearing the name "Okinawa."

The ship, the USS Wharton, traveled in a convoy, with mine-sweepers on either side of it. By the time they arrived at Okinawa, the battle for the island had begun. "You could see our ships in the distance gunning the shore. At night especially. It was just like fireworks."

The nurses disembarked at Orange Beach and were met by a weapons carrier that would transport them to their camp. As they rode along, Steele said, she noticed a Marine running ahead of them. He began to shout: "Women in the area!" As if on cue, from out of the bushes and undergrowth all around them, American troops emerged, running up to the vehicle.

"The boys wanted to talk to us," Steele said. "They just wanted to find out where we were from, things like that. ... (Women) were more of a novelty then than we are today," she laughed.

No time to be afraid

Between the sounds of ship guns firing and the nightly air raids, no one would have blamed the new nurses for feeling more than a little nervous. But "I don't remember that I was ever scared," Steele said. "I probably should've been. I knew nothing about war."

"Really, we just didn't have time to take it all in. From the time we arrived, things were happening so fast and you were kept so busy."

The work was hard. And as a nurse, you had to stay emotionally detached, she said. The patients were brought in with battle wounds of all kinds and to all parts of the body.

"You couldn't let it affect you," she said. "You just had to put them back together. Some days were worse than others," she said of the number of casualties coming in.

"One thing that always amazed me: The boys that were not injured seriously, they would pitch in wherever they could. They would help in the wards. That was very helpful."

With the demands of the job, there was never much time for conversation. But Steele would talk to the patients when she could.

"Mom. Their memories of home. Food. They especially liked to talk about food," she said of the young men's favorite topics. "They were just boys, many of them — away from home for the first time in their lives."

Many nights after her shift, Steele would stay behind to write letters for patients who were physically unable to do so. She remembers writing regularly for one young man, who liked to send a weekly letter home to his parents.

She usually would add a line or two of her own to the letters she wrote — to let the recipients know how their wounded warrior was faring. Being "very truthful" by nature, Steele said, she didn't gloss over reality.

A battle star

Steele has a lot of other memories from her time on Okinawa. Like the island's residents, with whom she had occasional interaction.

The Okinawans "were very poor," she said. "The Japanese had kept them that way. They were very friendly and very glad we had come."

One time, a typhoon hit the island. It lasted a few days, bringing in heavy wind and rain. "You could hardly walk in it," Steele said. "You put your helmet on" in case you were hit by a flying object. The storm took out a number of tents. But Steele's hospi-

Virginia Steele served as a nurse in Okinawa, Japan. COURTESY

tal came through mostly OK, she said. "I remember us hanging onto the poles so it wouldn't blow off. As if we could've prevented that."

After the war ended in August 1945, Steele had occasion to fly over Hiroshima and Nagasaki, the Japanese cities that had been leveled by atomic bombs.

"You could see the damage that was done," she said. "There were big holes. I don't know how else to describe it." Say what you will about the decision to drop the bomb, she added, but by making invasion unnecessary it "certainly saved a lot of lives."

Steele met and married her late husband, Byron, after finishing her Army service. They eventually settled in Tulsa, raising their family here while he enjoyed a long career as a surgeon.

Steele didn't talk about the war for many years. She began to share memories, though, with one of her brothers who had served. "It was helpful for him to talk about it," she said.

Later, one of her daughters asked her about the war. It surprised her — the realization that her children were interested, too. Nowadays, Steele finds interested people wherever she goes. She even gives occasional talks to groups.

Steele is not one to overstate her own part in the war. But one memento from it does fill her with a sense of satisfaction: the battle star she received for serving in the Battle of Okinawa. She still has it.

"You'll see these generals with a whole row of them. This is my only one. And I'm very proud of it."

Blood brothers

Local siblings served in same Army Air Corps squadron

From his place in the formation, Cecil Terrill could make out the other B-26 — see its left engine smoking where it had been shot out.

But what happened to it next he had no idea. His own plane, also in bad shape, had to pull out of the group to find a place to land. In fact, until he arrived back at base later, Terrill had no clue that his brother's plane had failed to return.

"I didn't know whether he was dead or alive," Terrill said. "I thought he'd died." If true, then fate had finally achieved what no one, not even the Army, had been able to do up to that point: separate Cecil and Jim Terrill. "That was pretty hard to take," Cecil Terrill added. "I was ... scared. I couldn't see staying over there without him."

Bond of brothers

Serving in the same 9th Air Force squadron during World War

II, both of them on B-26 bomber crews, Cecil and Jim Terrill stuck together in war like they had in peace. The siblings — natives of Collinsville and their parents' only surviving children — had grown up in Tulsa. Cecil was the older by a year and three months, and graduated from Will Rogers High School in 1941, a year before Jim.

From there, both studied aircraft mechanics at Spartan School of Aeronautics before joining the Army Air Corps together March 1, 1943.

"They didn't like to keep brothers together," said Cecil, 92, during a 2015 interview in Broken Arrow. But with "much pleading and arguing" the Terrills would be permitted to do so.

Cecil recalls that his parents, Everett and Ida Terrill, were supportive and proud. Undoubtedly they were afraid for their boys, he added. But they never showed it, and seemed happy that they were going together.

Same squadron

After training stints at Wichita Falls, Texas, and Fort Myers,

Brothers Jim and Cecil Terrill sit by a pile of German bombs in 1945 during their service together in the Army Air Corps in Europe. COURTESY

Florida, the Terrills arrived in England in October 1944. There, they started out in different units, Cecil in the 387th Bomb Group and Jim in the 323rd.

Later, after several missions, Cecil was moved to a crew in the same squadron as his brother, the 455th. Engineers on their respective bomber crews, they also manned the planes' guns at times.

The reality of war hit home early for Cecil, who before he'd gone on his first mission witnessed a terrifying sight — a bomber crash-landing and exploding on the runway at his base. It blew up, he said, as crews were trying to put out the fires.

"I had to go around and pick up the (body) pieces," Cecil added. "I began to wonder if I wanted to fly or not." He swallowed his misgivings, though, and went on to be part of 15 successful missions.

Aerial warfare "was pretty hectic," Cecil said. "It wasn't no picnic. But we came out all in one piece." Living under such conditions, the Terrill brothers relished their off-duty time, taking their leaves, like everything else, together. Their favorite, Cecil said, was a trip to "Gay Paree."

Paris, he said, "was about the only place to go. And it was really lively, I'll put it that way. We watched the risque shows. ... Women, songs and laughter. ... Lots of champagne."

Bailing out

The mission that Cecil remembers most happened on March 16, 1945. The anti-aircraft fire was especially heavy that day, he said, and, in formation with his brother's and other planes, he saw that his brother's plane had been hit. But his own plane had taken hits, too, and running low on fuel, it had to leave the group.

"We almost ran out (of fuel), but we found an airfield and landed safely."

Jim's plane, however, was not so fortunate. Arriving back at his base later, Cecil was stunned to find out his brother's aircraft had not made it back. Jim and his crew were missing in action. But after three days with no news, the story would end happily. Cecil learned his brother was safe.

When the two were reunited: "I was overjoyed," he said. He breaks down for a moment at the memory, unable to continue, the emotions still real for him after 70 years.

"We hugged each other, kissed each other's cheeks. We were overjoyed. That war was pretty rough at that time."

Jim filled his brother in on what had happened. Their plane going down, he and the crew had been able to parachute to safety. In fact, everyone except the pilot, who died in the crash, survived. Jim landed in a tree. There, suspended by his chute cords, he would be found and cut down by resistance fighters. He broke his wrist but otherwise was OK. Jim would go on to fly 23 total missions during the war.

Making headlines

In 1945, articles about the Terrill brothers appeared in both the Tulsa Tribune and Tulsa World, remarking on their virtual inseparability. At one point, in France, the two were assigned to bases a few miles apart. The action was so heavy that they lost contact with each other briefly. But after two months, they were back together again.

When the war ended, Cecil would concede the medal count to his younger sibling. Among their various decorations, Jim had four Air Medals to Cecil's two. Jim also received three Bronze Stars. Both achieved the rank of sergeant.

Back in Tulsa, where they soon married and raised families, they continued to do everything in tandem, careers included. Both went to work for American Airlines, Cecil retiring after 36 years, Jim after 45. Jim died in 1996. He was 71.

Reflecting on their military service, Cecil says he is proud of what he and his brother did to help stop "Ol' Hitler." They joined, he added, out of "loyalty to the country."

"It was the proper thing to do. I believe in my country. I wouldn't have had it any other way." Still, he has no use for war.

"I think wars are terrible because they mess up so many people. Bombs and all that. Wars are caused by greed, I think. If I had my way," Cecil added, "we'd have no more wars."

Shot out of the sky

Tail gunner Wally Tipsword was shot down over Germany

As he hurtled toward the earth below, his plane in pieces after exploding at 25,000 feet, Wally Tipsword could at least be thankful for one thing. Despite all the ribbing, he hadn't given up his parachute.

"My crew mates used to joke me about it," he said, explaining that as a tail gunner he'd always dragged one along in crawling to and from his post.

His buddies had a little fun with that. But now, free-falling through space, he was glad he had made a habit of it.

Just wearing a parachute, though, did not guarantee him a safe landing, he knew. And sure enough, Tipsword's chances looked suddenly doubtful when he yanked the rip cord — and got no response. The chute, he realized in alarm, had already partially deployed,

probably from the force of the explosion. Partially doesn't do much good with parachutes, Tipsword said.

"I've often joked that I gained altitude, when I started climbing those stringers to get up there to open that parachute," he said, laughing.

Out of the frying pan

Tipsword, who was part of a B-17 crew during World War II, talked about his experiences with the Tulsa World in 2015 at his office across from Guthrie Green.

At 91, the Tulsa native still owns and operates three companies, including Baird Manufacturing in Tulsa. He's climbed high and far in the years since being shot down over Germany. But that — and his subsequent tenure as a prisoner of war — are still with him every day.

Of his B-17's nine-member crew, only five would survive. It was a miracle, he said, that anyone did. It happened on Sept. 8, 1944, during what was just Tipsword's fifth mission. The target was a manufacturing plant in Ludwigshafen, Germany. Tipsword and company arrived and, despite anti-aircraft fire exploding all around, successfully dropped their bombs.

But then, he said, everything went wrong at once. Taking a direct hit, the airplane rolled to the right and into a downward spiral. The explosion followed seconds after that. Before Tipsword knew what was happening, he was falling through the air, blown clear of the plane.

Luckily, he never lost consciousness. Able to finally open his partially deployed chute, he executed a safe landing. But for Tipsword, the adventure was just beginning. He was still trying to collect his wits when he saw them: the mob of angry men. They were civilians from the town, and they were coming toward him, carrying a rope, ladder and waving a big scythe.

"They came out to do me in, I guess," he said.

Fortunately, Tipsword had come down just a few yards from an anti-aircraft battery, possibly the same one that had shot his plane down. A captain from the battery quickly intervened, he said, and putting his Luger pistol right to the forehead of the lead "lyncher," ordered them to clear out: He was taking Tipsword prisoner, he told them.

"I never got his name," Tipsword said. "That man saved my life. I

would've loved to have told him (thank you) at some future date."

Stalag Luft IV

Born and raised in Tulsa, Tipsword was just 11 when his father, a railroad section foreman, died. To support Wally and two older brothers, his mother went to work in a cafeteria.

"Somehow she got all three of us through college," Tipsword said proudly.

For everything the family had already endured, though, nothing would try them quite like the news that Wally, the youngest son, was a prisoner of war.

After he was shot down, Tipsword said, he was taken to Frankfurt for interrogation. There, he was reunited with two of his surviving crew mates. Together they would be shipped to Stalag Luft IV, a prison camp for captured Allied airmen located near Kolberg, Germany.

Marching in with other new arrivals, Tipsword would learn what a small world — indeed, small world war — it was: "I hear someone yelling 'Wally! What the hell are you doing here?' And I looked, and it was Ernie Woods."

A fellow Tulsan, Woods just a couple of years earlier had played basketball against Tipsword in school. Now, the pair were both

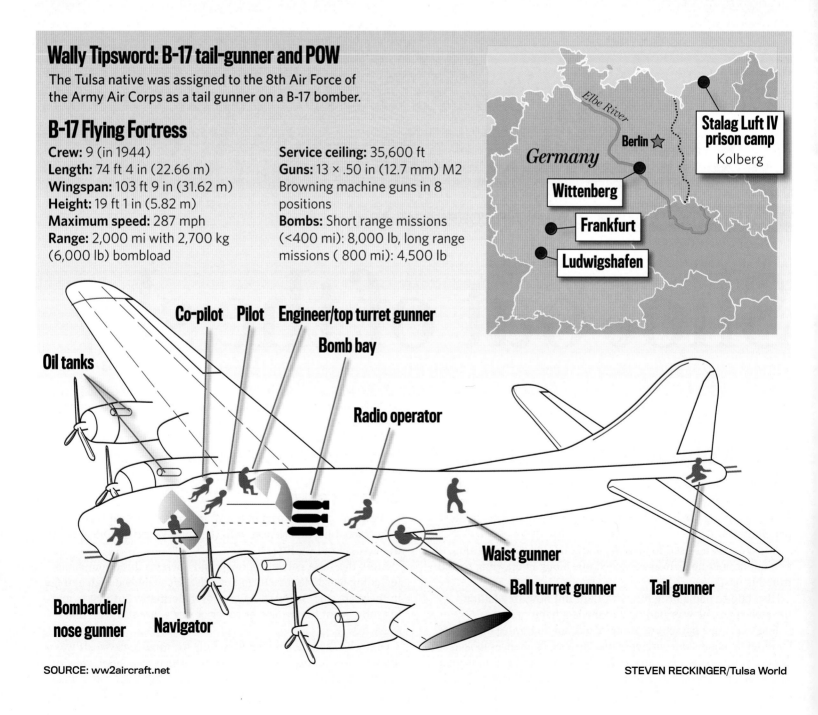

Wally Tipsword: B-17 tail-gunner and POW
The Tulsa native was assigned to the 8th Air Force of the Army Air Corps as a tail gunner on a B-17 bomber.

B-17 Flying Fortress
Crew: 9 (in 1944)
Length: 74 ft 4 in (22.66 m)
Wingspan: 103 ft 9 in (31.62 m)
Height: 19 ft 1 in (5.82 m)
Maximum speed: 287 mph
Range: 2,000 mi with 2,700 kg (6,000 lb) bombload

Service ceiling: 35,600 ft
Guns: 13 × .50 in (12.7 mm) M2 Browning machine guns in 8 positions
Bombs: Short range missions (<400 mi): 8,000 lb, long range missions (800 mi): 4,500 lb

SOURCE: ww2aircraft.net

STEVEN RECKINGER/Tulsa World

captured warriors.

POW life was monotonous, Tipsword said. The Germans broke rules here and there, he added, but for the most part observed Geneva Convention standards for treatment of POWs.

Still, it didn't mean comfort: prisoners were given little food — less and less, as supplies waned — and little coal, just a few pieces a day per stove to keep warm.

Some prisoners played softball. Others formed a jazz band with instruments brought in. A daily church service, held, Tipsword recalls, by a preacher and fellow POW from Buffalo, Oklahoma, was usually packed.

"Everyone was thinking they were going to die. We wanted all the help we could get."

Tipsword would remain at Stalag Luft IV for five months. Then, on Feb. 6, 1945, the next phase of his POW experience began.

With Soviet troops drawing near, the Germans herded the prisoners together and abandoned the camp, beginning a forced march that would last weeks and cover hundreds of miles. Tipsword remembers scrounging in fields for food, or trying to trade with housewives. Conditions were miserable: Temperatures dropped well below zero at night.

"We laughed at most of the (hardships)," though, Tipsword said.

Eventually the POWs would be turned over to U.S. 3rd Army forces across the Elbe River near Wittenberg.

Tipsword, a staff sergeant, was discharged in October 1945. Among his decorations, he would receive a Purple Heart, and in 2005, an Oklahoma Cross of Valor.

The hands of time

On Tipsword's left arm, visible when he unbuttons the sleeve of the dress shirts he still wears to work every day, is a vintage Longines wristwatch. A high school graduation gift from his oldest brother in 1941, he has worn it ever since, including through the war.

The only time he didn't was in prison camp, when the camp officials took it from him. They later returned it. Not even during the march, when he might've traded it for food, could he bring himself to part with it.

Besides the sentimental value, Tipsword added, "it's always been a terrific watch."

One thing it cannot do, he admits, is turn back time. Otherwise, the fates of his fellow crewmen — the ones who didn't come home from the war — might be different.

In an old black-and-white photo of his plane's crew, he can quickly point the four of them out.

After he got home, he said, the mother of one used to call him weekly from Chicago.

"Every Sunday morning. God bless her. ... She just wanted to know 'Can't you tell me anything? What could've happened to him? Could there be any chance he escaped?'" But there was little comfort Tipsword could offer.

Of the five crewmen who did come home, Tipsword is now the

Wally Tipsword (bottom right) poses with the other crew members of his B-17G bomber that was shot down on a mission over Germany in 1944. Tipsword was the tail-gunner and was one of five who survived the downing, only to be captured by the Germans. COURTESY

sole survivor.

"I just found out last week, the guy who was our engineer passed on," he said.

More to life

Except for his hearing, which was never quite the same after the exploding plane, Tipsword came home largely unscathed, including emotionally, he said.

"Those people who fought on the front lines and saw so much brutal death — I didn't get in on any of that."

If the war changed him in any way, it was simply in seeing that there was "more to life than basketball."

The sport had been his obsession: At Central High School, he had starred for legendary coach Grady Skillern, who became a father figure to him. From there he played at Long Beach State in California, which is where he was when he got his draft notice.

But after the war, Tipsword accepted that basketball was not his future. Graduating from the University of Tulsa, he would raise a family with his wife, Betty, who he's still married to after 68 years.

It took his generation two years of losing battles, Tipsword notes, before they got it together and won the war. He believes today's young people would also step up.

If faced with a world war, "I don't question at all that they would come forward."

All about his bass

Vivion served in a band playing his bass at dances and parades

Walking up the gangplank — his Army duffle bag on one shoulder, his upright bass on the other — Wayne Vivion couldn't wait to get the voyage home underway. But first he had to officially board the ship. And standing in his way at the top was a potential obstacle — a naval officer.

"Where are you going with that?" the officer asked, indicating the bulky 6-foot-long musical instrument. "He told me," Vivion added, "I couldn't go down in the hold with it."

Not about to leave his bass behind, Vivion worked it out to store it in the ship's pilothouse. On the ship ride home, he would retrieve it daily to play for his fellow passengers.

Back in the states the special accommodations for Vivion's bass would continue. Trying to get back to Oklahoma after his discharge,

he was again told, "You can't haul that around."

So he had a special wooden case made for it, then shipped it on ahead. When he finally arrived home in Wagoner, "there it was, waiting on me," he said.

Today, 70 years after coming home from World War II, Vivion, 89, and his bass are still together. And still making music. Every Monday at his retirement home, Vivion sits in with a visiting bluegrass group.

'You're in an Air Corps band now'

Vivion, who served in the Pacific with the Army Air Corps, playing for the 746th Air Force Band, started out with the intention of becoming a pilot.

While at Wagoner High School, he joined a reserve flight program, which allowed him to stay in school. But it was shut down, he said, when the demand for pilots declined. That's when an officer looking over his papers proposed another way of fulfilling his duty, Vivion said.

Wayne Vivion (right) and the Round Up Boys play for the Friday lunch crowd at Nelson's Buffeteria in downtown Tulsa in 2001. Vivion's bass is the same one he used as a musician during World War II. TULSA WORLD FILE

"He asked, 'You are a musician?' And I said, 'Well, I was in the high school band.' And he said, 'You're in an Air Corps band now.'"

The bass wasn't Vivion's first choice, either. At Wagoner High, he'd played the tuba. But after his assignment to the newly formed 746th, he was told to learn the bass, as well. He was needed for a dance band that was being organized.

For the rest of the war, Vivion would divide his time between playing tuba for the 746th and bass at military dances.

"It was on-the-job training," he said of learning the new instrument.

Manila nights

Sent to Washington state initially, Vivion played at Moses Lake and Ephrata air bases before shipping out for the Pacific with the 746th.

Their first stop was New Guinea. From there, 11 months later, it was on to the Philippines. In Manila, where he would spend the rest of the war, Vivion played weekly dances on base.

His favorite memories, he said, are of "being able to watch the troops enjoy the music."

The musicians didn't get to mingle with the dancers, who included young women bused in from the Women's Army Corps. As soon as a show was over, Vivion said, "they would load us up and take us back to the barracks."

In the 746th, Vivion played his tuba alongside "what we called big-time musicians," he said — fellow troops who as civilians had played in some of the era's famed big bands. Among them, he added, were musicians who had played with Benny Goodman and Woody Herman.

The 746th played parades, ceremonies and concerts, and helped out with USO shows.

"If some big shot was coming through, we'd play a military concert for them," he said.

It was in Manila that he would find the bass he would bring home. He was looking through a pile of instruments that were about to be dumped in the ocean — "(the military) did that a lot" to dispose of things — when a beautiful bass caught his eye, he said.

"It was brand-spanking new."

He swapped the one he had for the new one and played it for the rest of the war. It's the bass he still plays. When he left the service, he didn't ask permission to keep it. He figured it was his, he said.

A man's job

For Vivion, the military was an eye-opening experience.

"I was 18 and didn't know 'come here' from 'sic 'em' about anything," he said. "I went from being a kid growing up to overnight starting a job that a man's supposed to do. ... It made me grow up real quick."

Vivion and his wife, Norma, have been married for 67 years. They married after he returned from the war and raised two sons together.

After graduating from Northeastern State University in Tahlequah, Vivion went on to a long career as a sales manager for Kellogg's. He remained an Army reservist, rising to the rank of staff sergeant. He was recalled for the Korean War, although he did not go overseas.

In his spare time, Vivion strummed his bass.

After retiring, he played nearly two decades with Tulsa's Round Up Boys, including a long-running gig at Nelson's Buffeteria in downtown Tulsa, playing Western swing and gospel for the lunch-hour crowds.

Vivion thought once about having his well-worn bass restored. But when told it would never sound the same afterward, he didn't do it. And anyway, a little wear and tear never hurt anything.

"I've done a lot of music with it," he said of his bass. "And I enjoyed all of it."

'He was only 22'

Pietje Wall joined Marines to honor her fallen brother

The name Peleliu had never come up in Pietje Wall's high school geography class. But from the time she first heard it — after her older brother John was killed there — that "dot on a map" would loom very large, she said.

Buried initially on the tiny Pacific island with other fallen Marines, it would be four more years — 1948 — before John Smits was returned to his family in Paris, Kentucky, for final burial.

"As I like to say, he slept in the sand for four years," Wall said.

In the interim, she honored his memory in what she felt was the most fitting way: She joined the Marines.

"I did it to honor my brother who was killed," Wall said.

Kentucky farm girl

Welcoming the Tulsa World to her home in 2015, Wall, 90, a long-time Tulsa resident, talked about the war and her contributions to it, as an Army civilian employee and then with the Marines.

The third of four children and only girl, the former Pietje Gertruda Smits grew up on a farm in Kentucky, where her parents settled after immigrating from Holland.

"I'm full-blood Dutch," she said, hence her name, Pietje. It's pronounced "Pee-chee," though most know her as "Petey" or just "Pete."

After graduating from high school, Wall took what was a big step, she said, for a Kentucky farm girl: She left home for Washington, D.C., and a job at the Pentagon. She still remembers her father seeing her off at the train station. Handing her $50, Wall said, "he told me 'If you don't like it in Washington, you can come home.' "

"I was as green as the bluegrass I left," Wall admitted. But she was determined to make it work.

Wall's job at the Pentagon was with the Army Signal Corps, keeping records on radio communications equipment. When a ship was sunk in the Pacific, she said, "we knew exactly what and how many parts were on that ship."

While Wall was contributing to the war effort in D.C., her brothers were doing their parts abroad. Like John, her oldest brother, Bill, had also left home to fight. He served with the Army in Europe and would fight in the Battle of the Bulge. Bill came home, she said, but carried shrapnel in his body for the rest of his life.

John was not so lucky. Serving with the 1st Marine Division in the Pacific, he was killed on Peleliu Island. It happened at night, Wall said.

"They told him not to go (leave his foxhole) — it was too dangerous," she said. "But he said 'I have to check on my men.' So he went out. He was shot in the head."

For the 1st Marines on Peleliu, the dead and injured would number 6,500, a third of the division.

'They came back men'

After getting the heartbreaking news, Wall, still in D.C., headed straight for the nearest Marine recruiting office.

"I told them my brother had died, and I wanted to join," she said.

Accepted into the Marine Corps Women's Reserve, Wall completed boot camp and eventually was sent to San Diego. There, she worked in the office that gave troops returning from combat their new orders.

"They went over there as young boys and came back men," she said. "We tried to put them as close to their home as possible."

Marines returning from the Pacific would stay on base six days awaiting new orders, she said. "Some had minor wounds, some serious wounds," she said.

Others had wounds that were not so obvious. Wall remembers one young Marine who died while she was there — possibly of suicide. His body was found in the water where the ships came in.

"They gave me his wallet to inventory," Wall said. "There were pictures of his family. Very little money."

Being a woman on a base with so many men could be a challenge in itself. Once in her office, when a sergeant who sat next to her tried to pull up her skirt, Wall took matters into her own hands.

"I knew that if I hit him in any way, I was in trouble," she said. "But I did it! All of a sudden I'd had enough ... so I just backhanded him in his chest so that his chair rolled back."

The captain in charge demanded an explanation.

"'He will not keep his hands to himself when I'm trying to do my job,' " she told him.

Wall was demoted to the typing pool. But three weeks later she was back. As for the sergeant, he evidently was sent packing. She never heard his name or saw him on base again, she said.

Wall remained on active duty with the Marines for 13 months, before returning to the Pentagon, this time working in military photography. She remained a Marine reservist for four more years, earning the rank of sergeant, and when a new law in 1948 incorporated all women's corps into their regular military branches, she enjoyed the status of a full-fledged Marine.

It was also in D.C. that Wall would meet her future husband: Cpl. T.J. Wall, a fellow Marine and Oklahoma native, who had fought in the Pacific and was stationed at Quantico, Virginia.

After the couple married, they settled in Tulsa and raised three children together.

'Our best man'

Wall remembers a letter from her brother's lieutenant she received after his death.

"'We lost our best man,' " he told her John's men had said. "It still affects me," she added, her 90-year-old eyes tearing up. "He was

Marine John Smits was killed during the invasion of Peleliu in World War II, prompting his sister, Pietje, to joined the Marine Corps Women's Reserve in 1945. COURTESY

only 22."

In her mind, John is still just a boy, catching fish in the creek that ran by their farm.

Wall remembers well the day everything changed — when the world and its affairs, once seemingly so far away, invaded the lives of farm families everywhere. The news that Japan had attacked Pearl Harbor broke suddenly on a Sunday morning. Wall heard about it over the radio while doing homework at the kitchen table.

John, who was working on the farm, came into the house. He wanted her to tell him more news, but she knew only what she'd just heard.

"He immediately wanted to join (the military)," Wall said. "We didn't see him again from the day he left home. They sent him immediately overseas."

'War is futile'

Wall has lived in the same midtown Tulsa house for the last 52 years. She is a longtime active member of the Oklahoma Women Veterans Tulsa chapter, and in 2014, returned to Washington with the Oklahoma Honor Flights program. Wall downplays her own contributions to the war effort, though.

A couple of years ago, she turned down a seat on the reviewing stand at Tulsa's Veteran's Day parade. She said she told them, "I went from a typewriter in Washington, D.C., to a typewriter in San Diego. Take me off, and put one of the men who carried a gun there."

As Marine Corps Women's Reservists, Wall said, their motto had been "Free a man to fight." But it could just as easily have been "Free a man to die."

After her brother's death, in the text of his high school history book, Wall discovered three words underlined in pencil: "War is futile."

"I don't know what was going through his mind" when he marked those words, she said; it was well before he found himself in a war. But, Wall added, she can't agree more.

"'War is futile.' And it is! What do we gain from a war? So many lives were lost."

Life by design

Ward fought his way from Utah Beach to Battle of the Bulge

He had come to Reims looking for leftover Germans. But instead, all 1st Lt. Charles Ward found was a humble priest.

Just hours after German troops evacuated the French city, Ward and his sergeant became the first Americans to set foot in Reims' fabled 700-year-old cathedral in four years, since the occupation began.

The priest there was ecstatic to meet them. He gave them each a rosary medallion, and for years afterward, Ward would keep and treasure it. The medallion wasn't the most influential thing he would take with him from Reims, however. The cathedral itself gets that honor.

Together with the other architectural splendors of France, the impression its majestic spires made on Ward would last, inspiring him later in his choice of careers.

In search of adventure

Before Ward could come home to design beautiful buildings of his own, though, there was a war to win.

The renowned Tulsa architect and decorated veteran, now 90, in 2015 talked about World War II with the Tulsa World, including how it all started for him.

As a 17-year-old military boarding-school student in Tennessee, he was too young to join up when the U.S. entered the war. But "adventure" wouldn't stop calling, he said. As soon as he turned 18, after briefly attending the University of Oklahoma, he enlisted.

More than a year would pass, though, before he'd see the action he craved. That would come with D-Day, June 6, 1944. A platoon leader by then with the Army's 5th Infantry Division, Ward landed at Utah Beach, Normandy, three days after the Allied invasion of France began. From there, assigned to Gen. George Patton's 3rd Army, he and the 5th Division would fight through the region's famously forbidding hedgerows, and then, in the subsequent advance, help push the Germans back across France.

As he witnessed firsthand the liberation of French cities and towns, a kind of euphoria kept building inside him, Ward recalled; he was sure the end of the war was at hand. But any illusions that the Germans were beaten would be shattered in short order. Metz would see to that.

'A horrendous place to attack'

In war — if you're lucky and you keep surviving — you begin to wonder, " 'Why me, and not other people?' " Ward said. No place made him ask that question more than Metz.

Commencing in September 1944, the battle to capture the heavily fortified city would take weeks of brutal fighting and cost many American lives.

"Metz was a horrendous place to attack," Ward recalled.

Of his own men, he lost "lots, I'm afraid. ... And I was one of only a few officers who made it through. I don't know why. It wasn't anything I did."

In early December, the horrors of Metz at last behind them, Ward and his men crossed into Germany. But they found no respite — only snow and bitter cold. And then, in a few days, the Battle of the Bulge. During the Allied response to this final German offensive, Ward would distinguish himself, leading his men in the capture of several entrenched enemy positions in Luxembourg. He would be awarded a Silver Star for valor, with Gen. Patton himself pinning it on him.

The legendary warrior "had a bearing about him," Ward recalled. "He looked like he was in charge."

After the Bulge, Ward, now commanding a company, resumed his advance into Germany. But things were different now. Everywhere they turned, German civilians were waving white sheets or garments. The end, at last, was near.

Germany's official surrender would follow in May, with Ward's company joining in the ensuing occupation. Ward, now a captain, was briefly assigned to serve as mayor of a town. The oddness of the situation, he said, struck him.

"Just a few days earlier you were trying to kill these people. Now we were taking care of them." But he didn't mind. "Really, I came away with no hatred for the Germans, no animosity."

Reims revisited

In December 1945, after three years of service, Ward received his discharge.

Among his many decorations, along with the Silver Star, he brought home a Bronze Star, a Purple Heart and the French Croix de Guerre.

Returning to OU, he devoted himself to the study of architecture, going on to make a name for himself in the field.

While proud of his part in the war and holding no regrets, Ward admits he still has questions. For the most part, they are unanswerable.

"I shot several people (in combat situations) standing no further away than me to you. ... At least four face to face. ... And let me tell you, that stays in your mind. You ask yourself, 'Would society have been better off if I had died and he had lived? What might he have become?' "

Charles Ward pauses during his war service in Europe with Gen. Patton's army. COURTESY

Through the years, Ward made several trips back to the scenes of the war, including in 1994 for the 50th anniversary of D-Day. It was an opportunity to enjoy the company of fellow veterans. And it was a good reminder that even in all the ugliness of war, there were moments of beauty, the worst that humanity has to offer never quite vanquishing the best.

Revisiting the Reims Cathedral, which so many years earlier had inspired him to become an architect, was a special treat.

"Without knowing it (during the war)," Ward said, "it changed my life really."

SAM WARD   MARINES 1942-45

'It had to be done'

Sam Ward saw action at Saipan, Okinawa

He's "still the same ol' Sam."

It was true then, when Sam Ward came home from the war. And, for the most part — making some allowances for wear and tear — it's true now. But as much as Ward might insist World War II didn't change him, it's not entirely true. The nightmares, for one, are just too real.

"I've been lucky — I haven't dreamed about it in quite a while," the Sand Springs resident told the Tulsa World. "But I used to, boy. I'd wake up, scared to death. Or almost to death."

Haunted by some of the things he saw and did, Ward made it a point over the years not to talk much about the war. Even with two of his late brothers, Bob and Ralph, who also served in World War II, the subject wasn't brought up much.

"You wanted to get it out of your mind," Ward said. And keep it

out. "I try not to think about the war," he said. "I was just glad to get home."

'We hit it to get it'

As much as it's not a favorite subject, Ward graciously agreed to talk about his war experience at his home in 2015.

A member of the 29th Marines, an infantry regiment of the 6th Marine Division, Ward fought in the Pacific, where American forces took on the Japanese one island at a time, an unenviable task. He remembers coming off the landing crafts onto the islands.

"When we hit the beach, we just spread out, made a line across the island and took it over," he said. "It wasn't as easy doing it, though, as it is talking about it."

"We fought till it was all over with, as long as any (Japanese soldiers) were still there. We stayed right there till the island was secured. We didn't ever think about losing," Ward added. "We hit it to get it, and we got it."

Ward's primary weapon was a Browning automatic rifle. It weighed about 15 pounds and could fire 500 rounds a minute. He became intimately acquainted with his BAR, as they were called, in the battles for Saipan and Okinawa.

At Saipan, Ward's 29th regiment — he was in 1st Battalion, Company C — initially fought alongside the 2nd Marine Division. But in September 1944, it was added to the newly forming 6th Division on Guadalcanal to train for the invasion of Okinawa.

Sugar Loaf Hill

The invasion began April 1, 1945, and Ward's unit was involved from the start. The fiercest combat he would see was the fight to take Sugar Loaf Hill, from May 11-18 — possibly the hardest-fought battle of the entire 12-week Okinawa campaign. The small hill, 50 feet high and 300 yards long, was on the southern end of Okinawa.

Ward was part of the final push to overtake and secure the hill. He remembers how the

Japanese hid and fought from caves in the terrain.

"I called them 'tombs,'" he said of the caves. "We had to get them out of there, one way or another. Throw some dynamite in there. That would get them."

More than 1,650 Marines were killed in the epic fight for Sugar Loaf Hill. Another 7,400 were wounded. Ward came through without a scratch.

"I was one of the lucky ones," he said.

The battle for Okinawa ended on June 21. The 6th Division, which would be awarded a Presidential Unit Citation for its role there, was credited with helping to capture two-thirds of the island, killing or capturing some 24,000 enemy troops in the process.

"Okinawa was as bad (an experience) as I had," Ward said.

After Okinawa, the 6th prepared for the invasion of Japan. But with the atomic bomb making that unnecessary, it moved on to Tsingtao,

Japanese soldiers surrender to U.S. forces under a white flag during World War II. COURTESY

A photo from Sam Ward's scrapbook shows destroyed Japanese tanks. COURTESY

China. It remained there from October 1945 to April 1946, when it was disbanded. It was the only Marine division to never set foot in the U.S., spending its time entirely overseas.

Shooting to kill

The youngest of four brothers, Ward grew up in Sand Springs and attended school there. He quit after the eighth grade. He remembers his dad, who ran a fruit stand, saying to him: "If you're going to do that, you might as well join (the military)."

Eventually Ward would. But first he went to work. He was able to earn a dollar a rick cutting wood, he said — "pretty good money in those days."

He joined the Marines in December 1942. Two of his brothers did their part as well — Bob Ward in the Army, Ralph Ward in the Navy. All three would survive to come home again.

About the war, Ward said, "There's a lot I don't want to remember. You're shooting people, you know. You had that ol' (Browning)" — he raises his hands, imitating firing a gun — "and down they'd go."

"It didn't bother me then. But it bothers me now. The only way I'd shoot anybody now is if they were breaking in my house."

Ward didn't keep a tally on how many enemy soldiers he killed. But it included "anybody that got in front of me," he said. "Or we'd go in a house (where the enemy was holed up) and we'd just shoot them and go on."

At one shack, on Okinawa, he had started in the door when he spied a Japanese soldier sitting in one corner.

"I ran back outside and I knew where he was sitting and I shot through the wall. ... I saw the blood running out. I got him good."

While recalling these things, Ward has to squint his eyes a couple of times, fighting back the tears. Killing, he said, was the hardest part of the war for him.

"But it had to be done."

If he had to go back

Ward turned 91 in Dec. 4, 2015. He fully intends, he said, to make it to 100.

In a lot of ways, Ward, who raised five children with his late wife, Pauline, is still the "same ol' Sam." He still likes to keep things light, for one, always ready with a joke or a quip, or to flirt with a pretty girl.

And he still enjoys a good chew of tobacco: Red Man is his brand and he tries to keep a pouch handy — usually, the back right pocket of his blue jeans. Then there's his fishing. An avid bass fisherman who has won many tournaments, Ward still likes to go whenever he gets the chance. And like any good angler he still keeps his favorite spots to himself.

Another thing that hasn't changed is Ward's favorite branch of service. The Marines were "a good outfit, a good branch," said Ward, who was discharged in December 1945 as a private first class. "If I had to go back, I'd take the Marines again."

"I don't think I'll have to go back," he added with a chuckle, "but if I did."

A photo from Sam Ward's scrap book shows Marines and equipment on a beach landing during Ward's service in the Marines. COURTESY

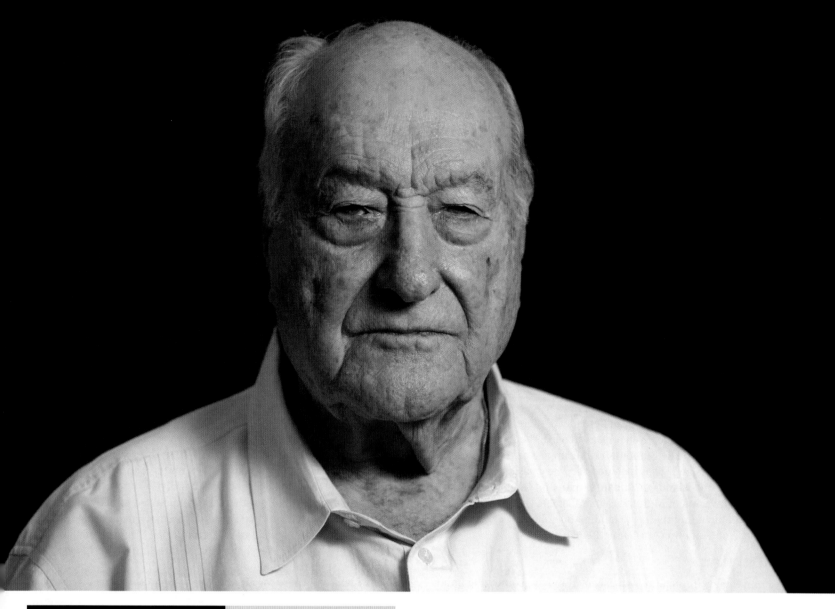

Luck of the Lang

Weber was a gunnery officer on a destroyer in the Pacific

When he moved into his daughter's home in Broken Arrow a couple of years ago, Al Weber didn't come unaccompanied.

He brought along his radio.

More than 80 years since his family acquired the old Montgomery Ward "Airline," it just didn't seem right to part with it. "It was the first radio we ever owned," he said. A console unit, it came with AM and shortwave dials, and most important, was battery-powered — the family had no electricity.

"We listened to Jack Benny, Bob Hope. The 'Hit Parade.' ... My mother liked gospel music," Weber said. The radio became his family's link, he said, to the big world beyond their small farm.

Of course, not everything they heard over it was welcomed, Weber added. Like on Dec. 7, 1941. That was the day — an otherwise peaceful Sunday — that the family radio brought the news about Pearl Harbor.

'Curtains of dust'

Before going on to serve on a Navy destroyer in World War II, Weber, his parents' only child, grew up on a farm near Elk City in western Oklahoma. From an early age, "it was my ambition to get off the farm," Weber, 91, told the World during a 2016 interview.

It was hard and unforgiving work, for one thing. Then, there was the Dust Bowl to contend with. As the storms rolled in, "big, black curtains of dust" swallowed everything, Weber said.

To keep it out of your mouth and lungs, you tied a wet bandana around your face, he said. "It was terrible and frightening," he said, adding that as a boy he couldn't help wondering if it was the end of the world.

After graduating from high school in Sayre, Weber began putting farm life behind him. He went to junior college and then to the University of Oklahoma. Fulfilling a school requirement for male students at the time, he signed up for the Navy ROTC. Commissioned an ensign, he was soon called up for duty and had to put his education on hold.

There was only one problem with his assignment, the destroyer USS Lang: He had to catch it first. "The Navy would assign you to a ship," Weber said, "but it was up to you to get there."

There, in this case, was somewhere in the Pacific. From San Francisco, where he waited a few weeks, Weber boarded a Navy transport to try to catch up to the Lang in New Caledonia. But after crossing the Pacific, he arrived to learn he had just missed it. Following the Lang back to the States, he missed it again before finally, hopping a plane for Pearl Harbor, he caught up to it there.

Weber officially began his duty on the Lang in May 1944. He served as a gunnery torpedo officer. But with torpedoes rarely called on, he would deal mostly with the guns and their crews.

The Lang and other destroyers played primarily a protective role, forming a ring around Navy aircraft carriers and other ships in order to head off enemy threats, including from submarines and aircraft. Weber said, "We tried to destroy the enemy before they could get in to the bigger ships."

In a sense, a destroyer's role was to make a target of itself. But that didn't bother Weber. "That's just the job," he said. "You didn't really think about it much."

With many months of fierce action ahead, there would be a lot not to think about. After Weber came aboard, the Lang returned to the Pacific and provided firepower and support as the Allies fought from island to island. That included the Marianas campaign, and the fights for the islands of Saipan, Tinian and Guam (June-July 1944); the invasion of Morotai (September 1944); the Philippines campaign, including the Leyte landing (October 1944); and finally, the Battle of Okinawa (April-June 1945).

The Lucky Lang

From the beginning, the Lang seemed to have something going for it. "We began to call our ship the 'Lucky Lang,'" Weber said, adding that it showed a knack for coming through trouble unscathed.

And it wasn't just the enemy they were up against. On its way to

Navy veteran Al Weber (third from left) served aboard the USS Lang. COURTESY

the invasion of the Philippines, the Lang had to weather a typhoon.

"It was my first experience with anything like that," Weber said. "The winds were very strong, whipping up great big waves, and the ship was rocking back and forth." A ship instrument that measures "angle of dip" reported it at 70 degrees during the storm. "The floor you were standing on was getting close to vertical," Weber said.

The waves, in some ways, were more of a threat than flesh-and-blood foes. In fact, the only man killed on the Lang while Weber was there, he said, was washed overboard.

In the conflicts to follow, the Lang would need all its luck. The battle for Okinawa would be the most intense. The last island battle of the war, it would last 82 days — from April through much of June 1945 — with the Navy suffering its largest number of casualties in any single engagement.

The Lang was there for all of it. For some of the time, it was part of a radar picket — a defensive perimeter of destroyers and smaller ships that encircled the island. Ships on the picket line worked in pairs. The Lang's partner ship was the destroyer USS Stanly.

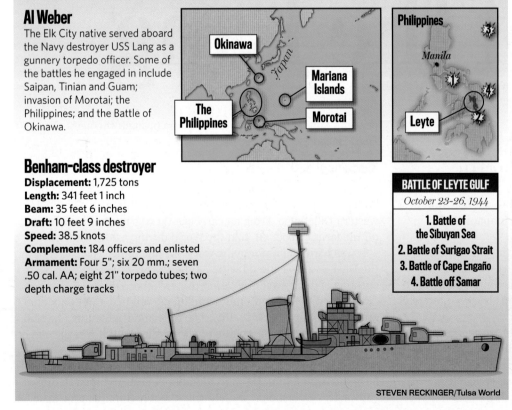

Al Weber
The Elk City native served aboard the Navy destroyer USS Lang as a gunnery torpedo officer. Some of the battles he engaged in include Saipan, Tinian and Guam; invasion of Morotai; the Philippines; and the Battle of Okinawa.

Benham-class destroyer
Displacement: 1,725 tons
Length: 341 feet 1 inch
Beam: 35 feet 6 inches
Draft: 10 feet 9 inches
Speed: 38.5 knots
Complement: 184 officers and enlisted
Armament: Four 5"; six 20 mm.; seven .50 cal. AA; eight 21" torpedo tubes; two depth charge tracks

BATTLE OF LEYTE GULF
October 23-26, 1944
1. Battle of the Sibuyan Sea
2. Battle of Surigao Strait
3. Battle of Cape Engaño
4. Battle off Samar

STEVEN RECKINGER/Tulsa World

Sailors load a torpedo onto the USS Lang in the Pacific. COURTESY

Sailors move
about the deck
of the USS
Lang, where
Navy vet-
eran Al Weber
served.
COURTESY

A torpedo is launched from the USS Lang. COURTESY

The job again was to head off enemy attackers. "Our assigned duty was to use radar to detect enemy planes and ships attacking from Japan. But our other important job turned out to be drawing the kamikaze planes to attack us before they could hit our main fleet." Picket ships stood about an 80 percent chance of being attacked, and at Okinawa there were plenty of kamikazes ready to oblige.

"The Lang was assigned to two of the most exposed and hardest-hit stations on the line," Weber said, "where several ships were sunk or damaged by the suicide planes." But the Lang's luck continued to hold up.

Still, "it was really stressful — our worst ordeal. Everybody was at their battle stations most of the time, ready to fight if they had to."

Luck rubs off

Being ready to fight, though, meant knowing what you were fighting. Which wasn't the case with the Ohka.

A recently developed rocket-powered suicide plane, the Ohka made its first appearance at Okinawa, offering a new twist on the dreaded kamikaze attack.

"Essentially it was a flying torpedo," Weber said. The manned plane — or "Baka bomb" as the Americans dubbed it — was carried underneath a larger bomber aircraft, then released near its target ship. Ohkas were much faster than the propeller kamikazes and could reach up to 620 miles per hour in a dive.

Weber recalls the exact date, April 12, 1945, when he and his Lang crewmates had their first experience with an Ohka.

They saw the bombers first. "They were flying pretty high," Weber recalled. "So I wasn't too worried." But then, they released their deadly payloads.

"Suddenly," Weber said, "we saw these planes streaking across the sky, four of them."

The Lang had faced down many incoming enemy aircraft before, Weber said — "you start firing when they get in range and you keep firing as long as you can. ... But these were moving so fast we couldn't track them." The next thing they knew one of the attackers had hit their partner ship, the Stanly.

"We saw this tremendous cloud of smoke and water," Weber recalled. What appeared at first to be a direct hit, though, was not. To everyone's relief and amazement, Weber said, the speeding plane had gone right through the Stanly's hull, exploding on the other side in the water. "It was like a little of the Lang luck must have rubbed off on the Stanly," Weber said.

It was the closest any of the four attack planes came. Of the others, one grazed the Stanly, while the other two, targeting the Lang, were off target and plunged into the sea.

More than luck

After the Japanese surrender in August 1945, Weber finished his service aboard the USS George. Then, it was back to Oklahoma and to school. Taking advantage of the G.I. Bill, he got his master's degree in physics and enjoyed a long career with Exxon as a reservoir petroleum engineer.

Weber and his wife, Betty, met after the war and raised three children together. Betty died in 2012.

Weber, a regular at reunions through the years, kept up with his former shipmates. He remains a proud "Lucky Lang" veteran. He knows, though, it took more than luck to survive. And it will take more than luck to continue to.

The country has enemies, Weber said, "and you need to try to estimate what your enemy is up to and try to stay ahead of the game. (We must) stay forever vigilant."

Hunting in secret

Army special agent tracked down Nazi war criminals

"Can you handle a Thompson (submachine gun)?"

The question, whispered under cover of darkness, was simple and direct. And Newell West didn't hesitate: Yes, he whispered back. He could.

It was a moment the Tulsan would never forget. Just seconds later, with one of the weapons in hand, he would participate in his first raid as an Army special agent — at a German inn where it was believed Nazi SS officers were hiding.

It was "my baptism" into field work, West said, recalling the incident in a 2015 interview. At first, he added, the operation didn't look promising. Kicking in the inn door and shouting for the sleeping occupants to get on their feet, the agent-in-charge got only groans and insults in return. He repeated the order, but still, nobody got up. "Well, I'm the guy with the Thompson," West recalled.

"So I put it on full automatic" and fired away, spraying rounds down the middle of the room and up to the ceiling.

He said that got them up. From there, the outing would be productive. Hiding among the guests at that inn in Ingolstadt, Germany, were two SS men, who West's team would find and arrest.

Nazi hunters

West has lived in the same midtown home, which he designed himself, for 70 years. He opened it to the Tulsa World to talk about his experiences in World War II.

The longtime Tulsa attorney served with the Army's Counterintelligence Corps — work that was not only important but at times exciting. As a special agent, he said, his duties included investigating and tracking down suspected Nazi war criminals, many of them connected to the notorious Dachau concentration camp and the atrocities committed there.

Assigned to Region 4 of the 970th CIC Detachment in Germany, West first arrived on the scene after the surrender, he said. By that time, the countryside was crawling with Nazis on the run.

Many of the most wanted were former members of the SS, the Nazis' elite paramilitary force. SS men could be quickly identified, West said, by a tattoo (of their blood type) under their arms. Some tried to conceal it with skin-colored ink, he added; but he and other agents carried a device that would reveal the tattoos using ultraviolet light.

Among the most sought-after Nazis that West helped track was Martin Bormann, Adolf Hitler's private secretary. West was part of a house-to-house search for Bormann in Munich that took six days. But Bormann was never found. Later, it was determined that he probably committed suicide. His remains were finally identified in 1972.

Dachau

After its liberation on April 29, 1945, Dachau concentration camp became a holding area for captured SS members from the region.

West can still describe the layout of the sprawling facility like it was yesterday. One part is especially hard to forget: the small, crudely furnished room — just one table and two chairs — where he and a partner interrogated prisoners.

In gathering evidence for the war crimes trials, West questioned dozens of SS officers. Typically, they were "very arrogant ... very stoic," he said. West said he and his partner eventually helped bring 59 indictments, with 21 of those tried receiving death sentences.

All told, the Dachau trials — held between November 1945 and August 1948 — would yield more than 1,400 convictions and almost 300 death sentences.

While interrogation was necessary, West said, he isn't proud of all the tactics used. Like with one SS captain, who repeatedly refused to answer questions. West said he warned him that if he didn't cooperate, his wife and son would be brought in and held as security suspects. At that, West said, the captain "jumped up and threw the table over — and my buddy shot him in the kneecap." The man, writhing on the floor in pain, was then told to talk or he'd be shot in the other knee, as well.

Incidents like that were rare, West said. "At the time, I didn't feel any remorse," he said, adding that, although there were rules, it was generally understood that "we could do what we needed to do."

Despite regrets about some tactics, West is proud of the part he played in helping bring justice after the war. He remembers one case involving an SS guard who had stashed away jewelry and other valuables taken from prisoners bound for the gas chambers. With the help of a liberated survivor they interviewed, West and his partner were able to recover the items — they had been buried in a canister in a garden — and build a case against the guard.

'Worst situation'

Besides investigating war criminals, West's unit also participated in joint operations in their region. A major one, Operation Nursery, targeted an effort to reorganize former members of the Hitler Youth.

It was during this operation that West experienced what he called the "worst situation" of his service. In an effort to spy on a secret meeting in progress in a wooded area, West was ordered to swim across the Amper River. But West didn't swim well and he was swept downstream.

He was eventually able to reach safety, grabbing ahold of a pontoon bridge. But the river was a drainage site for several

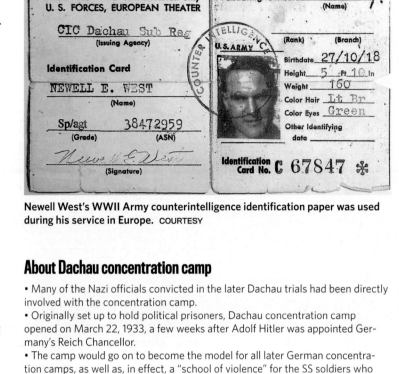

Newell West's WWII Army counterintelligence identification paper was used during his service in Europe. COURTESY

About Dachau concentration camp

• Many of the Nazi officials convicted in the later Dachau trials had been directly involved with the concentration camp.
• Originally set up to hold political prisoners, Dachau concentration camp opened on March 22, 1933, a few weeks after Adolf Hitler was appointed Germany's Reich Chancellor.
• The camp would go on to become the model for all later German concentration camps, as well as, in effect, a "school of violence" for the SS soldiers who oversaw it.
• Over its 12 years in operation, more than 200,000 people from across Europe were imprisoned in Dachau and its subsidiary camps. Ultimately, some 40,500 of them would be murdered.

Source: kz-gedenkstaette-dachau.de/index-e.html

local sewer systems and he developed a serious staph infection in one lung.

Worth the cost

After finishing his service, West returned to Tulsa. He would earn a law degree from the University of Tulsa and enjoy a long career practicing law while raising a family with his wife. In his spare time, West enjoyed flying. In fact, up until a stroke in 2013, he continued to pilot his own plane.

West's thoughts still take flight frequently. And when he reflects on the war, sometimes he can't help wondering:

Was it worth the cost?

"The world is no better off. (People are) blowing themselves up, killing their own people, killing our people. ... What did we prove?" For his part, West has tried to make the world a better place. He's still a member of the Oklahoma Bar Association and does pro bono work, helping immigrants attain legal status.

Despite occasional doubts, in the end West believes the war was worth fighting. "One of the better thoughts I have about the time I spent in the military is the fact that nobody in America is (goose-stepping), saluting, saying, 'Heil Hitler.' We can worship ... freely. We can cuss Obama if we want to. That part of it ... that this country still has the process of its Constitution, I feel good about what little I did."

Combat medic

45th Division fought from Sicily to Germany

Arms missing. Legs blown off. Brains oozing from shattered skulls. As a World War II combat medic in Europe, Joe Wilson "saw everything," he said.

"And it was just horrible."

But as much carnage as Wilson witnessed — and it was considerable, with his unit fighting more than 500 days in Sicily, Italy, France and Germany — none of it prepared him for Dachau. "We came out of the woods and there it was," he said of his first sight of the infamous German concentration camp.

In a 2015 interview, Wilson talked to the Tulsa World about the war and the action he saw with the Army's 45th Infantry Division. Made up of units from Oklahoma and other Southwestern states, the Oklahoma-based 45th was one of the first National Guard units activated in the war, and among its many accomplishments would

be liberating Dachau on April 29, 1945.

"The Germans (at the camp) at first were ready to put up a fight," Wilson said. But after a brief firefight that left several of them dead, "they saw the writing on the wall and surrendered."

About 32,000 prisoners were in the camp when the 45th arrived. They were glad to see their liberators, Wilson said — at least those who weren't so emaciated they were unable to speak. For Wilson, the images remain fresh. He still recalls the starving faces staring out from behind barbed wire. Little more than skeletons, some would die even as they were being freed.

After securing the camp, Wilson said, the horror just continued to unfold for the soldiers. Wilson said they found boxcars that had once hauled coal stacked instead with rotting corpses.

"Bodies were everywhere," he said.

'A bunch of greenhorns'

Just 17 when he joined the National Guard in 1938, Wilson had to lie about his age to get in. It was the Depression and times were hard, said Wilson, who grew up in Cushing. "We'd do anything for a little change in our pocket," he said.

The teenager had no idea then what lay ahead — that war was coming, and the guard would be mobilized for action overseas.

Wilson's first taste of combat came in Sicily, when the Allies invaded in July 1943. "We were a bunch of greenhorns," he said. "We didn't know what to expect." The landing craft hit the beach, the front ramp lowered and just like that "you're facing the Germans," he said. "The ones who made it, made it; those who didn't, didn't."

His job as a combat medic, he said, "was to take care of all the boys who were wounded." When possible, he engaged in a little preventative care. His memories of the location and circumstances that earned him a Silver Star are a little fuzzy now. But he knows it happened when his unit was taking heavy artillery fire. Instead of jumping for cover, Wilson risked his life to make sure other soldiers were safe.

Bobby

One soldier Wilson met holds a permanent place in his heart: An 18-year-old from Indiana named Bobby.

Bobby, whom Wilson befriended and shared a foxhole with, apparently mentioned Wilson once when he wrote home. A short time later, Wilson said, he received a letter from Bobby's father. "He asked me if I could look after him. He said, 'Bobby is the only boy I've got, the only family I've got left.' "

Not long after Wilson received the letter, Bobby was killed.

"Boy, that's what hurts — losing a friend like that," Wilson said. It has haunted him over the years, that he couldn't honor the father's request. The experience of loss was something everybody had to deal with, though, Wilson added.

"You have a buddy and you're going along, then you turn around and he's gone — laying on the ground back there. It's shocking."

Ultimately, the former medic added, the only cure for war is "brotherly love." If the experience taught him anything, that was it.

After finishing his service, Wilson returned to Oklahoma. He would raise three children with his wife, but he never talked much about the war — and even less about Dachau — until late in life, still coming to terms with he saw. Five years ago, a trip on one of

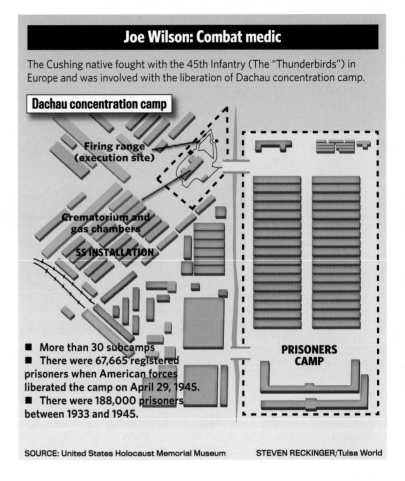

Joe Wilson: Combat medic

The Cushing native fought with the 45th Infantry (The "Thunderbirds") in Europe and was involved with the liberation of Dachau concentration camp.

Dachau concentration camp

Firing range (execution site)

Crematorium and gas chambers

SS INSTALLATION

PRISONERS CAMP

■ More than 30 subcamps
■ There were 67,665 registered prisoners when American forces liberated the camp on April 29, 1945.
■ There were 188,000 prisoners between 1933 and 1945.

SOURCE: United States Holocaust Memorial Museum   STEVEN RECKINGER/Tulsa World

Oklahoma's Honor Flights to the WWII memorial in Washington, D.C., helped him to do that.

As Wilson has gotten older, the nightmares have been less frequent. But sometimes, still, the faces converge on him, hollow eyes peering out from behind barbed-wire fences. When they come to him in his sleep, he said, he usually wakes up.

"I sit up in bed, and say, 'Joe, you're crazy. You're home in bed.' "

About the 45th Infantry Division

Joe Wilson, who was with the 157th Infantry Regiment, G Company, fought in Europe with the celebrated 45th Infantry Division.

Nicknamed the "Thunderbirds," the 45th was originally organized as a National Guard unit in Oklahoma, Arizona, Colorado and New Mexico.

During World War II, the division spent 511 total days in combat, fighting its way from Sicily to Germany. After its performance in Sicily with Gen. George Patton's 7th Army, Patton gave the unit high praise, calling it "one of the best, if not actually the best division in the history of American arms."

The 45th would continue to make its mark in combat, earning seven Distinguished Unit Citations before, finally, near the war's end, arriving to help liberate 32,000 captives at Dachau concentration camp.

The 45th Infantry Museum in Oklahoma City honors the memory of the unit.

A Silver Star decorates the ball cap of Joe Wilson, a World War II veteran who risked his life to make sure other soldiers were safe while his unit was under heavy artillery fire.

MICHAEL WYKE/ Tulsa World

A guard tower at Dachau concentration camp is seen in 2015. TIM CHAMBERLIN/Tulsa World

The Battle of Normandy began on June 6, 1944. U.S. NAVY

North Africa/European Theater

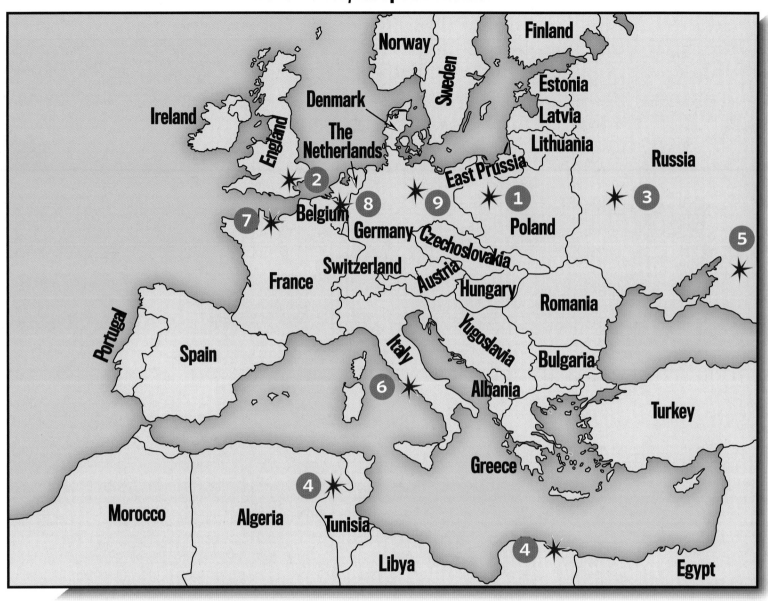

Timeline of significant military events of World War II

Pacific Theater

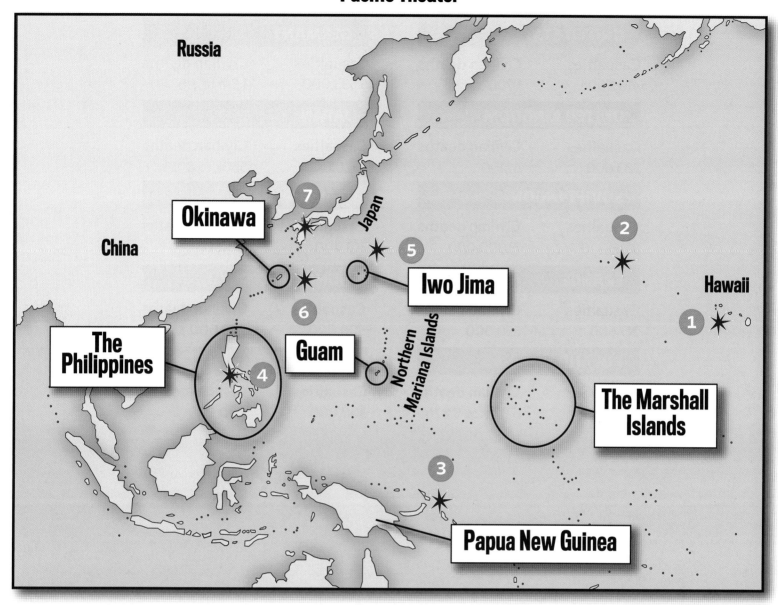

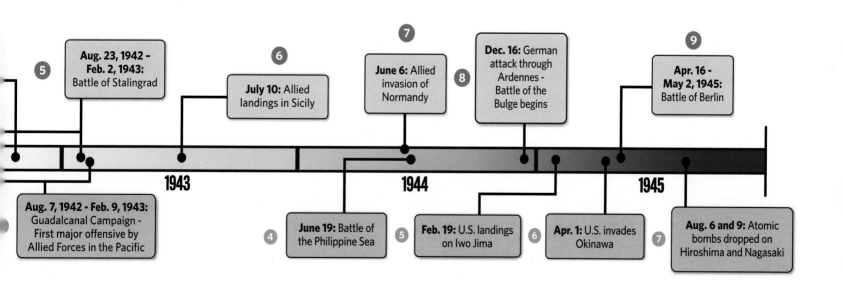

World War II casualties and civilian deaths

Allied Powers

UNITED STATES

Casualties	Civilian deaths
416,800	1,700

UNITED KINGDOM

Casualties	Civilian deaths
383,600	67,100

SOVIET UNION

Casualties	Civilian deaths
8.8m - 10.7m	13,300,000

FRANCE

Casualties	Civilian deaths
217,600	350,000

POLAND

Casualties	Civilian deaths
240,000	5.62m to 5.82m

Axis Powers

GERMANY

Casualties	Civilian deaths
5,533,000	1.5m to 3m

JAPAN

Casualties	Civilian deaths
2,120,000	550k to 800k

ITALY

Casualties	Civilian deaths
301,400	155,600

HUNGARY

Casualties	Civilian deaths
300,000	280,000

ROMANIA

Casualties	Civilian deaths
300,000	200,000

Effects of the atomic bomb on Hiroshima are seen.

At right, The mushroom cloud is seen over Nagasaki.
U.S. MILITARY

INDEX

INDEX

INDEX